Executive Leadership

HOW TO GET IT & MAKE IT WORK

Mary E. Tramel
Helen Reynolds

A SPECTRUM BOOK

PRENTICE-HALL, INC., ENGLEWOOD CLIFFS, N.J. 07632

Library of Congress Cataloging in Publication Data

TRAMEL, MARY E
    Executive leadership.

    (A Spectrum Book)
    1. Executives. 2. Leadership. I. Reynolds,
Helen, 1919-   joint author. II. Title.
HF5500.2.T73   658.4'092   80-26350
ISBN 0-13-294132-5
ISBN 0-13-294124-4 (pbk.)

The authors have chosen to write in the traditional style of using the male personal pronoun, fully recognizing that there are achievement leaders among both men and women.

Editorial/production supervision and interior design by Donald Chanfrau
Illustrations by Billie Jean Staehle
Cover design by Ira Shapiro
Manufacturing buyer: Barbara A. Frick

10 9 8 7 6 5 4 3 2

Printed in the United States of America

PRENTICE-HALL INTERNATIONAL, INC., *London*
PRENTICE-HALL OF AUSTRALIA PTY. LIMITED, *Sydney*
PRENTICE-HALL OF CANADA, LTD., *Toronto*
PRENTICE-HALL OF INDIA PRIVATE LIMITED, *New Delhi*
PRENTICE-HALL OF JAPAN, INC., *Tokyo*
PRENTICE-HALL OF SOUTHEAST ASIA PTE. LTD., *Singapore*
WHITEHALL BOOKS LIMITED, *Wellington, New Zealand*

Contents

one
LEADERSHIP IN GENERAL

1   *What Makes a Person a Leader?*   3

2   *Interpersonal Relations of Leaders*   12

3   *Personal Power Tools*   33

two
MANAGERIAL LEADERSHIP

4   *What Makes a Manager a Leader?*   57

5   *Managerial Leadership Power*   64

6   *Leadership Styles*   68

three

BUILDING A PRODUCTIVE TEAM

7 *The Leadership Team*   *79*

8 *Developing Your Leadership Team and Staff People*   *93*

9 *Staffing for Productivity*   *106*

10 *Upgrading Achievement*   *117*

11 *Building Team Loyalty*   *136*

four

LEADERSHIP METHODS

12 *Managing Creativity*   *147*

13 *Using Executive Time*   *151*

14 *Delegating for Achievement*   *163*

15 *Planning for Achievement*   *170*

16 *Leading in Problem Solving and Decision Making*   *174*

17 *Communicating for Achievement*   *184*

18 *Coaching and Counseling Employees*   *201*

19 *Change Leadership*   *210*

20 *Discipline: A Function of Leadership*   *219*

five

MAKING LEADERSHIP SEEN, HEARD, AND FELT WITH CREDIBILITY AND POWER

21 *Communicating Leadership*   *229*

22 *Leadership Ethics*   *241*

23 *Enhancing Your Image*   *252*

one

LEADERSHIP
IN GENERAL

1
What Makes
A Person A Leader

One has only to read the numerous texts that have been written on leadership to realize there is not a common definition of leadership. The subject is too complex to include all facets of it in a single definition. Not all leaders are alike. Each one has his own personality traits, talents, and methods.

To better understand what makes a person a leader, we can draw a parallel between a leader and an automotible engine, like this:

Automobile Engine	Leader
1. Ignition	1. Motivation
2. Power	2. Power
3. Motor runs	3. Action
Goal: To move the automobile	Goal: To move people

Because an engine is an inanimate object, someone has to put a key into the ignition and turn it to start the engine's power flowing. The driver of the automobile is the spark igniter. However, the leader ignites his own spark to get leader power flowing. The leader is his own motivator, although he may have been inspired by an outside source.

Hitler was a leader of the German people of his day. He was motivated by the desire for power to enslave others. Albert Schweitzer, the great medical missionary who worked for years to combat disease in Africa, was motivated by a desire to give himself to the service of others. Both were powerful leaders. Both were motivated to act. Both of them had their ignitions turned on.

To do anything requires action and action requires power. Without power an engine cannot run. Without power to act a person cannot act. Different kinds of engines require different kinds of power. Some run on diesel fuel while others run on gasoline, gasohol, or electric power. Similarly, different kinds of people require different kinds of power. We can begin to understand what makes a leader, then, by discovering what kinds of power are common among leaders. Most of these leader powers are ones that give the follower some kind of power which he didn't have before.

LEADER POWERS

Think back to your earliest remembrance of other people in your life. Think of all the people by whom you have been led, that is, influenced to take some action, whether physical, mental, or spiritual. Can you find a common denominator among these people? Did they all have power of some sort over you?

Leader Power

When you were a child, most of the people leading you had power over you. Sometimes it was physical power (position power), sometimes it was a "Mother knows best" power, which could be translated to the follower as either *follower self-preservation-power* or *follower model power*. Mother said I should chew my food; Mother knows everything; therefore, I will chew my food (model power). Mother said I should chew my food because if I don't, I may get a stomachache; Mother knows everything; therefore, I will chew my food so as not to get a stomachache (follower self-preservation-power). Effective leaders use their leader power to stimulate some kind of power within their followers.

Goal Power

When you were old enough to have playmates you began to interact with a peer group. You may have had a similar experience to mine. When I was eight or nine years old I was one of four girls who played together. I remember Ruth who made most of the decisions for us. We didn't think of Ruth as our leader, but we always willingly followed her lead. Why? Because Ruth always had the most exciting ideas of what to do with our time. Not only that, but she had a special talent—she could sew doll clothes and she could teach us how to make doll clothes. Actually, what Ruth did was to fill two of our needs: (1) she gave us a goal by deciding what to do, and (2) she showed us how to do it.

Deciding what to do (play with our dolls or roller-skate) could have developed into a big argument with each one wanting to do something different. If three of us were followers and Ruth the only leader, there would be no problem. However, in any group of four youngsters there is likely to be more than one who wants to lead. But Ruth was the strongest leader and so the rest of us were willing to follow her. What made Ruth the strongest leader? She always gave us a specific goal. Playing with dolls was not just playing with dolls in a general sense. It was accomplishing something very specific like making doll clothes. Roller-skating was not just roller-skating. It was seeing how far we could coast on one foot or it was skating in such a way as not to roll over any cracks in the pavement. Ruth knew a lot of different ways to skate. Like every effective leader, Ruth recognized options and she gave us specific goals and helped us to achieve them. Ruth gave us *follower goal power* and *follower achievement power.*

Follower Power

Popularity often seems to breed popularity. A person with many followers seems to be able to attract still more followers without even trying. The popular person may have originally become popular for any number of good or bad reasons, but his or her popularity grows to some extent simply because others want to be associated with a popular person. Most people want to be on the winning side. The leader with follower power, regardless of how he became leader, often maintains leadership by offering *follower belonging power* to his followers. Unconsciously perhaps, the message the leader is giving to would-be followers is "Follow me and you will belong to the in group." Effective leaders attract followers.

Communication Power

A leader can have leader power and goal power, but unless he has communication power, he will not have follower power. A leader must be able to get his message across to those who would follow. There are many effective and ineffective ways to communicate. A person who attempts suicide communicates to the world the message "I hurt—I am in need of something." Suicide, although the person involved may know of no other way, is not an effective means of communicating. While it may effectively get the message across, if the suicidal act is carried out, it is self-destructing to the communicator and therefore worse than merely ineffective. If the suicidal act is not carried out, future messages from this communicator will tend to be ignored.

Even among effective ways of communicating there are varying degrees of effectiveness. The degree of *follower understanding power* that the follower receives from the leader depends on the skill of the leader in using leader communication power.

So far we have seen that leaders have in common:

Motivation

Power of four kinds:
    Leader power
    Goal power
    Follower power
    Communication power

In using these four powers, leaders give certain other powers to their followers. A leader's position is maintained and grows stronger when followers have follower power because they enhance the leader's power.

It is important to bear in mind that someone is a true leader only when his followers are *able to follow* and when they follow *willingly*. Followers will cease to follow a leader who has become a dictator or a tyrant. Circumstances may force them to obey. But then they are not being led, they are being driven. Their leader is no longer leading, but driving—a situation that is not effective and usually ends in defeat for all persons involved.

NEEDS OF FOLLOWERS

Even though the driver of an automobile has turned on the ignition and the motor is running, the engine may not arrive at its goal of moving the car, or the car might start moving and then stall, if the driver has not kept the automobile in good repair by giving attention to proper maintenance such as having a tune-up, the oil changed, the parts lubricated, and so forth. Similarly, even though the leader is motivated and the followers are moving toward the goal, they may not reach the goal if the leader has neglected the finer points of leadership which consist of recognizing and filling the needs of the followers.

Dr. Abraham Maslow in his research on motivation theory developed an order in which man fulfills his needs.[1] This order of needs is commonly referred to as Maslow's Needs Hierarchy. Maslow's Needs Hierarchy can be pictured as steps starting with man's physical needs and rising to man's self-actualization needs which, when met, allow a person to be the best that he can be. He is self-fulfilled. (See Figure 1-1.)

Physical Needs

Physical needs are basic needs for clothing, food, and shelter. A person must have these things before being able to give much attention to anything else. In our society today, especially among workers, these needs are met.

Safety Needs

The second level of need, safety needs, has to do with security. A person must feel that life is secure in order to work well. He will strive for job security, seniority rights, and fringe benefits in order to satisfy safety needs.

[1] Abraham Maslow, *Motivation and Personality*, New York, Harper & Row, 1954.

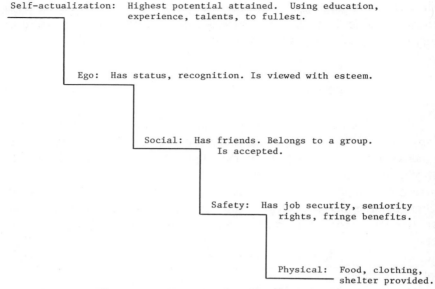

Figure 1-1 *Steps in Man's Fulfillment of Needs*

Social Needs

Man is by nature a social being. A normal person wants to associate with other people, to feel that he belongs to a group and is accepted by the group.

Ego Needs

To satisfy ego needs a person must have status. He must feel recognized, appreciated, and respected. Others must view him as a person of worth in order for his ego needs to be satisfied.

Self-actualization Needs

Self-actualization needs are those which, when met, allow a person to attain his highest potential. When self-actualization needs are being met a person is using his education, experiences, talents, and abilities to their fullest.

Maslow maintains that the physical and safety needs of man are relatively well satisfied in current Western societies. Man will not concern himself with anything beyond safety needs until his physical and safety needs have been met. Ego needs are only moderately satisfied, according to Maslow, and self-actualization needs are rarely ever satisfied.

If a leader will keep in mind the social and ego needs of his followers and do all that he can to satisfy those needs, he will have willing followers. The more he can provide an atmosphere wherein self-actualization can take root and grow, the more motivated his followers will be.

Again, summarizing what we have discovered so far, leaders have in common:

> Motivation
> Power of four kinds:
> > Leader power
> > Goal power
> > Follower power
> > Communication power

By using these four powers, leaders transmit to their followers certain follower powers:

> Self-preservation power
>
> Model power
>
> Goal power
>
> Achievement power
>
> Belonging power
>
> Understanding power

We have also discovered that followers have certain needs in common:

> *Basic needs*: food, clothing, shelter
>
> *Safety needs*: security
>
> *Social needs*: acceptance by others
>
> *Ego needs*: status, recognition
>
> *Self-actualization needs*: opportunity to realize full potential

When followers find their needs being met by their leader they become willing and motivated followers.

DEFENSIVE LEADERSHIP

We can extend the parallel between an automobile engine and a leader to understand what defensive leadership is. So far we have:

Automobile Engine	*Leader*
Ignition started	Leader motivated
Power flowing to all parts of engine	Power flowing to followers
Motor running	Followers performing
Goal: To move the automobile— being accomplished	Goal: To move people— being accomplished

It looks as though everything is going along smoothly. But, as every driver of an automobile knows, unexpected situations develop from time to time. Approaching an intersection you have a green light but you are confronted by someone running a red light. Or rounding a bend on the highway you meet oncoming traffic in your lane. Or a tire blows on the freeway. Leaders, too, are confronted by unexpected situations. A key employee resigns, an emergency comes up, a change becomes necessary, or an employee fails to perform as expected.

Good drivers drive defensively. They take certain precautions to forestall the occurrence of emergency situations. Therefore, they are prepared when the unexpected occurs. Of course, it is not always possible to avert an accident. But we know that defensive drivers have fewer accidents.

Good leaders recognize problems before they become emergencies. They lead defensively, so to speak. By various methods they stay alert to both the job to be done and the workers who do the work. They anticipate problems that are likely to occur and take preventive action. As with driving an automobile, it is not always possible to avert a problem. But we know that leaders who spend time preventing problems have fewer problems to solve.

One defensive action leaders sometimes take is to record information about their encounters with people. A written record made immediately after their encounter is a more accurate reference later on than a memory that can become dimmed after several encounters with different people. Figure 1-2 is a form that you can use

```
        RELATIONSHIP RECORD


Date: _____ Today I talked with: _____
_____

Where? _____ How long? _____

Subject of Conversation: _____
_____
_____
_____

What was accomplished by this conversation? _____
_____
_____

What did I learn about this person?
_____
_____

Degree of this person's openess to me: _____
   (Using a scale of 1 to 5:  1 = closed (hostile)
                              5 = very open (very receptive to me)

Other things I want to remember about this person or this encounter:
_____
_____
_____
```

Figure 1-2

to record significant information concerning your encounters with specific persons. Then, when you are going to converse with one of these individuals again, you can prepare yourself for more success by looking over what transpired the first time you met. You may want to fill out another record after the second meeting if it appears the relationship will continue for a while.

2

Interpersonal Relations
of Leaders

Leadership is a social function. Leaders depend on other people who are their followers to get things done. Therefore, leadership involves a special kind of relationship with other people. In order to have followers, leaders must be able to draw people to them. In this chapter we will discuss how successful leaders use drawing power to establish and keep followers.

FIRST IMPRESSIONS

First of all, a leader has to make a good first impression in any contact he makes with another person. Leonard Zunin, in his book *Contact: The First Four Minutes*, lists what he calls the four Cs always present in a good contact situation.[1] Other elements, such as humor, may also be involved, but these four elements are basic to

---

[1] Leonard Zunin, with Natalie Zunin, *Contact: The First Four Minutes*, New York, Ballantine Books, 1972, p. 12.

a good first impression: confidence, creativity, caring, and consideration.

Confidence

Successful leaders display confidence at all times and especially upon their first encounter with another person. Self-confidence
is not egoism or conceit. Rather, it is a quiet, unassuming attitude of
being in control of oneself and expecting the best outcome of one's
efforts. It is a leader power that comes from within. It is knowing
what you believe and why you believe it. It is knowing where you are
headed and how you plan to get there. Self-confidence is indicative
of inner strength and it is a drawing power. People feel secure around
a person who has inner strength.

Creativity

Leaders with creativity power find ways to tune in on the
thoughts and feelings of others. This is not easy on meeting someone
for the first time; but careful attention to the way the person is
dressed, facial expression, language or vocabulary being used, and the
overall impression the person makes on you will usually give you
some indication of what the person is like and what he may be feeling at that particular moment. It may be boredom, self-doubt, hope,
delight, indecision, or confidence. The more accurate your reading of
the other person, the more appropriate your reaction to him will be
and the more you can draw him to be your follower.

Caring

All successful leaders use lots of caring power. They know
that people want to be heard. The more inept people are at expressing themselves, the less likely they are to be listened to. Some people
go through life without anyone ever having taken time to really listen
to them. These are usually frustrated, unhappy, unfulfilled people. A
successful leader will listen to the other person regardless of who he
or she is, young or old, rich or poor, successful or unsuccessful. We
left out important or unimportant because, as every successful leader
knows, there is no such person as an unimportant person. A person
may not be of very great importance to a given situation. He may not
be a key factor in the solving of a specific problem. But every individual is the most important person in the whole world to himself.

When someone listens to him, he feels drawn to that person. When he is listened to, he feels good about himself, even when the other person has not agreed with his point of view. It helps to build self-esteem.

Consideration

Power-filled leaders radiate a sincere concern that makes one feel better about one's self even in just a brief meeting. Leaders with consideration power know the truth of Goethe's maxim, "Treat people as if they are what they ought to be and you help them to become what they are capable of being." Consideration power is really made up of all the other Cs: confidence, creativity, and caring.

Successful leaders who have drawing power can rouse in any individual a desire to be a better person. And the individual instinctively knows that this desire can be fulfilled in the presence of such a leader.

POWER TOOLS
FOR EXPRESSING LEADERSHIP

As the words to a popular song go, little things mean a lot. There are little things that one uses in everyday interacting with other people that mean a lot. If ignored, they spell disaster to effective leader-follower relationships. But if attended to and used to their best advantage, they are power tools for creating effective leader-follower relationships. These power tools can be grouped into four main categories: nonverbal power tools, verbal power tools, personal power tools, and operational power tools.

Nonverbal Power Tools

Sexuality. Sexuality is a nonverbal power tool available to both men and women who are discreet enough to recognize it. Society has never had a problem with women leading women's groups, such as a sorority, a women's club, the Soroptimist Club, or the PTA whose membership for years was predominantly women teachers and mothers. Why shouldn't a woman lead a women's group? Such a situation entails no competition for leadership between male and female. However, now that more and more women are moving into leadership roles in business, civic, and religious organizations, sexuality becomes an acute problem for many men and women. There are still men and women followers who prefer to work for a man and have difficulty taking orders from a woman. There are women in leadership positions who still feel somewhat out of character leading male followers. There are male leaders who find it hard to accept women as peers.

The problem has two prongs: change and sexuality. While change in the traditional role of women is a change that can affect one emotionally and therefore is more difficult to accept, it is being accepted and handled successfully by men and women leaders. Chapter 19 deals with how effective leaders handle change.

Sexuality, in this context, means the inherent female personality and the inherent male personality. As a rule women are more intuitive than men while men tend to rely more on logic. Women freely express feelings of fear, frustration, and insecurity; men have been taught to hide these feelings. Generally speaking, men are not condemned for showing anger in speech or action; women are expected to be more ladylike and speak in soft tones even when angry.

Effective leaders use sexuality as a power tool by recognizing that men and women *are* different. They seek to complement their own inherent strengths with the inherent strengths of their followers and peers who are of the opposite sex. For example, a male leader may be able to solve a problem using logic, but he would be wise to weigh the ideas of female peers and staff members that may be based on intuition alone. A female leader would do well to weigh the ideas of males offering logical input.

Leaders are assertive. Assertiveness is a trait that most women in leadership roles have had to learn. Effective women leaders have learned how to be assertive without losing any of their femininity. Women who step into a leadership role and think they must act like a man by showing authority, using foul language like some men do, and attempting to emulate male characteristics in dress or mannerisms will have difficulty leading most followers, especially men. Men leaders who rely on nonassertive feminine characteristics usually do not gain the respect of followers. The section on assertiveness under verbal power tools later in this chapter applies equally to men and women leaders.

It is important to remember that other people want to be recognized for their contributions to group achievement. Men and women will always want to feel important. If leaders will keep this human relations fact in mind and conduct themselves accordingly, competition between the sexes because of sex will be negligible.

Posture. Leader posture is a power tool for attracting awareness of you as a leader. Leader posture is the result of your attitude. A successful leader sees himself as immune to disparagement, unfearful of challenge, and beneath nothing and no one. H. W. Gabriel, in his book *Power, Influence, and Control over People,* says the only sure technique so far found that truly brings forth your self-power attitude (leader attitude) is the see-and-be technique.[2] It works like this. Instead of concentrating on a fault, concentrate on yourself as you want to be. See yourself as immune to disparagement, unfearful of challenge, and beneath nothing and no one. If you see yourself in your mind's eye as the successful leader you want to be, you will automatically look the part, feel the part, and behave the part without conscious effort. You will sit straight but comfortably, you will hold your head up, you will have eye contact with people—if this is how you visualize yourself to be.

Recognition. Recognition is another leader tool successful leaders use. Successful leaders form the habit of recognizing others—not necessarily knowing who they are (unless they have met before), but accepting them and giving recognition to their presence.

Stop reading and think about the last stranger you encountered. Could you describe him or her? More important than wearing apparel, do you remember the facial expression? Or is that person someone you were barely conscious of at the time and now is just a blur in your memory?

Recognition power is a big plus in drawing followers. It portrays you as one who is approachable and receptive, one who cares about other people.

To acquire recognition power, become a caring person. To become a caring person, think more about others than you do about yourself and your own activities when you are in the presence of other people. Act as if you are interested in people and you will soon find that you really are. Then recognition power will be a natural part of your personality. Francis Bacon said,

> If a man be gracious and courteous to strangers, it shows he is a citizen of the world, and that his heart is no island cut off from other lands, but a continent that joins them.

[2]H. W. Gabriel, *Twenty Steps to Power, Influence, and Control over People*, Englewood Cliffs, N.J., Prentice-Hall, 1962, p. 38.

Smile. A smile is a power tool that anyone can use. Dale Carnegie says in *How to Win Friends and Influence People* that you must have a good time meeting people if you expect them to have a good time meeting you.[3] No one can deny the drawing power of a sincere, heart-warming smile. A synthetic smile won't do. It must be a natural smile that is evidence of a smiling spirit within. Who can resist the joyous greeting a dog gives his master when he returns home after being gone only a short time? Your smile should be as sincere as that. If you are smiling inside, you won't have to be concerned about your facial expression. Your face will smile if you smile.

The only trouble with that theory is that often we are not smiling on the inside and certainly don't feel like smiling on the outside. Perhaps we are too preoccupied with other things to muster up a smile. Can one smile sincerely when one doesn't feel like smiling? Think back and try to remember the times when you were happy and smiling was easy. Perhaps it was just yesterday when you were engrossed in whatever you were doing and your enthusiasm was high. Were you ever enthused about something and did not feel like smiling about it?

Smile power is acquired in the same way recognition power is acquired—by becoming a caring person. Get enthused about meeting people. Start caring enthusiastically about the people you meet. A smile enriches those who receive it. Get enthused about enriching the lives of other people and you will have enough smile power and to spare. And if they don't smile back? Well, no one needs a smile so much as the one who has no smile to give. So keep on smiling and people will be warmed by your smiles and drawn to you.

Of course, there are times when a smile would be entirely inappropriate, as when expressing sympathy. At such times a warm, sincere attitude has the same effect as a smile—because it is born out of caring for the other person.

Handshake. People shake hands for numerous reasons—as a greeting, to say goodbye, to confirm a pact, to congratulate, to accept a challenge, to end a disagreement, to comply with simple courtesy, and so forth. A handshake is a communicating device. It is most often used with words but it is a powerful communication tool even without words. Sometimes it communicates in spite of words and sends a different message than the words that are spoken.

A minister stands at the door of the church building to

[3] Dale Carnegie, *How to Win Friends and Influence People*, New York, Simon and Schuster, 1936, p. 68.

shake hands with the parishioners as they leave the service. Why? Too often only because it is customary. A customary handshake is no better than a hand-powered lawn mower. It's sheer tedium. On the other hand (no pun intended), a purposeful handshake can be likened to a power mower. It's easier and it accomplishes more in less time.

If the handshake is to be used as a power tool, it must have power in it. It can't be limp, wishy-washy, cold, or clammy. It should be as warm as your smile ought to be, and as firm as the sincerity of your purpose. If your purpose as a parishioner is to congratulate the preacher on the eloquence of his oration, shake hands as though you are really impressed with the sermon. If your purpose is to thank the preacher for bringing inspiration to you, shake hands as though you are really inspired. If your purpose, as the preacher, is to convey your love and goodwill to the parishioners, be really interested in the person attached to each hand you shake. This means that you will give that person your full attention while shaking his hand. You will not be looking over his shoulder at someone else. You will not allow someone else to engage you in conversation. I have known ministers who appreciate the response of individual members of the congregation after the service and who wonder why some individuals never bother to go through the line to shake their hands. One reason might be that these individuals have found the handshake to be perfunctory and, therefore, they feel it is not important.

In *Contact: The First Four Minutes*, Leonard Zunin says:

> The one type of handshake which inevitably turns people off is usually termed "the dead fish." Whether the hand is dry or clammy, a flaccid grip connotes indifference, an impression that may be reinforced in far less than four minutes. However, a moist palm may merely show someone is nervous, a symbol which automatically eliminates any job applicant at at least one large company of which I am aware. Its personnel director once told me that regardless of the qualifications of a man he interviews, "if his handshake is weak and clammy, he's out." Such reaction to body language is probably far more prevalent than we realize, as others assume many things about our glance, stance, or advance.[4]

The handshake is a power tool used by successful leaders of both sexes. Most women now feel that either sex should have the

[4] Zunin, *Contact*, p. 106.

option of being first to extend a hand when meeting or departing. The long-established custom was for the woman to initiate a handshake, but that custom is disappearing. In a poll of over 500 women it was noted that most women prefer a moderately firm handshake from a man. The main thrust of the grip should be on the hand, not on the fingers. Women, and sometimes men, often wear rings that cause pain when the fingers are squeezed together too tightly.

Dress. John T. Malloy in *Dress for Success* says one should always use clothing as a tool.[5] Just as packaging is important to the sale of a product, the way you package yourself is equally important to selling yourself. Others pay attention to the one who is dressed appropriately for the place and the activity, the one whose clothes fit, the one who is groomed and neat.

Here are some dress rules you can follow that will help establish your credibility as a leader in whatever business or nonbusiness leadership role you may have. These rules apply equally to men and women.

1. Do not fall prey to designers' seasonal styles. Just because a certain style is in vogue is no reason to go out and stock up on clothing of that style. In the first place, it may be entirely unsuitable for you, your physical build, and/or your personality. It may not be suitable for the places you go or the leadership position you hold.

2. Have a basic wardrobe which you can dress up or dress down to suit the occasion. Women can add fashion to a basic dress or suit by selecting appropriate accessories. Men can do the same to a basic suit by careful selection of shirt, tie, and so forth.

One of the best buys for a well-rounded wardrobe for men or women is a navy blue blazer. A man can wear it with tan or gray trousers for business, over an open-necked shirt for a casual dinner, or even with white pants and shoes at a resort. A woman can wear it over a dress, with a skirt, or with pants.

A woman would be wise to buy two suits of coordinating colors for business. She could then combine the suit blazers with dressy pants and blouse for evening wear.

3. Select materials with care. A blend of wool and polyester (usually 45/55 percent) wears well. Most uniforms are made from such a blend. It is comfortable and wrinkle-resistant—a very practical fiber. Linings are important, especially in suits. The lining

[5] John T. Molloy, *Dress for Success*, New York, Peter H. Wyden, 1975, p. 237.

helps the garment hold its shape. It is well worth the extra cost.

4. Select accessories that will give you a well-coordinated look. For men, belt, shoes, and socks should be the same color. However, black socks can be worn with any color shoe. Do not adorn yourself with too much jewelry. Better to wear no jewelry than jewelry that draws attention to itself and away from the wearer by being too flashy or too noisy.

5. Be sure clothes fit properly. Too-tight clothes portray sexuality and too-loose clothing results in a sloppy look. Clothes that fit properly help the wearer's leadership image.

Looking sharp is feeling sharp. If you want to feel confident and have credibility, wardrobe planning is well worth the effort.

Verbal Power Tools

Nothing will make or break a leader quicker than the use or misuse of verbal power tools. It is by what you say and how you say it that people judge you most often.

To use verbal power effectively, it is necessary to understand how verbal power functions. The basic fact that must be understood to comprehend how verbal power functions is that *communication is not a one-person act*. It takes both a sender and a receiver; and both sender and receiver must function according to the rules of communication. In a forward pass on the gridiron the ball is thrown by a back to an eligible receiver running downfield. If the receiver fails to catch the ball, the pass is termed incomplete. Similarly, in communication a person sends a message to another person. If the other person fails to receive or "catch" the message that was sent, communication is incomplete. But unlike football where there is only one ball to catch or not catch, in communication the receiver may receive a message that is not the message sent by the sender. In other words, the message sent may be misunderstood by the receiver, in which case again communication is incomplete.

Even though the receiver has received the identical message that was sent by the sender, in the game of communication there is still one more play to be played. The receiver now must in some way let the sender know that he has received the message. This play is called "feedback." In football, the back knows the receiver has received the ball when he runs with it. In communication the sender knows the receiver has received the message when he feeds it back to the sender. Feedback is illustrated in Figure 2-1.

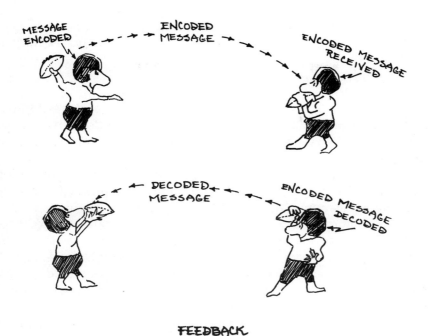

Figure 2-1

In the illustration, the sender encoded a message and directed it to the receiver. The receiver received a message, decoded it, and directed it to the sender. If the decoded message is identical to the encoded message, communication has been completed. But if the decoded message is different from the encoded message, communication is incomplete. The sender now tries again to encode the message in such a way as the receiver will be able to decode it and come up with the same message. Conversationally, the process may sound like this:

> *Sender*: Jones suggested to Smith that he drive his car. So he'll pick you up at nine o'clock.
>
> *Receiver*: Smith will pick me up at nine in Jones' car.
>
> *Sender*: No. Jones will pick you up at nine.
>
> *Receiver*: Jones is driving Smith's car and he'll pick me up at nine.
>
> *Sender*: No! No! Jones is driving his own car. Smith will pick you up at nine with Jones.
>
> *Receiver*: That's what I thought you said. Smith will pick me up at nine in Jones' car.

> *Sender*: No, that's not it! Smith and Jones, er, I mean, Smith or Jones—somebody will be by for you. Just be ready at nine!
>
> *Receiver*: Gotcha! I'll be ready at nine.

Purpose, Editing, and Timing. Effective conversation is a matter of purpose, editing, and timing. The biblical Book of Proverbs admonishes, "Seest thou a man that is hasty in his words? There is more hope of a fool than of him."[6]

Conversation can be divided into impromptu conversation and planned conversation. Both impromptu and planned conversations are made more effective by careful editing and timing.

Impromptu conversation is the small talk we exchange with friends and acquaintances on coffee breaks, at a party, in the supermarket, or wherever we happen to meet them. Often small talk is of little value as far as real communication is concerned. At the end of the conversation it is doubtful that either person has acquired any new information. Successful leaders, however, recognize and seize every opportunity to draw people to them. A chance meeting is a good opportunity to learn something about another person or to influence another person favorably toward yourself.

To have purpose behind every conversation is good, but if conversation rambles, as it so often does unless you have edited your conversation beforehand, you are not likely to fulfill your purpose. To edit your conversation simply means to think before you speak. If you start your automobile engine running, it will merely idle and the car will go nowhere unless you give it direction by putting it in gear. It is the same with conversation. Compare the following conversations between Mary Munro, personnel director for XYZ Company, and Hal Harris, data-processing director for ABC Company, who meet unexpectedly at a subway station and have about three minutes to chat.

First Conversation:

> *Hal*: Well, if it isn't Mary Monro! Hi! How are you anyway?
>
> *Mary*: Hal! I never thought I'd be meeting you today!
>
> *Hal*: Small world, isn't it?
>
> *Mary*: Let's see. I guess the last time we saw each other was six months ago at the Kiwanis convention. Remember? Ted and I ran into you and Jane in the hotel lobby.

[6] Proverbs, 29:20.

Hal: Yes, I remember. How is Ted?

Mary: Oh, he's doing great. How about Jane?

The conversation rambles on in this vein until Mary's train arrives. As the train starts up and Mary staggers to a seat she remembers that she has been meaning to talk to Hal about an applicant who was in her office yesterday.

Second Conversation:

Hal: Well, if it isn't Mary Monro!

Mary: Hal, it's good to see you. What a coincidence—I need to talk with you.

Hal: Really? What about?

Mary: Chris Curtis applied for a position we have open in our Data-processing Department. Says she worked for you as a keypunch operator before her present job. How do you feel about her as an employee?

Hal: She was dependable—a little slow, but always accurate. Nice kid. Where is she working now?

Mary: She's head keypunch operator with Smith and Company. She's going to night school and wants to advance. We're considering her as a programmer.

Hal: She's a learner and an eager one. If she says she can do the job, I'd be willing to bet she can do it a hundred percent.

Mary: Thanks, Hal. Sure glad I ran into you today. There's my train. Say hello to Jane for me.

As the train pulled out of the station Mary leaned back in her seat, smiled, and thought, There's one of tomorrow's objectives taken care of.

Timing is also important. To know when to talk and when not to talk is as important as knowing what to say. Suppose Hal's and Mary's conversation had gone like this:

Hal: Well, if it isn't Mary Monro from XYZ!

Mary: Hello, Hal. It's nice to see you again.

Hal: Well, I'm glad I recognized you. I'd hardly recognize my own mother after a day like today.

Mary: You had a bad day.

> *Hal*: Anything that could go wrong went wrong, believe me. Do you ever have days like that, Mary?
>
> *Mary*: I guess we all have a bad day now and then. Can I do anything to help?
>
> *Hal*: Well, not really, I guess. It helps just to know you can have a bad day, too.
>
> *Mary*: Yes, and when I do, I feel like you're feeling now. But one thing about it—tomorrow is a clean page to make a fresh start.
>
> *Hal*: Well, at least that's good to кnow. Thanks for listening, Mary. I feel better already.
>
> *Mary*: I'm glad. There's my train. Give Jane my love.

Mary wisely avoided the subject of Chris Curtis at this meeting because obviously Hal could not have been objective in his evaluation of Chris at this particular time. He was too concerned with his own problems.

Well-planned conversation pays high dividends in leader power. People notice and respect a person who can carry on an effective conversation with ease. An effective conversation is one where both parties feel they have been understood by the other person and where useful information has been exchanged. Preplanning conversation will usually result in an effective exchange. When planning for a conversation give attention to purpose, editing, and timing. The following suggestions are aimed at helping you do this:

1. Putting purpose in your conversation is knowing what you want to say, saying it, and omitting everything else. Without purpose you may ramble, forget what you want to say, repeat what you have already said, or never come to the point. With purpose you will come across as one who has purpose and direction—a leader in any conversation situation.

2. Part of editing conversation is talking to the right person, in the right place, and in the right way. If your utilities bill seems unreasonable, don't talk to the switchboard operator at the utility company about it (except to inquire to whom you should talk). To explain or complain to the switchboard operator would be a waste of your time and the operator's. Such conversation would be totally ineffective because the switchboard operator could do nothing about the situation. Save your conversation for the person who has the authority to do something about the situation.

Also, consider whether the telephone is the right place for the conversation to take place. Might better results be attained by an eyeball-to-eyeball conversation? If so, should the conversation occur in your office or in the other person's office; in a formal setting such as an office or in an informal setting such as the employees' lunchroom or on the fifteenth hole? Choosing the right place to converse on a specific topic sets the desired mood and helps make the other person receptive to what you have to say.

Tactfully is the right way to talk to anyone. Tact is a sixth sense that makes you aware of what is appropriate at a given moment. Tact involves empathy—a feeling for the other person's needs and desires. Effective leaders use a lot of tact in their conversations. Tact is a must if you want to draw people to you. You are using tact when

1. You attack the issue and not the person.
2. You discuss and don't argue.
3. You are careful about your tone.

To improve your tone develop empathy. If you feel what the other person is feeling, you will be less apt to speak in a tone that would be downgrading to the other person or inappropriate for the situation.

Editing conversation also consists of organizing your thoughts. If a conversation is not impromptu, take time to write down on a slip of paper or 3 X 5 card key words to help you present your thoughts in logical order without overlooking important points. If you will practice doing this when you know you are going to converse with someone, you will soon be able to organize your thoughts mentally even in impromptu situations. You will find fewer deadly "uh's" and "er's" cluttering up your conversation.

3. Timing is talking to the right person at the right time. To help yourself do this keep a pocket-size notebook with you at all times. As subjects about which you want to talk to specific individuals occur to you, jot them down in your notebook. Review your notebook several times a day to keep these thoughts in your mind. You can glance at your notebook while waiting for an elevator, your car, or for your party to come on the line when using the telephone. When you meet one of the people for whom you have recorded a topic in your notebook, either by appointment or impromptu (as

Mary did in our previous example), you will have in mind an important topic of conversation.

Perceiving the Other Person. Webster offers the following definitions:

- To hear: to perceive (sounds) by the ear
- To listen: to attend closely, so as to hear
- To perceive: to obtain knowledge through the senses . . . to understand.

One person turns on the stereo and only hears music. Another person turns on the stereo, hears the same music, but listens to the sopranos, tenors, and basses. Still another person turns on the stereo, hears the same music, listens to the same tones, but also perceives the message and the feeling of the musical arrangement. This last person, the perceiver, feels through all his senses to get a complete understanding of the music. A successful leader uses his power of perception in every conversation to gain as much knowledge and understanding as he can, not only of what is being said, but of the other person as well.

To perceive in conversation you need not only your ears, but your eyes, heart, and mind as well. Perceiving is accomplished by observing what is said, how it is said, what is left unsaid, and other nonverbal signs such as facial expression, posture, grooming, and so forth.

Like the automobile driver, the perceiver keeps an eye out for traffic lights. These are his listener's signals of enjoyment, attentiveness, and receptiveness, or of boredom, irritation, and frustration.

Aggressive Perception. One of the verbal power tools used by successful leaders is aggressive perception. Aggressive perception is controlling how people talk to you. You can do this by:

1. Asking questions such as "How do you know that?" "Who are the 'they' you refer to?" "Can you cite a specific instance?" Sometimes people will attempt to give you information not based on fact. They do this because of a need to feel important and knowledgeable and the desire to have you recognize them as important and knowledgeable. Don't swallow information that does not seem reasonable to you. If you do, it will make you appear gullible to the other person and lessen your leadership status.

2. Not allowing people to gossip to you. When you listen

to a gossiper you bond with him and put yourself on his level. Again, ask questions: "Where did you hear it?" "Do you believe it?" "Why?" "Who started the rumor?" "What was the purpose?" "Why are you telling me this?"

3. Not letting people advise you. People enjoy giving advice, asked for or not, from how to treat a cold to how to invest your money. You may have hired some of these people to advise you, such as your lawyer, broker, agent, or assistant. Actually, what you want from such people is facts and possibly opinions based on technical knowledge which you may not have. The successful leader welcomes facts and opinions, but not advice. Facts and opinions are the basis upon which a leader makes up his own mind—not advice.

Persuasion. To get people to follow you—to think the way you think or do what you want them to do—use persuasion tools. Here are some persuasion rules successful leaders use as tools to bring people around to their point of view.

1. Always avoid an argument. Discuss but don't argue. If the other person seems bent on having an argument rather than a discussion and you cannot bring him around to calmly discussing the issue, it reveals greater leadership for you to walk away from the argument than it does for you to join in the argument. If the issue is of great importance to the other person, he will broach the subject again when calmed down and will let you take the lead in setting the tone of the discussion. If you are the one to whom the issue is of great importance and the other person insists on arguing, it is still better to walk away from the argument and find another way to get your point across later. Keep your discussion impersonal. Attack the issue, not the person. It never helps your leadership image to run down another person no matter how wrong he may be.

2. Never tell a person he is wrong even if it's true. All that would accomplish is a deflation of the other person's ego. A true leader tries to fulfill the needs of followers, not create needs. The most persuasive leaders are those who can satisfy the ego needs of other people. Rather than saying, "You are wrong," say, "You may be right but what do you think of this, . . ." In other words, show respect for the other person's opinions.

3. If you are wrong, admit it quickly. You will not be blamed for being wrong as much as you will be admired for admitting an error.

4. Begin friendly. A smile never hurt a sale.

5. Begin with agreement. Open the discussion with a statement with which the other person must agree. If you can get the other person to agree with you, it will be harder for him to disagree with you when you broach the main issue.

6. Let the other person talk. He may talk himself right into your point of view.

7. Give credit even where it's not due. You may have done such a good job of persuading that the other person gets the notion that the idea you have been trying to get across is his. Your goal was to change someone's thinking. You have accomplished your goal and that is far more important than who gets the credit for the idea.

8. Use plenty of empathy. Honestly try to see things from the other person's point of view. Be sympathetic to his ideas and wants. By doing so you may learn something that will make your task of persuasion easier.

9. Throw a stimulating question into the discussion—one that will cause the other person to think and perhaps come up with an answer that convinces him that you are right after all.

10. Dramatize your idea. If your idea lends itself to a story, tell a short story that will bring out the point you want to make.

11. Fill a need. Every human act is a response to a personal need. The more intense the need, the more intense the response. Therefore, to persuade one to your way of thinking, show that person how he will benefit by thinking as you do or by doing what you want him to do. A person will react as you want him to if he recognizes his own need to do so.

12. Be enthusiastic. Enthusiasm based on the power of conviction can perform miracles. Believe what you are saying and your conviction will be evident in your enthusiasm. By enthusiasm we do not mean high-pressure loud or fast talking. This is simulated enthusiasm that often creates resistance rather than confidence. It may sway some people temporarily but its effect is short-lived. We are talking about sincere enthusiasm based on your inner belief in what you are selling, whether that be an idea or a product. This kind of enthusiasm is a drawing power that can influence your most stubborn opponent.

Assertion. It is important to make a distinction among nonassertive, assertive, and aggressive behavior.

A nonassertive person is one who is self-denying, inhibited, anxious, easily hurt. A nonassertive person allows others to choose for him and seldom achieves a desired goal. He feels guilty when criticized and will usually find personal fault with the critic.

An aggressive person is at the extreme opposite end of the scale from the nonassertive person. An aggressive person is self-enhancing at the expense of others, critical of others, and chooses for others. He achieves goals by hurting others. When criticized the aggressive person will not admit mistakes and seeks to place blame elsewhere.

In the middle is the assertive person. This person feels good about himself and is outgoing and self-enhancing, but not at the expense of others. He makes his own decisions and usually achieves desired goals. He learns from criticism and can discuss the criticism openly with his critic.

It is obvious that the nonassertive person is no leader. But what about the aggressive personality? History records many aggressive individuals who have led a people or ruled an empire. But such people are tyrants, dictators, drivers—not leaders as we have defined a leader. We have said a leader is one who has willing followers. Hitler was a leader for only as long as the German people thought he was filling their need. His true role of tyrant or dictator later became evident even to his own people.

Obviously the assertive personality is the only kind of personality that becomes effective leadership. You can express assertive leadership verbally in the following ways:

1. By listening to find out what is interesting or important to the other person. This will give you more self-assurance when entering into conversation. It will help you to prompt others to talk more easily about themselves. Assertive leaders usually wait a few seconds before speaking, even to answer a question. This makes them appear thoughtful and gives more credibility to what they say.

2. By disciplining yourself to accept and disclose information about how you think and feel and what is important to you.

3. By calmly and repetitively saying what you want. Often others will try to manipulate your desires to match their own. Calmly repeating your desire will make you feel comfortable in ignoring manipulative traps, arguments, and irrelevant logic. For example, suppose you want to return a purchase and receive a refund. The store clerk or manager does not want to refund your money and tries to interest you in an exchange. Simply repeat as often as necessary, "I want a refund."

4. By being open, honest, and direct with people when you criticize. Suppose someone has an irritating habit of interrupting you when you are telling a story or making a point. Realize that *you* have the problem, not the person who interrupts. He is likely unaware that there is a problem. So the problem is yours. Approach the problem by stating how it makes you feel—not by putting down the other person or telling him how to act. Instead of saying, "You have a bad habit of interrupting," say, "I get irritated when you interrupt me." The first statement puts the other person on the defensive. No one likes to be criticized, and so he feels hurt and put down. In the second statement, you have not put him down. You have only said how his action makes you feel. The second statement, while still a criticism, lets the other person save face and leaves the door open for him to change.

SPEECH: THE LUBRICANT
FOR YOUR VERBAL POWER TOOLS

Your ability to speak confidently, concisely, and convincingly is vital to your success as a leader. No matter how you assemble your phrases and sentences, if your pronunciation is faulty, if your tone is tarnished, or if your grammar is unclear, your leadership qualities will not come across to those who hear you. Your voice can make you sound older than you are, tired, frustrated, discouraged. But it can also make you sound young, vibrant, clear, and optimistic. The choice is yours.

Self-evaluation

Do you know how you sound to others? Chances are you don't unless you have heard a recording of your voice. Most people upon hearing a recording of their voice for the first time are astonished at how it sounds. We simply don't hear ourselves as others hear us.

The first step to evaluate your speech is to record it. You can record your own voice while reading or talking with someone. A better way would be to have a friend record your voice when you don't know it is being recorded. This way your natural speech will be recorded. If you know you are being recorded, you are apt to correct some speech flaws which you habitually make. Also, if you know you are being recorded, a certain amount of nervousness or self-consciousness will show up and you will not get a recording of your natural voice.

Negative characteristics to watch for when you play back the recording are nasality, stridency, hoarseness, mumbling, slurring, lack of projection (do your sentences fade away before reaching the end?), monotony of pitch, speed (do you speak too fast? or too slow?), and speech tics such as "oh's," "er's," and "ya know's."

Just being aware of some of these characteristics is half the battle of correcting them. You may need professional help to correct some others. There are helpful speech books available at the public library and at your bookstore. *Speech Can Change Your Life* by Dorothy Sarnoff, published by Doubleday, is one, and there are many others.

Vocabulary

An easy flowing, easily understood vocabulary is a mark of a leader. If you can express yourself vividly, confidently, and concisely, people will listen. Your selection of words is important. Here are some thoughts to keep in mind as you choose your words.

1. A familiar word is better than an unfamiliar word.

2. A short word is better than a long one.

3. Pompous words and phrases will turn off your hearers.

4. Watch for feedback from the people you converse with. If they seem to be puzzled or if you have to explain too often, you may be using terminology unfamiliar to them.

5. If possible, use the terminology that is familiar to your listener. For example, if you are a salesperson talking to a prospective customer who is in the hardware business, talk in hardware language.

6. Give attention to proper pronunciation. Improper pronunciation confuses your listener and lessens your credibility.

7. If you have an accent, keep it if you like; but eliminate the part that is disagreeable to most people or that is difficult for them to understand. Some regional accents are pleasant to the ear and are often an asset if they are clearly understood. Ivy in *The Grapes of Wrath* expressed it well when she said, "Everybody says words different, Arkansas folks say 'em different, and Oklahomy

folks says 'em different. And we seen a lady from Massachusetts, an'
she said 'em differentest of all. Couldn't hardly make out what she
was sayin'."[7]

8. Avoid using profanity. Some people think this kind of
language adds emphasis or expression to what they say. Actually, all
it does is reveal a poor vocabulary and a dependence on feeling rather
than logic. It connotes poor leadership qualities in the speaker.

9. Watch for monotony. Are you using the same words or
phrases over and over?

10. Learn a new word every day and use it in your conversation until it is at home in your vocabulary.

Dorothy Sarnoff, in *Speech Can Change Your Life*, says:

> A positive speech image can help you as much as a negative one can
> hurt you. Advertising tycoon Mary Wells, who took Madison Avenue
> by storm, is unexcelled at creating fresh, effective advertising cam-
> paigns; but her rise would not have been so meteoric were it not, as
> columnist Eugenia Sheppard remarked, that "Her soft, thrilling voice
> makes the maddest ideas seem perfectly possible." Your speech
> image can be your greatest asset—or your worst liability. Make it
> work for you, not against you.[8]

---

[7]John Steinbeck, *The Grapes of Wrath*, New York, Viking Press, 1939, p. 184. ©1939 by
John Steinbeck. Copyright © renewed by John Steinbeck, 1967.

[8]Dorothy Sarnoff, *Speech Can Change Your Life*, Garden City, N.Y., Doubleday, 1970,
p. 7.

3

Personal
Power Tools

In Chapter 2 we discussed how verbal power and nonverbal power affect leader-follower relationships. In this chapter personal power will be discussed.

There are six personal power tools that effective leaders use to establish and maintain leader effectiveness in any group situation. Think of them as the six Ps: possibility thinking, political sense, prior achievement, poise, pliability, and principles.

POSSIBILITY THINKING

Possibility thinking is not false optimism. The person who cheerily says, "Cheer up—everything will turn out all right" is not necessarily using possibility thinking. The possibility thinker can see, very specifically, the opportunities in any situation. Helen Keller once said, "When one door closes, another opens; but often we look so long at the closed door that we do not see the one that has been opened for us." The possibility thinker can see alternatives in most situations. This is sometimes called lateral thinking as opposed to vertical thinking. Vertical thinkers see black and white and think in terms of yes and no. Lateral thinkers see a rainbow of colors and think in terms of either and or. The possibility thinker recognizes human worth. He knows there is creative power in every individual. He brings out the good in people and helps them to see their own worth.

Possibility thinking might also be termed creative anticipation. It's the ability to expect the best of oneself and others. Emerson once said that what you deeply expect is what you tend to get. Creatively imagine the result you want to achieve and you will probably achieve it.

Possibility thinking results in enthusiasm. Enthusiam results in possibility thinking. Effective leaders look for the best, expect the best, and work enthusiastically for the best.

POLITICAL SENSE

For some people the word *politics* carries a connotation of something scheming and dishonest. The many are often labeled by the actions of the few and in this manner politicians, political practices, and politics have often been labeled. Aristotle said that man is a political animal; and indeed, wherever people interact with one another within a group, in a club or organization, politics is present. If you want to be the leader of a group, you must have some political acumen, not so much to become leader for that could be bestowed upon you by appointment, but to maintain leadership effectively.

Games people play, sometimes innocently but often with intent, are aimed at either dethroning the leader, slowing progress, frustrating group goals, or establishing leadership power with themselves or someone other than the one who is currently leading.

Whether you are the director of a volunteer organization, the president of a service club, or a corporate executive, you need to be able to recognize politics when it is being used by others and know how to use politics to your own advantage.

Political games used by group members are innumerable and new ones are invented every day. Here are a few of the more common ones that a leader should be aware of and the action a leader can take to neutralize their effects.

The Look-at-Me Game

There are few groups that do not have at least one person who plays the "look-at-me" game. This person never misses an opportunity to point out to everyone how much he or she contributes to the group. This person usually gets into an important spot in the group—does a specific job no one else wants to do or can do, but one that must be done—then constantly reminds the other group members how important this function is and how much he does for the group. This person becomes powerful whenever the group wants to take an action that is dependent or related to the responsibility that this person holds. The look-at-me player can help or hinder the cause and no one does anything about it because he is, or is believed to be, indispensable.

A wise leader will be certain that there is a backup person for each major job to be done. If there is only one person who can do an important job and that person becomes indisposed for any reason, the job cannot be done if there is not a backup person to step in and fill the gap.

The Foot-dragging Game

Some group members, given an assignment, will not follow through or will do so at a snail's pace, thus slowing the progress of the entire group. A group member may muff an assignment for a number of reasons: failure to understand the assignment, unsure of authority to go ahead, no deadline established for completion of assignment, or lack of interest in the assignment.

The group leader can usually avoid foot dragging by making the proper assignments. Be sure to assign the job to someone who is actively interested in the group's goals, someone who wants to see the group succeed. Pick someone who can do the job. For example, don't assign a letter-writing project to someone who cannot put words together clearly, can't spell, or hates letter writing. Be sure the assignment is thoroughly understood by the assignee. Get feedback from the assignee when you delegate the job to be certain the assignee understands what the assignment is, what result is desired, and what authority the assignee has to do the job (such as the authority to appoint other group members to help or the authority to make decisions). The leader should establish, alone or with the group's or assignee's help, a date for completion of the assignment. This is of utmost importance if the assignment is not to drag on indefinitely. If it is a long assignment, one that will take several weeks to complete, mid-assignment dates for the assignee to report progress to the group or to the leader should be established along with the final completion date.

The Grapevine Game

Rumors often get started innocently by a misunderstanding of something someone heard. However, malicious gossip, that is, gossip aimed at destroying, is usually started with forethought and purpose. Rumor and gossip are carried by the grapevine. These juicy fruits grow bigger and bigger as the vine grows and entwines itself around every group member.

You cannot suppress a grapevine. You may as well resign yourself to living with it and attempting to do something about the poisonous rumors and half-truths spread by the grapevine. What can you do?

Use the grapevine to your own advantage. Listen to your group members. Find out what they really think, what they want to know, and how they feel about things. Make a checklist of subjects in which your group members are interested. Then graft facts into the grapevine. Pure, organic fact is the best pesticide for killing rumors.

There are two ways to graft a grapevine. You can graft it yourself by simply telling group members the information you want them to have and pass on. Or you can be more selective as to which branch on which to graft your information. This is a better approach if the grapevine is already circulating a rumor about you personally. If you were to announce to everyone that the rumor is false, you might be believed and you might not. "After all," some might say, "he is trying to cover up, make excuses, or defend himself." The person you pick to start your factual information growing on the grapevine should be someone the other group members respect. This person should not be your best friend. Choose a person who is noncontroversial, one whom you believe is open-minded, fair, and objective. If he is a person you would trust, in all probability your group members will trust him also.

The Clique Game

In large groups cliques sometimes form. There may be one clique recognized as the "in" group and everyone else is on the outside. This clique may be nothing more than a social group that has drawn a circle around itself and has as little to do as possible with anyone outside the circle. The social clique may be ever so harmless today, but it could become dangerous tomorrow. Most cliques are self-centered, with their own desires above that of the entire group. All a clique needs is a cause that is contrary to the group's goal or a target (leader or other group member) to pounce on, and you have a real leadership problem.

The best approach a leader can take to this game is, of course, to prevent it from happening in the first place. This is not always possible, but a few precautionary steps on the part of the leader will help ensure the unity of the group.

1. Identify the people in your group to whom others seem to be attracted. These are the potential clique leaders. Remember that all cliques do not have ulterior motives for the group, but all cliques tend to divide the group.
2. Give these potential clique leaders something to do. Include them in planning and decision making. Appoint them chairpersons of committees. Keep them busy so that they do not have time to develop their own "axe to grind."
3. Involve as many group members as possible in planning sessions. People tend to support what they have helped create. Involve as many group members as possible in decision making. They will stand behind their own decisions.
4. When it is not possible to include all group members in planning and decision making, be sure those that will be affected by a decision are included at least to the extent that their opinions have been asked for.
5. Whenever you take action as a leader, be sure the what, why, when, who, where, and how of your action are thoroughly understood by all.
6. Take a personal interest in individual group members. If they regard you as a friend, they will not be as apt to join someone who opposes you or your goals.

Suppose a clique has formed and is proving to be destructive to group unity. The worst thing you, as the group's leader, could do is to sit on the fence. Like Humpty Dumpty you will have a great fall if you do because you will likely alienate both sides. It would be equally dangerous to take sides because in doing so you would be abdicating leadership of the other side. Some things you could do are:

1. Be aware of the dispute but not a part of it. In other words, don't pretend it doesn't exist.
2. Clear any communication channel that may have become clogged so that information can flow from leader to group members and from members to leader freely.
3. Reemphasize the group's purposes and goals to all group members.
4. Don't let the dispute continue without taking some action to check it. The longer you wait to take action, the bigger the dispute will grow, more people will become involved, more damage to group morale will result, and the more difficult it will be to deal with the cause of the dispute.

The action you take will, of course, depend on the situation. But it is safe to say that face-to-face encounter offers the best chance for successful resolution of conflict. Plan a meeting with the leaders of the dispute. The most important word in the previous sentence is *plan*. A meeting to resolve conflict must be thoroughly planned ahead. This does not mean that the leader has predetermined the outcome of the meeting. It does mean that the leader has prepared himself with the proper attitude with which to engage in the meeting. It means that the proper place, time, persons, and so forth have been determined prior to the actual meeting. Without preplanning a leader could be drawn into the argument and wind up on one side or the other.

The leader's attitude is the most important aspect of the meeting. If the leader goes into such a meeting determined to be the "boss" and lays down the law and makes demands, he may get an alleviation of the conflict temporarily but he will not have resolved the problem. The old feelings will remain and be intensified. Consider an automobile that has stalled. You can push it and it will move as long as you keep pushing it. But if you want it to move when you stop pushing it, the power to move it must come from its own engine.

When an automobile has stalled you sometimes need to give it a push to get it started. Similarly, you may need to push a little to influence the persons in the meeting to exert their own power to resolve the conflict. Begin by being very clear and honest about the conflict. Point out the effect it is having on the group as a whole, on you as the group leader, and on the effectiveness of the entire group. In doing this be impersonal. The conflict is the cause of the problem, not the people involved. It will be easier for both sides to look at the conflict objectively than to look at themselves as the problem.

After you have laid out the problem, let others talk. In a 45-minute discussion, you should be talking about 10 minutes. You cannot convince people to change. They convince themselves. Your role in the meeting should be one of discussion leader, keeping the conversation on the subject under discussion, and keeping the discussion on an impersonal basis as much as possible.

The language you use is important. It can help unite meeting participants in one objective, which should be to resolve the conflict.

1. Don't talk about individuals. Do describe the situation.
2. Don't interpret the behavior of others. Do observe and report without your personal interpretation.
3. Don't judge. Describe without evaluating.
4. Don't talk about the past. Talk about the here and now.
5. Don't give advice or answers. Share ideas and explore options.
6. Don't ask, "Why?" Ask, "How can we . . .?"

Sometimes an argument will arise between two group members, neither a part of any clique. As long as the productivity of your group is not being adversely affected by the argument, the leader should stay out of it. The two group members will likely be able to iron out their difficulty themselves. If the leader gets involved, the members have the added problem of saving face in front of the leader. It will be harder for the difficulty to be resolved, and if it is resolved in favor of one over the other, resentment is apt to remain with the other. However, if the effectiveness of the group as a whole is being adversely affected by the disagreement between two members of the group, then the leader should meet with the two members in much the same way as if a clique were involved.

If a clique or individual member sets out to undermine your position as leader of the group, meet with that individual. Lay the problem on the table and try to get at the cause. Why does he feel the way he does about you? The answer to this question may reveal that a basic need is not being met. It may be a need for recognition.

If this is the problem, you can relieve the difficulty by "positive stroking"—praise him for what he does well. Be sure your praise is for something specific and is given in all honesty. Insincere flattery would be recognized immediately and result in a worsening of the situation. It may be that the cause of the hostility is a misunderstanding of some information he received directly or indirectly. This should be easy to straighten out. The main thing is not to place blame.

The discussion may bring out that his feelings are justified. Perhaps you have been at fault. If so, admit it quickly. Show that you have the good of the individual group members and the group as a whole at heart, that you are sincere in wanting the group to succeed even if it means you must change.

PRIOR ACHIEVEMENT

Leaders who have already achieved a goal have a momentum to achieve the next goal. This momentum comes from within the leader as well as from without. An old French proverb says, "Nothing succeeds like success." A person who has succeeded is encouraged within himself to succeed again. Achievement builds up one's creative anticipation.

Prior achievement also builds a reputation for success. People tend to follow the person who has already demonstrated that he can achieve. That is why prior experience is a part of any job application. That is why previous accomplishments are included in one's resume. Effective leaders do not hide their light under a bushel, but rather let their prior achievements be known. Is this not the basis of most successful advertising campaigns? It works equally well in leadership if handled in a factual and nonboastful way.

POISE

I attended the annual meeting of a large apartment owners' association for two consecutive years. The first year I found the meeting boring, uninspiring, long, and tiring. The president of the association, who was also the master of ceremonies of the evening, was rather dull. He did not seem to enjoy the position he was in. He showed much annoyance when the mikes failed to work at first and spoke sarcastically to the hotel employee who came in to adjust them. The meeting dragged on through speaker after speaker, some of whom may have seemed more inspiring if the tone of the whole meeting had been more exciting. I went to the annual meeting the second year on the urging of a friend. I was not anxious to go and I went prepared to be bored. By this time, the association had a new president and she was a real live wire. She was behind the association 100 percent. She was enthusiastic. She enjoyed her spot on the program as the emcee. She introduced each speaker with relish so that we could hardly wait to hear what a speaker had to say. She kept us informed on what was coming up next on the program so we could look forward to it, and we did with anticipation. The evening seemed to be over before it had hardly started.

The difference between the two presidents was simply a matter of poise. The first one was concerned with himself, his position, his feelings. The second was concerned with the audience, their enjoyment, their attitude toward the association.

From the standpoint of leadership poise is essential. The person who cannot handle himself in any given situation is in a poor position to lead others. The would-be leader who, under pressure, fails to plan, or gives up when a job becomes difficult or boring, or vacillates between contrary objectives, will have little success in leading others toward achievement of goals.

Self-discipline in regard to emotions is also essential for effective leadership. A person who is defeated by discouragement, anger, hate, prejudice, or a bad temper is hardly able to lead others to victory.

PLIABILITY

Pliability or flexibility has to do with change. To be an effective leader one must be able to change. One must be able to handle change in himself and in his followers. In all of life change is inevitable. This is especially true today when changes of all kinds—social, technological, scientific, moral, economic—are occurring so rapidly. There are few people who have the same life style today that they had just 10 or 15 years ago. Therefore, since leadership involves dealing with people, leaders have to be able to change to meet the changing demands placed upon leadership of people.

Some of these demands are in the areas of communication, power relationships, leader-group relationships, success channels, conflict management, and problem solving.

Communications

Don't wait for a breakdown in communication to occur before evaluating your communication effectiveness. Communication is one of your primary leadership tools. Review what has been said about nonverbal and verbal power tools in Chapter 2.

Messages are very often misconstrued. Others will often infer what you did not imply. This is partly because words don't have the same meanings for all people. People come from different geographic areas, have lived in different economic and social environments, and have had different experiences. Misinterpretation of tone also plays a part in miscommunication. Sometimes "silence gives consent" when consent was not intended. What you fail to say can communicate a message you did not intend to send.

Here are some questions leaders can ask themselves to find out what the chances are that their communication might be misunderstood:

1. Is your conversation sincere and friendly?
2. Can more than one meaning be inferred from what you say?
3. Do your actions match your talk? For example, do you talk to group members about being punctual when you are often late?
4. Are your instructions clear and at the level of the listener?
5. Do your written communications convey the tone you want them to? Might the reader read a different message between the lines?
6. Is your telephone conversation as cordial as your face-to-face conversation?
7. In meetings do you ask for suggestions while giving the impression you want your own ideas approved?
8. What message do those outside your group get concerning your group from what you say about it? Is it the message you want to broadcast?

Phraseology is a part of communication that effective leaders give constant attention to. How you phrase your thoughts can either build motivation or destroy it. An effective leader will avoid discouraging phrases such as these:

> We tried that before.
> A swell idea, but . . .
> You haven't considered . . .
> It costs too much.
> It's too radical.
> Too hard to administer.
> Too early
> Let's shelve it for now.
> We've never done it before.
> That's not our responsibility.
> There are better ways.
> Somebody would have suggested it before if it were any good.
> Top management will never go for it.
> We're not ready for that.

Effective leaders use encouraging phrases like these:

> Fantastic!
> I know it will work.
> Good for you!
> You're brilliant!
> I'm glad you brought that up.
> That's the first time I've heard that idea.
> Let's get right on it.
> I appreciate what you've done.
> Keep up the good work.
> Great idea!
> That's an interesting idea.
> We can always depend on you.
> Good work!
> You're on the right track.

Power Relationships

Power relationships within your group have significant influence on how well your group functions. As a leader, study your group to be aware which group members have the greatest influence on the rest of the group. These people can help you get across the message you want your group to hear. Sometimes group members place more credibility with a peer leader than with the group's official leader.

Leader-Group Relationships

An effective leader knows his group members individually. He studies them to understand their individual characteristics. He knows which ones have initiative and can work well alone, which ones need constant supervision or encouragement, and which leadership style each one responds to the best at any given time.

Individual group members can change as they adjust to the group as a whole. Therefore, a leader should review the status of each group member from time to time. Group members become more experienced in their individual roles within the group and they grow older. Their life goals may change. Their values may change. Their personal life styles change. Any of these changes may cause a group member to react differently in the group, and a wise leader keeps abreast of these changes so he can adjust his leadership pattern. (See "Leadership Styles" elsewhere in this chapter.)

Success Channels

Effective leaders keep abreast of the channels through which to get action in organizations. There are official channels and unofficial channels. Sometimes the unofficial channels are much more receptive and productive. It isn't always what you know, sometimes it's who you know. The organization chart might tell you the official procedure, but from experience you know you have obtained faster or more positive action by using an unofficial channel.

Nancy Jamison heads up a fund-raising drive for her service club. She wants a substantial contribution from a certain business organization in her town. Mr. Smith is in charge of public relations for the firm and is the official person to approach for a contribution. But for three consecutive years Nancy has not been able to get more than a "We'll consider it" from Mr. Smith. Nancy is talking about this problem to her neighbor, Frank Getsit.

> *Nancy*: Didn't you tell me last year that ABC Company donated heavily to your Christmas project for handicapped children?

Frank: Yes, in fact, we've received a substantial contribution from ABC for three years in a row.

Nancy: How do you do it? I have gone to them every year but I never get more than a promise that they'll consider it.

Frank: Who do you talk to at ABC?

Nancy: Mr. Smith. The information clerk told me Mr. Smith was the person to see.

Frank: Well, officially he is. His department makes the recommendations to their board concerning charitable contributions. But he relies heavily on his administrative assistant, Mrs. Stevens. She makes up the list of all requests that the company receives. And she stars the ones that she feels are most deserving—sometimes even adds a comment of her own.

Nancy: You mean if I were to talk to Mrs. Stevens about our project, she might be impressed enough to recommend it to Mr. Smith?

Frank: That's what I did three years ago and all I've had to do each year since is talk to Mrs. Stevens on the phone and remind her about our Christmas project and she puts it high on the list.

Nancy: But I thought Mrs. Stevens was only the secretary . . .

Frank: Oh, but never underestimate the power of a secretary!

Conflict Management

Whenever human beings are involved in working together conflict cannot be entirely avoided. There are bound to be misunderstandings, conflicting interests, personality clashes. But not all conflict is bad. As Dr. Thomas Gordon, in his book, *Leader Effectiveness Training*, points out:

> It would be naive for any leader to hope that conflicts will never develop in relationships with others. In fact, as I have said, a good case can be made for the position that the absence of conflict may be symptomatic of an organization or group that is not functioning effectively—not growing, changing, adapting, improving, or creatively meeting new challenges. Experience convinces me the *number* of conflicts in groups (including families) is not at all indicative of how "healthy" they are. The true index is whether the conflicts get resolved and by what method they get resolved. Whether they get

resolved is critical because some leaders have a tendency to avoid resolution of conflict by walking away from it, hoping that the conflict will go away by itself.[1]

Some conflicts can be prevented, or at least kept from developing into a full-blown eye-for-an-eye, tooth-for-a-tooth struggle. Use of the relationship record mentioned in Chapter 1 (Figure 1-2) will assist a leader in both preventing and resolving conflict. If a person is involved in a conflict situation, either with another group member or with the leader, having a record of previous encounters with this person or persons will enable the leader to better understand the person(s) and resolve the conflict sooner.

The effective use of listening skills is a good preventive measure that leaders use. A leader who is competent in recognizing and understanding problems of group members can help the group members solve their problems before they become problems for the leader or develop into conflict among group members. In Chapter 2 we discussed perceiving the other person. Suppose as the superintendent of a volunteer organization you notice that one of your volunteer workers—one of the best on your staff as far as sincerity of purpose and ability is concerned—begins arriving at the last minute, distraught and unprepared. You perceive that this person has a problem. At an appropriate time you might approach the person this way: "I notice that lately you are having a problem getting to your assignment on time. You do not seem to be as interested as you used to be and I am concerned that the quality of your work may suffer because of this. Is there any way I can help you with your problem?" Notice that you have not placed blame on the volunteer. You have stated that you have noticed a problem (the problem is the villain, not the volunteer), you have stated how the problem makes you feel (concerned), and you have offered to be of help.

When you say how you feel about a situation, or how a situation affects you, you send an "I" message. Leaders make use of this technique in resolving conflict to avoid placing blame. It usually results in the follower being willing to communicate his side of the problem and to cooperate in solving the problem.

In the case mentioned above, the volunteer would probably tell you what change had occurred to cause the problem, in

---

[1] Thomas Gordon, *Leader Effectiveness Training*, New York, Wyden Books, 1977, pp. 146-47.

which case you might be able to help solve the volunteer's problem. If the problem is unsolvable, at least for the present, you would know that the person would probably continue to arrive at the last minute unprepared to work. Then you would know that you have to take some action such as assigning temporary help, for example.

In this particular incident, the volunteer (who taught crafts to a class of senior adults) had started picking up one of the class members on the way to her assignment. Often this person was not ready on time and kept the volunteer waiting. The superintendent was able to find other means of transportation for this class member, thus relieving the volunteer of this responsibility.

If you cannot change a situation, you can change your response to the situation. For example, if you are studying a planet with a telescope and the planet you are studying changes position, you can't change the course of the planet, but you can turn your telescope in a different direction. The same principle applies to people. You cannot change a person, but you do have the power to change your response to the person or his behavior.

If conflict has developed within a group, as it will from time to time in spite of preventive measures, an effective leader will see that the conflict gets resolved. Some leaders feel very uncomfortable in the presence of conflict. They hope that it will go away, but often it won't. They don't want to get involved in the conflict for fear of being unable to resolve it and losing prestige with the group.

When conflicts are left unresolved, resentments build up and there is excessive griping among group members, undercover criticism of one another and of the leader, gossiping, hurt feelings, and a general breakdown of communication. The leader himself is affected by unresolved conflict. He becomes frustrated, resentful, and complaining, often taking out his feelings on family members or other innocent bystanders.

Most people think of the resolution of conflict as being either "I win—you lose" or "You win—I lose." In either outcome there are damaged relationships and a reduction in group effectiveness. There is a third way to resolve conflict and that is by what Dr. Gordon calls the "no-lose method."

The no-lose method involves searching for a solution to the conflict that does not require use of power, as with the win/lose methods, but does require creative thinking on both sides. The aim is to find a solution that will meet the needs of both sides so that everyone wins and no one loses. The no-lose method results in:

- Increased commitment to carry out the decision because both parties had a part in arriving at it
- Higher-quality decisions because there has been more input
- Warmer relationships
- Quicker decisions, because facts and feelings that otherwise would not be known to both parties are brought into the open
- No selling of the decision required because all parties have had a part in arriving at it

The no-lose method is a special kind of problem solving, discussed next.

Problem Solving

Problem solving relating to leadership usually involves people problems. Therefore, the no-lose method of resolving conflict proposed by Dr. Gordon in *Leader Effectiveness Training* is recommended here. The resolution of conflict usually results in one side winning and the other side losing. However, if both sides can win, good relationships are maintained or restored and individual and group effectiveness is enhanced. Dr. Gordon's method consists of six steps:

1. Identifying and defining the problem
2. Generating alternative solutions
3. Evaluating the alternative solutions
4. Decision making
5. Implementing the decision
6. Following up to evaluate the solution

Before using the no-lose method, all parties concerned should understand the goal, which is to arrive at a solution that is acceptable to all concerned, one in which there are no losers. Participants should understand each step of the process, and there should be agreement that each step be completed to the satisfaction of all before going to the next step. Naturally the leader has an important role to play. But this doesn't mean that the leader does most of the talking. The leader should, however, be skillful in drawing out others' feelings and ideas.

Step 1: Identifying and defining the problem is basic. This must be accomplished to the satisfaction of both sides. Obviously, a satisfactory solution will not be found if the wrong problem is being worked on. Be sure to get agreement on what the true problem is. This process cannot be hurried. Feelings must be brought out in the open. Often the real problem is not the one that set off the conflict. But open and frank discussion will uncover any hidden problem. The hidden problem is more likely to be the true problem and the one to be solved.

Step 2: Encourage others to suggest solutions. Offer your own suggestions for solving the problem, but be sure you do not leave the impression that you think your suggestions are better or that you expect others to agree to them. Avoid any evaluation of suggested solutions until the next step. Generate as many alternative solutions as possible.

Step 3: Evaluating alternative solutions requires honesty and objectivity on both sides. Encourage critical thinking about each alternative. Are there any flaws in it? Is there any reason why it wouldn't work? Is it fair to both sides? A brand-new solution may be thought of during this step or a combination of ideas might be proposed, or a modification of one of the alternative solutions. Be sure both sides are together in their thinking before moving to step 4.

Step 4: Make the decision. It is essential that a mutual commitment be made to the decision or solution decided upon. Mutual commitment, freely given, will help ensure that the decision will be carried out. The next step should follow immediately.

Step 5: Implement the decision by agreeing and deciding who will do what and when. Each side must show faith that the other will carry out whatever responsibilty he has in implementing the decision. If, however, someone fails in this responsibility, he should be confronted with "I" messages. While it should not be necessary to constantly remind a person to do what was agreed upon, you or someone else may have to confront him often until he gets the message that he is not going to be allowed to ignore his part of the agreement.

Don't overlook *Step 6*: Follow-up evaluation of the solution. Both sides should have an understanding that decisions can be revised, but that modifications must be agreed upon, just as the initial decision was. Decide now on a definite time when the solution will be evaluated.

Figure 3–1, the No-lose Agreement, may be used as a guideline as you and your group member(s) proceed through the steps of problem solving. There should be a copy for each person involved in the problem solving.

Section I is filled in upon completion of step 1 above. This is the problem definition agreed upon.

Figure 3-1

NO–LOSE AGREEMENT

I - The problem is:

II - The problem solution is:

III - The solution will be implemented as follows:

What	Who	When

IV - An evaluation of how the solution is working will be done after

_____ and before _____
(date)   (date)

by _____ and _____ .

V - Revision or modification suggested after evaluation:

_____
(Signature)

Section II is filled in upon completion of step 4. It is the solution or decision both sides have agreed to.

Section III follows step 5. It is simply to record who does what when. The last column purposely has no heading. Depending on the situation, you may want to use this column for each person listed under "Who" to initial to indicate his understanding of what his responsibilities are. However, if requiring an initial in this column would indicate to anyone that he is not trusted to follow through, it would be better to omit the initialing. If one side uses this column, be sure that the other also initials any commitment they have made.

Section IV sets down as a reminder a time for following up or evaluating the problem solution. After the word "by" enter all parties' names. This will ensure that both sides will evaluate how the solution is working. Fill in section IV after completing step 6.

Section V is for entering any revision that either side feels necessary. If either side wants to suggest a modification of the solution, they should record it in section V and notify the leader. If a significant revision is suggested by either side, schedule a time for another no-lose problem-solving session.

LEADERSHIP STYLES

There are three basic leadership styles:

1. *Tight Control*: The leader determines policy, makes decisions, and demands obedience from group members.
2. *Team Approach*: The leader encourages group members to participate in setting policies and making decisions for the group. The leader acts mostly as a moderator for the group.
3. *Free Rein*: The leader exercises a minimum of control. Group members are mainly on their own and the leader is on hand to supply information and provide materials.

Studies have indicated an effective leader needs to be an expert at using all three methods of leadership. While it is generally agreed that the team approach is usually the most effective under the right conditions, there are times when group climate or individual group member characteristics dictate use of either tight control or free rein leadership.

Leadership styles are a definite consideration of executive

leadership and will be discussed in more detail in Section II (Chapter 6). However, leaders of any kind of group (club, volunteer organization, church, private industry, government agency) should be aware of the three basic styles of leadership and be able to fit the style of leadership to the characteristics of the group being led. Usually leaders find that one style of leadership fits their own personality better than the other styles. If you find tight control leadership easiest for you and it seems to be accepted by your group members and your group is successful, then tight control leadership is right. Free rein leadership may be more comfortable for you. If so, and if your group is not frustrated by it and is successful, free rein is fine. But be sure to evaluate your group's response and success objectively. For a person who doesn't like to lead, free rein leadership is an easy out. Don't adopt free rein as your leadership style just to avoid leading. It can result in chaos.

By far the most effective overall leadership style is team approach. However, it is also the most challenging for the leader.

In choosing a leadership style, effective leaders consider not only their own personality and the group as a whole, but also the individual members of the group. While your overall leadership pattern for your group may be team approach, you may find that individual members in the group will function better in their respective roles if you use either a tight control or free rein style with them individually.

PRINCIPLES

On the eve of his first inauguration George Washington is reported to have said, "Integrity and firmness are all I can promise." If all leaders would promise and deliver as much, what a utopia this world would be! But promises are often easier to make than to keep.

How does one keep one's integrity and firmness in the face of the complex and often perplexing problems of leadership? Webster defines *integrity* as "uprightness, virtue, honesty, and soundness." Integrity, then, seems to imply adherence to certain moral principles.

Before you can have integrity you must have firm values. It is important that you establish a basis of conduct from which to operate. Without a firm knowledge of what to you is right and what to you is wrong, you will be wishy-washy in leadership situations, especially when a spur-of-the-moment decision is called for. You must have a clear-cut standard of behavior to guide your thoughts and actions in any situation. Without a standard you cannot hope to hold firmly to your integrity. For example, how much do you value honesty? Do you value it enough to determine that you will be honest with others no matter what happens? How much value do you place on people? Are your followers more important to you than the goal you are striving for? If so, you will place their needs above the desired goal whenever an occasion arises where you have to make that choice.

Here are some areas where you may unintentionally sacrifice integrity if you do not have a firm ethical standard to go by:

1. *Personal bias.* Do decisions you make grow out of your background, character, personality? In other words, do you decide on the basis of personal bias rather than facts? If you are not sure in a given situation, get an independent opinion from someone who doesn't have an interest in the outcome.
2. *Prejudice.* Are any of your acts or decisions based on your personal prejudices of race, color, creed, age, sex, or anything else?
3. *Trickery.* Is "Winning is everything" your motto—or is winning less important than *how* the goal is won?
4. *Quality of leadership.* Do you take your leadership function seriously and conscientiously try to be the kind of leader you know you should be? Do you strive for quality performance of your group and encourage group members to take pride in the way they perform in their individual functions? Do you welcome the input of group members and are you concerned whether they are being personally fulfilled in their jobs?
5. *Responsibility.* Are you quick to acknowledge your own mistakes? It has been said that "a good leader takes a little more than his share of blame; a little less than his share of credit" (Arnold H. Glasgow).
6. *Achievement model.* Are you a norm setter? Do you look for a reflection of yourself in your group members? Leaders who achieve produce followers who achieve.
7. *Definition of success.* Does your definition of success line up with that of Cyrus H. K. Curtis, founder of the *Saturday Evening Post*, who defined success as the ability to get everything one desires or needs without violating the rights of others?
8. *The golden rule of leadership.* Are you doing unto your followers as you would want them to do unto you if your roles were reversed?

two

MANAGERIAL LEADERSHIP

4

What Makes
A Manager A Leader?

Abraham Zaleznik, professor of social psychology of management at the Harvard Business School, writes that "managers and leaders are very different kinds of people. They differ in motivation, personal history, and in how they think and act."[1]

    A manager is like a good transportation car. A transportation car is good for taking you where you want to go—for getting the job done. This is its only motivation. It probably has a personal history of more than one owner. It very likely has a standard transmission. If you have a good transportation car, you value it because it takes you where you want to go and it does so economically. Organizations need good "transportation car" managers who can, with the help of a staff, get the job done efficiently and economically.

    A leader, on the other hand, is more like a luxury model car. A luxury car is geared to give comfort. It may be custom-designed with plush upholstering, lots of accessories, plenty of room, and automatic transmission. If you have one, you value it because of the feeling of affluence it gives you and the impression it makes on your friends

---

[1] Abraham Zaleznik, "Managers and Leaders: Are They Different?" *Harvard Business Review*, May/June 1977, p. 67.

Figure 4-1 *Transportation Car (The Manager)*

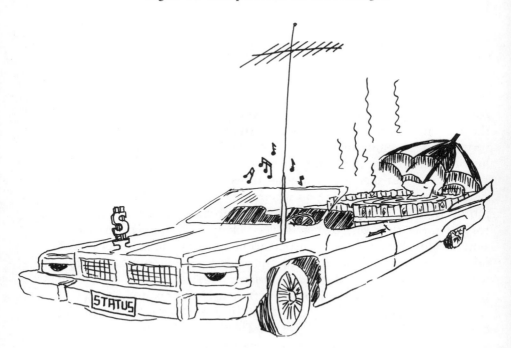

Figure 4-2 *Luxury Car (The Leader)*

and neighbors. Business organizations need leaders who are custom-designed with ability to change the status quo, to conceive and try out new innovations, and who are persuasive enough to impress others.

Some of the characteristics of managers and leaders are tabulated below to indicate how these kinds of roles differ from one another.

MANAGER	LEADER
How they view themselves:	
Managers have a strong sense of belonging to their organizations.	Leaders see themselves as separate from their organizations and the people of their organizations.
Managers see themselves as protectors of existing order with which they identify.	Leaders have strong personal mastery which impels them to struggle for change in existing order.
How they view their function:	
Managers work through other people within established organizational policies and practice to reach an organizational goal. They limit their choices to pre-established organizational goals, policies, and practices. Managers are concerned with process.	Leaders question established procedure and create new concepts. They inspire people to look at options. They are concerned with results.
Personality:	
Managers have a strong instinct for survival.	Leaders seek out risks, especially where rewards seem high.
Managers can tolerate mundane, practical work.	Leaders dislike mundane tasks.
Relationships:	
Managers relate to people according to their role, that is, boss, employee, peer, and so forth.	Leaders relate to people in an intuitive and empathetic way.
Primary Concern:	
Managers are concerned with achievement of organizational goals.	Leaders are concerned with achievement of personal goals.
Place in Organization:	
Managers are supervisors, department heads, administrators. They are usually considered the higher echelon.	Leaders may be found at any level in the plan of organization from technician to highest echelon.

MANAGER *(cont.)*	LEADER *(cont.)*
Power:	
Managers derive power from their positions.	Leaders derive power through personal relationships.
Goals:	
Managers are concerned with preestablished, organizational goals. Their personal and sub-goals arise out of necessity to conform to organizational structure, rather than a desire to change.	Leaders are concerned with personal goals. They are not comfortable with the status quo of established organizational goals and policies. They enjoy innovating.

A managerial leader is like a family car. It has the most effective features of both the transportation car and the luxury model. If you have a family car, you value it because it will take you and your family where you want to go fairly economically and with enough innovative accessories to make the trip enjoyable and even profitable in terms of relaxation and enjoyment. Organizations need "family car" executives to lead them in determining and reaching established goals and to persuade them into new concepts of better ways of doing things and better things to do.

We are living in an age of criticism, and it seems to be popular to look at our leaders to discover what they did or are doing

Figure 4-3 *Family Car (The Managerial Leader)*

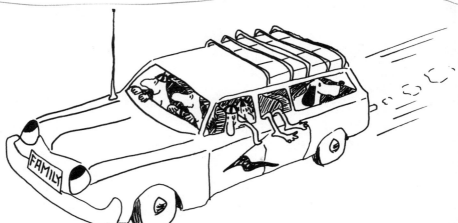

wrong. An inquiring mind is one of the marks of leadership; but we can learn little by inquiring negatively in the light of obvious success. So let us engage in some old-fashioned "learning from history" to discover what some of our past business leadership greats did right.

The National Business Hall of Fame, established in 1975 by Junior Achievement Inc., honors "outstanding and enduring contributions to improving the products, the processes, the efficiencies, or the human relations of business." Each year, at JA's request, the board of editors of *Fortune* magazine select a new group of laureates.

Studying the biographies of forty-five of these business leadership greats we found they differ in personality, talent, ability, and method. But we also found certain common threads running through the lives of all of them. By examining these similarities we can understand better the marks of an outstanding business leader.

All outstanding business leaders are hard workers, risk takers, decision makers (although they vary in decision-making methods), opportunity seekers, and, to some extent, loners.

They all are innovative, visionary, objective, persuasive, versatile (but usually expert in at least one field), and dollar-wise. Many of them have outstanding reputations for integrity and high ethical standards.

Their strengths are varied, but they all have at least one strong interest or ability that played a major part in their successful careers. For example, John D. Rockefeller didn't like disorder or waste. His *organizational skills* led him to the restructuring of the oil industry and, later, to his elaborately rationalized and institutionalized philanthropies. Walt Disney's *quest for excellence* inspired hundreds of talents brighter than his own to produce at levels of quality they could not have approached without him. His *business acumen* made him quick to see how his studio could use every technological advance. After World War II he told his brother and collaborator Roy, "If we try to coast, we'll go backward." With this thought in mind the Walt Disney Studio produced an ambitious and highly successful program of cartoons in the 1950s.

Harry Blair Cunningham had *political know-how* without which he may never have become the president of S. S. Kresge Co. In line for the presidency, Cunningham noticed that many corporate executives competed so intensely for the chief executive office that they didn't know what to do with it when they got it. He set out to find what the company needed. He visited all but 14 of the firm's

725 stores and found that the chain's customers had been moving to the suburbs, stranding central-city stores. Cunningham, searching for new directions for Kresge, studied discount stores that were booming in New England and concluded that Kresge with its strong national organization could carry this idea even further. But the company looked down on discounters. So with political wisdom Cunningham didn't toot his idea until after he became president of the company. He said, "If I had announced before being elected president my intention to take Kresge into discounting, I'm quite sure I would not have been elected president."

Known for his inventiveness, Thomas A. Edison also had impressive business ability. He had a sense of the market, and nearly all his inventions started from an idea of what people would use. Edison was *dollar-wise.*

C. R. Smith of American Airlines was perhaps the most *single-minded* and *hard-working* executive of his time. He rode the line as much as he could, chatting with pilots, mechanics, stewardesses, picking up ideas for better service. He had the line, its hopes, and its problems in his head. In the 1950s, John Naish of Convair said, "C. R. is one of the few businessmen left in America with whom you can close a $100 million deal on his word alone."

Florence Nightingale Graham, alias Elizabeth Arden, was a *risk taker* of the first order. Her track to success led through a series of dull office jobs in Canada to a daring gamble in New York in 1910, when she opened a Fifth Avenue beauty salon, furnishing it lavishly on $6000 borrowed from a relative. The loan was paid back in six months.

George Stevens Moore of New York's Citibank credits his early experience in journalism with his life-long habit of *getting the facts.* Moore had a great deal of enthusiasm, imagination, and boldness, and if it had not been for his habit of getting the facts first, his exuberance could have carried him to career disaster. But instead, Moore and his bank were in the forefront of the two most significant developments in United States banking in the last thirty years—broadening services and overseas expansion.

Stephen Davison Bechtel, Sr., president of Bechtel Corporation from 1933 to 1960, was able to *recognize an opportunity* when one came along. He wasn't a person to sit back and wait for projects to fall into his lap. For example, at a Los Angeles luncheon in 1949 he happened to be sitting next to Robert L. Minckler, an oilman who was talking about the new field near Edmonton, Alberta. Minckler said, "If they could ever run a pipeline from that field to the West Coast, I'd build a refinery up North, and I should think some other companies would want to do the same." Then and there, Bechtel and Minckler started drawing maps on the tablecloth and another Bechtel project was launched.

5

Managerial
Leadership Power

We know that effective managerial leaders have power. Without managerial leadership power, organizations would not develop or expand; there would be little dollar profit made; there would be little progress toward desired goals and no incentive to go beyond the status quo. What is this power that effective managerial leaders have? How do they get it and keep it, and how do they use it after they get it? This chapter will attempt to answer these questions.

WHAT IT IS

According to Peter Drucker, managerial leadership power lies in the managerial *leader's contribution to the results of the enterprise*, rather than in responsibility for the work of others.[1]

David C. McClelland and David H. Burnham in an article titled "Power Is the Great Motivator" express the same thought this way:

[1] Peter F. Drucker, *The Effective Executive*, New York, Harper & Row, 1966, p. 52.

Good managers are not motivated by a need for personal aggrandizement, or by a need to get along with subordinates, but rather by a need to influence others' behavior for the good of the whole organization.[2]

In Chapter 4, we compared a managerial leader to a family car. Let's think about the family car to see where it gets its power. We know the life of the car is in the battery. If the battery is dead, the whole car is dead as far as being able to perform or run is concerned. So the car's power is the life that is stored in the battery until needed. We know a car is an inanimate object and spiritless. But for the purpose of comparison, let's consider a car to be an animate object. We might say the car has a goal or powerful desire in its battery to influence other parts of the motor to achieve the goal of moving the car. To have a powerful desire indicates the presence of personal motivation. In the case of an automobile this personal motivation is electricity.

An achievement leader has a goal or powerful desire in his heart to influence other people of the organization to perform effectively for the good of the organization. This powerful desire is personal motivation.

With an automobile, other parts of the motor will not function minus the electricity in the battery. With the organization, other parts may function minus the personal motivation of the leader because there are other subpowers that influence. But the efficiency of the organization will be greatly hampered by the lack of personal motivation on the part of the manager/leader.

Thus in answer to the question "What is managerial leadership power?" we state: managerial leadership power is the *state of being personally motivated to influence others to achieve a goal.*

HOW TO GET IT AND KEEP IT

An automobile battery is charged by virtue of its chemical elements or recharged by accepting direct-current electrical energy from an outside source. An achievement leader, one whose group achieves goals, is similarly charged in two ways: by creation of motivation within himself and by influence or inspiration from a source outside himself.

[2] David C. McClelland and David H. Burnham, "Power Is the Great Motivator," *Harvard Business Review*, March/April 1976, p. 100.

Outside sources of influence include such things as: salary and the things salary can buy, threat of loss of job, social prestige, commendation, power over others, and so forth. These outside influential forces create a desire for personal gain in the leader.

Motivation created from within has its source in the human spirit. It is soul searching to find out if the organization's goals and your goals as a person are compatible. Unless you can say a fervent "Amen" to what your organization is attempting to do, you will never be motivated by anything other than personal gain; and you will be as ineffective as scores of others who think only, "What's in it for me?"

Assuming that you work for an organization whose beliefs and purposes you endorse, your next step is to examine your special skills and talents, your function, and your department to see how you can contribute to the achievement of organizational goals.

Peter Drucker says:

> The effective executive focuses on contribution. He looks up from his work and outward toward goals. He asks: "What can I contribute that will significantly affect the performance and the results of the institution I serve?" . . .

> The great majority of executives tend to focus downward. They are occupied with efforts rather than with results. They worry over what the organization and their superiors "owe" them and should do for them. And they are conscious above all of the authority they "should have." As a result, they render themselves ineffectual. . .

> The man who focuses on efforts and who stresses his downward authority is a subordinate no matter how exalted his title and rank. But the man who focuses on contribution and who takes responsibility for results, no matter how junior, is in the most literal sense of the phrase, "top management." He holds himself accountable for the performance of the whole.[3]

HOW TO USE IT

The battery's motivational power is used to start the engine running and to influence other parts of the motor to perform.

Leader power is used to spark enthusiasm among others in the organization and to influence them to become excited about their

---

[3] Drucker, *The Effective Executive*, Chap. 3.

individual contributions to the achievement of the organization's goals.

First of all, the powerful achievement leader focuses on his own contribution to the effectiveness of the organization. Effectiveness is not inborn like a gift for drawing beautiful pictures. Effectiveness can be learned, and it is largely a matter of systematizing. The powerful leader concentrates on doing a few jobs well, eliminating obsolete jobs and improving worn-out methods, making the most effective use of time, making productive decisions, and testing ideas. These and other leadership methods will be discussed fully in Section IV of this text. They are mentioned here only to indicate that they are focal points for manager/leader power.

Secondly, the powerful achievement leader focuses on the contributions his individual staff members can make to the effectiveness of the department and the overall effectiveness of the organization. It used to be, and still is in many organizations, that the structure of the organization and its official plan of organization dictated communication patterns and each person's sphere of responsibility. No one dared to step out of his own sphere or communicate any way but up or down on the plan of organization. This system ensured the manager/leader's position power, and he was solely responsible for the output of his work unit. He alone was supposed to do the thinking for his unit.

However, this strict adherence to the officially dictated plan of organization has given way in most successful organizations to a less formal structure. Today freedom of workers to contribute expertise and communicate laterally on the plan of organization enables them to be more effective in their overall contributions to the success of the organization. While the manager/leader still has position power, it is overshadowed by team effort. The manager/leader no longer merely gives orders—he induces others to contribute to the success of the department or organization.

Motivation and how to build a productive team will be discussed in Section III.

6

Leadership Styles

There are many different models of automobiles, and one chooses the model one wants according to purpose and the particular needs of the owner-to-be. The same is true with business leadership styles. There are many different styles of business leadership, and one chooses the style according to the result to be attained and the particular needs of the user.

Before choosing a specific model of automobile one usually learns as much as he can about all the different models in order to make a wise choice. It is just as wise to learn the pros and cons of various leadership styles.

Leadership styles range from very tight control of subordinates or group to practically no control at all, with many degrees and combinations of degrees in between.

Figure 6–1 indicates the characteristics of the tight control, team approach, and free rein styles in relation to certain areas of concern to the manager/leader function. Keep in mind the possible degrees of control in between. For example, in making decisions a leader may confer with his group but reserve actual decision making as his own function. Under delegation of authority a leader might establish certain limits of authority within which the group may operate freely.

Note also that regardless of leadership style, the final responsibility for the achievement of goals of the department or organization rests solely with the manager/leader. This is a responsibility that is nondelegatable. However, under the team approach style, the *feeling* of responsibility is shared among leader and all team members. When responsibility for achievement is felt by all (leader

Figure 6-1

COMPARISON OF LEADERSHIP STYLES			
Area of Concern:	Tight Control	Team Approach	Free Rein
Who does planning?	Leader	Ldr. + group	Individuals or group
Who does problem-solving?	Leader	Ldr. + group	Individuals or group
Who makes decisions?	Leader	Ldr. + group	Individuals or group
What is direction of communication?	Down	Down, up, and across	Across
Where is responsibility for achievement felt?	Leader	Ldr. + group	Not felt
Where does final responsibility actually lie?	Leader	Leader	Leader
Leader's confidence in subordinates	None	High	High
Leader's rapport with subordinates	Low	High	Questionable
Amount of delegation of authority by leader	None	Lots	Lots
Crisis management	Good	Poor	Chaotic
Change management	Poor	Good	Ineffective

and team members) there is more likelihood that achievement will be accomplished than if the responsibility is felt only by the leader.

SOME APPROACHES TO LEADERSHIP

There are many theories or approaches to managerial leadership. Paul Hersey and Kenneth Blanchard believe the appropriateness of a leader's behavior determines its effectiveness:

> The difference between the effective and the ineffective styles is often not the actual behavior of a leader, but the appropriateness of the behavior to the situation in which it is used.[1]

Gordon points out that task and relationship are two important dimensions of leadership behavior:

> The effective leader must be *both* a human relations specialist and a task specialist. Leader effectiveness requires treating people decently, while at the same time successfully motivating them toward high performance in their work. One without the other doesn't work.[2]

Burns says:

> Executive leaders have effective power (rather than merely formal authority) to the degree that they can activate the need and motivational bases of other leaders and subordinates in the organization.[3]

Tannenbaum and Schmidt state:

> The successful manager of men can be primarily characterized neither as a strong leader nor as a permissive one. Rather, he is one who maintains a high batting average in accurately assessing the forces that determine what his most appropriate behavior at any given time should be and in actually being able to behave accordingly.[4]

[1] Paul Hersey and Kenneth H. Blanchard, "Leader Effectiveness and Adaptability Description (LEAD)," in *The 1976 Annual Handbook for Group Facilitators*, San Diego University Associates, 1976, p. 87.

[2] Thomas Gordon, *Leader Effectiveness Training*, New York, Wyden Books, 1977, p. 6.

[3] James MacGregor Burns, *Leadership*, New York, Harper & Row, 1978, p. 373.

[4] Robert Tannenbaum and Warren H. Schmidt, "How to Choose a Leadership Pattern," *Harvard Business Review*, May/June 1973, pp. 1-10.

THE TRANSMISSION APPROACH

In Chapter 4 we said that a managerial leader is like a family car that will take you where you want to go fairly economically and with enough innovative accessories to make the trip enjoyable and profitable. "Family car" leaders use the *transmission approach* to leadership. In the transmission approach there are several leadership styles. They are like the gears in the transmission of a car. You use a different gear depending on the direction you want to go and road conditions. These are the things that help you determine which gear to use. For example, if you want to go up a steep hill, you may decide to use a low gear, or if you want to speed up to pass another vehicle you may decide to use a high or passing gear. You can brake going down an incline by using a low gear. In the transmission approach to managerial leadership the leader determines the style of leadership he will use based on certain determinants such as the situation, follower personalities, follower needs, leader personality, leader needs, the task to be done or goal to be reached, organizational climate, and group climate. All these things and others are what a leader bases his choice of leadership style on. He must be able to shift gears, so to speak, quickly and smoothly, perhaps several times a day. He must be able to shift from very tight control (autocratic) to practically no control (free rein) or to any leadership style in between these two extremes.

Which Gear to Use

The first determinant for a leader to consider in deciding the leadership gear (or style) to use in any given situation is his own personality. There are forces within each of us that cause us to react in certain ways, and knowing what these forces are and dealing with them objectively is the first step to effective managerial leadership. Here is a quiz that can help you understand the forces within you that are likely to affect your choice of leadership style. Answer these questions objectively in relation to yourself. There are no right or wrong answers—only objective and biased answers. Be as objective as you can be and check the column that most accurately expresses your personal feeling for each statement—A denoting that you strongly agree with the statement and E denoting that you strongly disagree with the statement.

| | Strongly Agree | | | | Strongly Disagree |
	A	B	C	D	E

1. Individuals are not entitled to help make decisions in matters that affect them.

2. People generally prefer direction and dislike responsibility.

3. Generally speaking, people must be threatened to get them to work.

4. People seldom exercise self-direction and self-control.

5. I can do a specific task better than my subordinate; therefore, I should do it.

6. Resolving problems and issuing orders are easy for me.

7. I feel nervous allowing subordinates to make decisions I cannot predict.

8. Rules and regulations should be written out and I and my subordinates should conform to them.

9. I believe "tried and true" ways of dealing with subordinates are better than "fresh and new" ways.

10. Employees' personal problems should not be considered when evaluating their job performance.

11. Working conditions and salary are greater motivators of employees than work satisfaction and feeling of personal growth on the job.

12. My needs and values are more important than my subordinates, needs and values.

	Strongly Agree				Strongly Disagree
	A	B	C	D	E

13. My decisions should be final and should not be questioned by my subordinates.

14. Differences of opinion within a work group indicate flaws in group unity.

15. Employees who violate rules should be punished.

Now look back at the columns you have checked to find out your personal leadership style. The more checks you have placed in the "Strongly Agree" column, the more you enjoy tight control; and the more checks you have placed in "Strongly Disagree" column, the more you tend toward free rein leadership. More checks in the middle columns indicate that you lean toward the team approach.

The second determinant in deciding the leadership style to use is the follower. Because people are so complex and often vary their attitudes and behaviors depending on the situation, it is difficult to label an individual as a certain kind of follower. The effective leader first diagnoses a subordinate's feelings about leadership, that is, how he expects his leader to lead.

Psychologists categorize followers into three types of personality: authoritarian, equalitarian, and libertarian.[5]

Personality Type	Characteristics	How this type views leadership
Authoritarian	• Tends to have a narrow outlook on most things	• Considers team approach and free rein leadership undesirable
	• Usually conservative	• Views any leadership that is not tight control as weak
	• Conforms to customs and manners and views those who don't with suspicion	• Expects tight control from superiors

[5] Auren Uris, *How to Be a Successful Leader*, New York, McGraw-Hill, 1953, pp. 46-47.

Personality Type	Characteristics	How this type views leadership
	• Dislikes weakness in individuals or groups	
Equalitarian	• Liberal-minded about most things	• Regards tight control leadership as dictatorial
	• Judges peoples on an individual basis	• Expects team approach from superiors
	• Doesn't like to be pushed around or see others pushed around	
Libertarian	• Somewhat of a loner	• Thinks of any amount of control as interference
	• Self-confident and self-directed	• Expects free rein leadership from superiors
	• Likely to be highly skilled, intellectual	

The leader who understands his subordinates' characteristics and the effect these characteristics have on how his subordinates expect him to act as their leader will be able to choose an overall leadership pattern that will be compatible with his subordinates.

But even though a leader accurately diagnoses subordinates and knows the leadership style a subordinate expects, it may not be best to use that particular style with that subordinate. Personality traits overlap, and it is unusual for a person to be completely authoritarian, equalitarian, or libertarian. Just as there are degrees of leadership types, there are degrees of followership types. Nor do followership styles remain constant. Many situations occur to change how a follower feels about leadership. Change in the difficulty of the work or the amount of work expected of the employee, competition with other employees, length of time on the job, age, change in work area, events away from the workplace, the contemporary spirit of demanding one's rights, and so on—all have their effect on the subordinate and how he responds to various leadership styles.

And that brings us to the third determinant in choosing a leadership style: the situation. Not only do situations occur to change how a follower feels about leadership style, but situations occur that make it necessary for the leader to change. An obvious example is the emergency situation where leadership action must be taken quickly and orders obeyed at once without question. In such situations even the most casual leadership must change to tight control to accommodate the emergency situation. Other situations that can occur and necessitate a change of leadership style include changes in organization, moving an office or department to a new location, changes in organizational philosophy and/or goals, a subordinate who becomes "stale" on the job, conflict within the work group—the list is endless.

The effective leader is one who is insightful and has empathy for both the follower and the situation and chooses the leadership style for each employee in each situation that will most likely have the desired result.

In all relationships, whether with subordinates, peers, or superiors, achievement leaders recognize differences in people. In your relationships with people take time to observe each one's uniqueness. Be a person watcher and you will strengthen your leadership power.

Remember that each person has areas of special sensitivity. Don't create an obstacle in your leadership role by infringing upon those sensitive areas. Also, be aware of your own sensitive areas and you will be less likely to take offense or overreact when someone trespasses on one of your sensitive areas.

three

BUILDING
A PRODUCTIVE TEAM

7

The Leadership Team

In Section III we will deal with the leader at all levels of management, from first-line supervisor to top management, and their staffs. We will begin in this chapter with the leader of subordinate leaders or managers.

Organizational leadership is not a one-person operation. It can rarely be done successfully by one person. It takes the coordinated efforts of a team of managers or leaders to achieve well-rounded leadership of an organization. The leadership team meets, usually on a regular basis, for formulating policy, solving problems, and making decisions.

CHOOSING THE LEADERSHIP TEAM

First, the leader chooses his leadership team. Usually the organizational chart will be the determinant in making these choices. For example, in Figure 7–1, suppose you are Leader A and you lead a group of five managers: Leaders B, C, D, E, and F. These five managers are directly responsible to you.

You may also have staff members responsible to you such as an assistant, a secretary, an office manager, and others with "staff" as opposed to "line" functions. You will need to decide which of these people, if any, will also be on your leadership team.

Here are some guide questions you can ask yourself to help you make this decision:

- Do any of my staff people have specialized knowledge that my line people do not have?
- Do any of them need to be aware of the management team's problems and decisions in order to function effectively?
- Do they want to attend regularly scheduled meetings?
- Is their attendance at leadership meetings affordable in time and money?
- Do any of them want to qualify themselves for more responsible positions in the organization and, if so, could they learn from the kind of leadership meetings we will have?

There are alternative methods you can consider to determine who shall be on your leadership team:

Figure 7-1 *The Leadership Team*

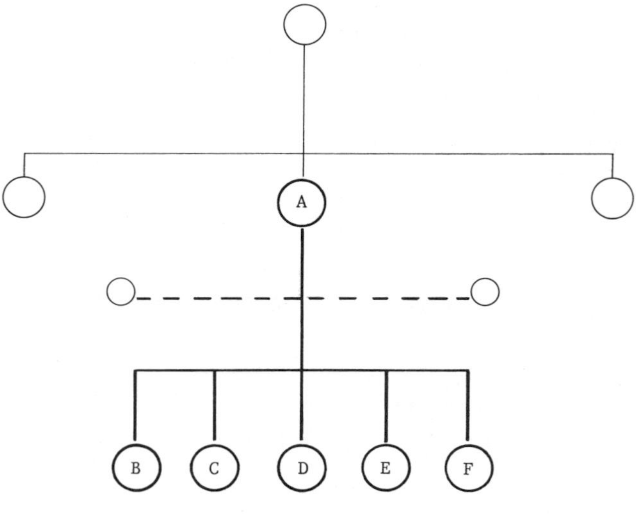

- Leave it up to each staff person to decide whether or not he wants to attend. Some people dislike meetings and would rather spend their time at their desk instead of in a meeting where they feel uncomfortable or have little to contribute.
- Extend an open invitation to staff people to attend management meetings when they want to. A staff member may have an interest in one specific topic but would not want to attend all leadership team meetings.
- Include all staff people. The problem with this is that you may create a group that is too large to function.
- Invite only those staff members who can contribute to an item on the agenda. They need not be present for the entire meeting but only for that part of the meeting where they have special expertise or relevant information.

After you have chosen your leadership team, you may wish to have each person assign an alternate in case he is unable to attend a meeting. In this way, all departments will always be represented. There will be no delay in decision making due to absence of a team member, and all departments will still have access to the information derived from the meeting.

In some large organizations the leadership team, even without staff people, could be too large to be practicable. One school superintendent who found this to be so arranged it so certain classifications of managers sent alternating representatives to leadership meetings. For example, all the high school principals elected a representative to serve on the superintendent's cabinet for three months, at the end of which time another high school principal was elected to serve for three months. The junior high school principals and the elementary school principals did likewise. In this way three people represented some twenty-six managers (principals), all of whom would eventually have an opportunity to serve on the cabinet.

HOW THE LEADERSHIP TEAM FUNCTIONS

The functioning of the leadership team focuses on leadership meetings. There are two types of leadership meetings: informational meetings and problem-solving/decision-making meetings. They can be called at regular intervals such as weekly, biweekly, or monthly, or they can be called as needed.

Leadership Meetings

Informational leadership team meetings are those which are for the purpose of exchanging information. Team members, including the team leader, bring reports from their departments or divisions, usually brief oral reports, so that all members of the leadership team know the progress of the whole organization. At this meeting problems may be presented but not solved. Problem solving and decision making should be reserved for that kind of meeting, unless it is a problem that must be handled immediately. If that is the case, the leader could call a special problem-solving meeting. This may or may not be the better course to take. The leader uses his own judgment depending on the situation. Even though rules have been established for each kind of meeting and for the general functioning of the leadership team, it must be remembered that rules shackle the team. Leadership team meetings are a tool to be used by the leadership team to achieve effective leadership.

Informational leadership team meetings may also be used for reporting by individuals on a conference or other meeting attended or a visit to another organization. They can also be used for training such as when a consultant or other authority in a job-related field is brought in. Whatever the purpose of the informational meeting, questions can be exchanged and answered.

If a problem should come to light through discussion held at an informational meeting, it should be placed on the agenda for the next problem-solving/decision-making meeting.

Problem-solving/decision-making meetings are called by the team leader whenever there is a problem to solve or a decision to make. If the problem or decision is not urgent, the team leader can wait until a number of small problems have accumulated and then call a problem-solving/decision-making meeting to take care of all of them at one meeting. However, it is best not to crowd one meeting with too many problems. It will cause the meeting to run too long, and the thinking of team members can become sluggish.

Depending on the magnitude of the problem, it may take several meetings to arrive at a decision concerning it. Some team leaders routinely break the problem-solving/decision-making process into three meetings, the first for problem identification, the second for generating alternative solutions, and the third for making decisions. This is a good practice because it assures that team members have ample time between meetings to mull the problem over in their minds, perhaps discuss it with their staff members if this is appropriate, and come back with more ideas than they could have generated in one meeting.

Meeting Pointers

The following pointers concerning leadership team meetings may not fit every situation. They are presented here as guidelines for the team leader to consider.

1. Leadership teams should be self-governing as much as possible. As a group they can determine how often to meet and where. A newly formed group may meet more frequently at first because of full agendas and because the members are learning each other's styles. Teams should reach the point where they can carry on even in the absence of the leader.

2. Meetings should have definite beginning and ending times. A new group may need to adjust the beginning time the first few meetings until all members' schedules can accommodate the meeting. Once a beginning time has been established it should be strictly observed. Always begin the meeting on time. The ending time can be more flexible and will depend on the length of the agenda. If the group has completed all items on the agenda, the leader should adjourn the meeting. If leftover time is used for informal discussion among team members, problems may surface that are not appropriate problems for group discussion. Individual members may become impatient to get back to their desks if they are being held in a meeting after the agenda has been completed.

If the agenda has not been completed when dismissal time arrives, the leader can (a) announce that the remainder of the agenda will be held over for the next meeting and adjourn this meeting; (b) complete only the item under discussion and then adjourn the meeting; (c) set a time for a special meeting to complete a specific item on the agenda (depending on the urgency of the item or items remaining); or (d) declare a recess for 10 minutes and reconvene the meeting after that time. In deciding what to do, the leader assesses the items and the team members. Are team members becoming tired? Do they feel an urgency about the item under discussion? Is rapport among team members still high or are nerves beginning to fray a bit? Ordinarily groups should not meet for longer than 2 hours without a break.

3. Team members should place a very high priority on leadership team meetings. Attendance at team meetings should nearly always have a higher priority than other functions. If it is necessary for a team member to forego a team meeting (this will happen occasionally), he should assign a representative to attend the team meeting. (See next point concerning representatives.)

Team members should make arrangements to have their phone calls held during team meetings. Team members should do as much preplanning as is necessary so they will not be called out of a meeting nor their attention diverted to other matters. The team leader and members may prefer to meet away from the workplace in order to cut down on interruptions.

4. Team members should agree on the appropriateness of attendance of persons other than regular team members. If there are confidential items on the agenda, it might be better for no one to represent an absent member. Some teams leave this up to the team leader. When the agenda is distributed prior to the meeting, the leader can note on the agenda if representatives are invited or if it is a closed meeting. If a representative does attend a meeting, he should have the authority to speak for the absent member of his department.

5. The meeting room should be equipped with any audio/visual aids that will be needed for the meeting. Seating should be arranged so each person can see and be seen by every other person. The leader should not sit at the head of the table, but vary his location among team members. In this way the idea of status will be lessened and team members will express themselves more freely. A round table serves better than a rectangular or square table.

6. Team members should strive for total agreement on all problems. However, this will not always be possible. If a group member does not feel particularly strong about his stance, he should be willing to go along with the majority. Team members should be sensitive to times when advocating their position further is not likely to change the position of the majority. If it is feasible to do so, team members should defer to those members who will have the most responsibility for implementing the decision or to those members in whose area of responsibility the problem logically falls.

7. Each team member should observe the confidentiality of leadership team meetings. In effective problem solving all team members need to feel confident that what they say or feelings they

express will not be repeated or discussed outside the group. If this confidence does not exist, discussion will be inhibited.

8. The team should decide what kind of minutes they want recorded and who is to do the recording. The team should also decide on the distribution of minutes following the meeting. (See the following sections on agendas and minutes.)

Agendas

Agendas for informational meetings will be different than agendas for problem-solving/decision-making meetings.

For informational meetings only the topic or topics to be presented and their presenters need to be listed on the agenda. An agenda for an informational meeting might look like the sample shown in Figure 7–2.

The format for agendas for other leadership team meetings will depend on whether you want to have problem solving and

Figure 7-2

```
                    LEADERSHIP TEAM MEETING

   Purpose:  Informational          Date: _____

   Place: _____      Time: _____


                          A G E N D A

   1.  Oral reports by department heads  (limit to 5 minutes each)

   2.  Question and answer period relating to above reports
       (limit to 15 minutes)

   3.  Presentation on Effective Communication

       Guest consultant:  John Doe

   4.  Question and answer period relating to above presentation.
```

decision making in the same meeting or whether you want to separate these functions into three meetings for the purposes of identifying problems, generating solutions, and making decisions.

If the problem is known and you are reasonably certain that there are no hidden problems, and if you believe it can be solved and a decision made all in one meeting, use the agenda format shown in Figure 7–3.

If the problem seems to be more complex, it would be better to use the three-meeting approach. For the first meeting use the agenda format shown in Figure 7–4. Since the problem is complex, there should not be more than one item per agenda. The item would be a statement of the unsatisfactory condition that exists—for example: "Profits for this quarter are down 1 percent from profits for the same quarter last year."

This condition is discussed at the problem identification meeting. Using the same example, the team might agree that the

Figure 7-3

```
                    LEADERSHIP TEAM MEETING

    Purpose:  Problem-solving/Decision-making  Date:  _____

    Place:       _____  Time:  _____


                          A G E N D A

    1.

    2.

    3.



```

reason for this condition is that the production rate is down from last year. However, this does not seem to be the root of the condition; and further discussion brings to light that morale among technical workers is low as evidenced by numerous cases of tardiness, absenteeism, and below-standard work. Now the problem has been identified as "low morale among technical workers."

This is the problem that will be carried forward to the meeting for generating solutions. If a few days elapse between the problem identification meeting and the solution-generating meeting, team members will have time to think over the problem and be ready to suggest solutions.

For the second meeting, the solution-generating meeting, use the agenda format shown in Figure 7–5. List the problem which was identified at the problem identification meeting. More than one problem may have been identified. If so, list each one. For example, besides finding that the morale of workers is low, the team may have

Figure 7-4

```
                    LEADERSHIP TEAM MEETING

    Purpose:  Identifying Problem         Date: _____

    Place: _____         Time: _____



                          A G E N D A

    1.  (Statement of unsatisfactory condition that exists)
```

discovered that workers have faulty and insufficient materials to work with. If this is the case, the problem of materials would be listed as the second problem on the solution-generating agenda.

At the solution-generating meeting team members should be encouraged to think of alternative solutions for each problem. The more solutions the team can think of, the more apt the team will be to choose the right solution at the next meeting.

For the next meeting, the decision-making meeting, use the agenda format shown in Figure 7-6. First restate the problem—"Low morale among technical workers"—and list the alternative solutions that were arrived at during the solution-generating meeting. This is item 1 on the agenda. Item 2 would be the next problem—"Faulty and insufficient materials"—and the alternative solutions for this problem that were arrived at during the solution-generating meeting.

During the decision-making meeting, the team will discuss each alternative solution and arrive at the best solution for the prob-

Figure 7-5

```
                    LEADERSHIP TEAM MEETING

  Purpose:  Generating Solutions        Date:  _____

  Place:    _____ Time:  _____


                         A G E N D A

  1.  (Description of first problem that originated in the Problem
      Identification meeting)

  2.  (Description of second problem that originated in the Problem
      Identification meeting)

  3.  (Description of third problem.......
```

lem. The best solution could turn out to be a combination of solutions.

There are different methods for developing the agenda for any leadership team meeting. Items for the agenda should come from individual members of the group, rather than from the leader only. Group members, including the leader, can give items in writing to the leader's assistant or secretary who can hold them in a file until it is time to send out an agenda.

Some leadership teams prefer to have members submit items at the beginning of the meeting, listing them on a chalkboard or flipchart and establishing priorities. This practice does not give team members an opportunity to study the problem prior to the meeting. However, last-minute items could be added in this manner to a previously distributed agenda. Whether the agenda is distributed before the meeting or established at the beginning of the meeting, the group should determine priorities for agenda items. If a team member's item is crucial, he should indicate this fact and the reason

Figure 7-6

```
                    LEADERSHIP TEAM MEETING

    Purpose:   Decision Making           Date:  _____

    Place:     _____     Time:  _____


                          A G E N D A

    1.  (Description of problem and alternative solutions that originated
        in Generating Solutions meeting)

    2.  (Description of second problem and alternative solutions......
```

on the agenda item sheet and the team can take this information into account when determining priorities. More than one member may consider his item to be of highest priority. This is why the group as a whole should determine priority order. If agreement cannot be reached, the leader would have the prerogative of determining priority order.

Each team member, including the leader, should tell the group what his item requires from the team. This could be a decision, the team's ideas for solutions so the member can pick the final solution, or a sounding board to test out the solution he had tentatively chosen.

Generally speaking, the problem that team members bring to the team should be only those that require data from team members, or those whose solutions may have to be implemented by the team, or those whose solutions affect team members. A team member should not bring a problem to the team if it affects only his area of responsibility. Team members should be alert to spot items on an agenda that are not appropriate for team discussion and assign them to others outside the team for resolution.

Minutes

Minutes of leadership team meetings can be recorded by a group-selected team member or by a secretary. If the minutes are recorded by a secretary, she or he should be instructed about the confidentiality of the meetings and the minutes.

Minutes should be typewritten and copies distributed to team members as soon as possible after the meeting. The team should set up rules regarding who should see the minutes and who in addition to the team members should receive copies of minutes.

Minutes can sometimes be misinterpreted. Therefore, team members should discuss important topics with their subordinates who see the minutes.

Minutes contain the following information:

- All decisions made by the team.
- A record of the disposition of every agenda item.
- A record of all task assignments made at the meeting—who does what when.
- The date, time, and place of the meeting.

- A list of those in attendance.
- A list of late arrivals (optional). This can help alleviate tardiness: no one wants his name appearing on a tardy list very often. Also, a list of late arrivals indicates who was absent during a specific discussion, so they can be filled in later if necessary.
- Background discussion leading to a decision (optional). At some time in the future when a decision is being reevaluated team members may want to refresh their memories by a review of the discussion.

Follow-up of Meetings

Whoever records the minutes (whether the secretary or your assistant) should redline individual copies of minutes going to individual members of the team to point up any task assigned to that member. This will serve as a reminder to team members who have a follow-up assignment to do, and will save time because the member does not have to read the entire minutes to pick out his assignment—if it is redlined, his attention is drawn to it immediately.

Another service the secretary or your assistant can perform, if the team considers it helpful, is to attach a summary to each agenda listing the tasks assigned at the previous meeting and noting the status of the task, that is, whether it has been completed or is still in the process of being completed. This, of course, requires communication between the secretary and the team members who were assigned tasks. Such a summary is one way of keeping all team members posted on progress and eliminating the necessity of having such reports presented orally at a meeting.

EVALUATION OF TEAM EFFECTIVENESS

Leadership teams do not always function effectively. Therefore, the team should adopt a method of evaluating its own performance. This evaluation should be done periodically. Some leadership teams evaluate their performance at the end of every meeting in order to give immediate feedback to team members. This can be done orally or in writing. Here are some questions team members can ask themselves. Answers can be summarized as a monthly, bimonthly, or quarterly group evaluation. If there is a great disparity among the answers group members give for any question, or if there is much negative feedback, a special meeting to discuss the team's effectiveness is in order.

Team Effectiveness Questions:

1. Are team members prepared for each meeting? Have individual members done their homework on problems they bring to the team?
2. How inhibited is discussion? Do members feel free to express their thoughts openly to one another?
3. Does discussion center on the agenda item being dealt with—or do members wander from the subject frequently?
4. Do all members participate actively in discussion?
5. Do any members engage in activities that disrupt the group, such as sarcasm, asides, digs, inappropriate humor, and so forth?
6. Do members follow up promptly on assigned tasks?
7. Do members refrain from complaining about decisions once the team has made them?
8. Do members refrain from appealing to the leader to change a decision the team has made?
9. Is the team leader accepted as a team member, as opposed to someone with more authority than other members and therefore someone to defer to?
10. Does the team leader refrain from preaching, lecturing, moralizing, and psychoanalyzing?
11. Is the leader willing to trust the combined wisdom of the team members as equal or superior to his own individual wisdom?
12. How well can the team function without the leader? Are decisions made in the leader's absence frequently returned to the agenda for restructuring?

8

Developing
Your Leadership Team
and Staff People

Each year, after selections for the Hall of Fame for Business Leadership have been completed, the editors of *Fortune* review the biographies of the business leaders selected for this honor to see if there is a common thread running through the lives of each of them. The 1979 theme turned out to be the importance of the learning process in business achievement. Writing about the 1979 Hall of Fame, Max Ways stated:

> Because business never sits still, the men who lead it must be learners and educators. To learn and help others to learn is what management is about. [1]

There are good reasons for organizations to invest time and money in development of their leaders. If an organization is to remain strong and competitive, it must be able not only to attract strong leaders, but also to hold them in the organization. Often an organization's most promising executives will migrate to other organizations when their self-actualization needs are unmet. The basic

[1] Max Ways, "The Hall of Fame for Business Leadership," *Fortune*, March 26, 1979, p. 43.

cause of high attrition among promising leaders who have career aspirations are underdevelopment and underutilization. Achieving top-level leaders identify subordinate leaders who have achievement potential and then invest time and money and personal nurturing to help them succeed in their careers within the organization.

THE EXPECTANCY CONCEPT
OF LEARNING

Hybrid leaders are the result of genetic seed (skills, talents) being sown in fertile soil (organization) and nourished by expectancy. Most employees have the genetic seed necessary to do at least average work. When an employee plants his genetic seed in an organization that is rich in opportunity, it may or may not grow depending on the initiative and drive of the employee. The ground may become hard and some seeds may never germinate. Criticism will rain like hail upon the young seedlings and break them. If the young plants grow at all, they will grow slowly and bloom late. But if the same seed is planted in the same soil, but placed in the care of a gardener who looks beyond the seed and visualizes a harvest of great value, the seed will be nurtured and will almost always meet or exceed the gardener's expectations. A leader's expectations are the key to a subordinate's performance and career success.

In George Bernard Shaw's *Pygmalion* (1912), Eliza Doolittle wisely says:

> You see, really and truly, apart from the things anyone can pick up, the dressing and the proper way of speaking, and so on, the difference between a lady and a flower girl is not how she behaves, but how she's treated. I shall always be a flower girl to Professor Higgins, because he always treats me as a flower girl, and always will; but I know I can be a lady to you, because you always treat me as a lady, and always will.

It takes more than positive thinking about an employee and a verbal pat on the back now and then for a leader to develop a subordinate's skills and talents. Helpful as these things are, they do not reach deeply enough. Used often without substance to back them up, they become superficial and ineffective. One executive thought that by promising career advancement to his subordinates he could keep them working at top performance in anticipation of advancement. The years rolled by and the promised advancements never materialized. One subordinate became discouraged and left the company to accept a position with another firm. Another subordinate just became discouraged, then bored, and finally became a less-than-average employee and a liability to the company.

What can a leader do to develop a subordinate? First, he must have confidence in his own ability to do so. The subordinate will interpret any lack of self-confidence in the leader as the leader's lack of confidence in the subordinate. Success breeds confidence. Confidence in yourself as a developer of people will come as you work at developing people. As you see the people you work at developing becoming more and more like what you know they can be, your confidence in your ability to develop people will grow.

Second, a leader must know how to develop people. It is not a natural talent—it is a learned skill.

How the Expectancy Concept Works

The expectancy concept works best when you hand-pick your protégés. The reason for this is that not everyone is career-minded or wants to advance to more responsibility. Some like what they are doing and have no wish to take on more responsibility. These persons are assets to the organization if they are placed in positions suitable to their talents, skills, and personality. There is nothing wrong with not wanting to advance to higher positions. There are excellent machinists who want to remain excellent machinists and have no desire to become managers or lead supervisors regardless of the increase in salary they would receive if they did move up. To advance these employees against their desire to advance would be denying them the freedom to pursue their self-actualization needs.

The achievement evaluation interview which we will mention in Chapter 10 will help you determine those subordinates who want to advance in their careers. An achievement-minded leader will work with all of those subordinates who want to advance. He may, however, give particular attention to those who seem to have greater potential. Look for your protégé among young men and women of the organization. Early career years are critical. They often determine the later success of the worker. Early successes lead to positive attitudes in the subordinate that will be an advantage to him when he leaves your tutelage and is on his own. Another place to look for your protégé is among your first-line managers and supervisors. These are important people to the organization. How they function determines the morale of workers under them, which in turn determines the productivity of the organization.

Having identified your protégé, have a career conference with him. This may be the annual performance evaluation or it may be a special conference. Tell your subordinate that you have high expectations concerning his abilities and that you want to help him achieve his potential. Be sure to let him tell you what his aspirations are and show a genuine interest in what he says. Point out how his aspirations can fit in with the organization's goals. Some leaders go as far as to give their protégé the lion's share of training money available and to risk future commitment.

The protégé must consider his superior's high expectations of him to be realistic and achievable. If he strives for what he believes to be unattainable results, he will give up and settle for lower performance than he is capable of. At the same time, expectations should not be set too low. There is no incentive when the goal is virtually certain to attain or virtually impossible to attain.

DEVELOPING YOUR SUBORDINATES

Here are some ideas for developing your subordinates. You may want to utilize those that fit your particular situation.

1. The first experiences of a young executive strongly influence his chances for achievement later in his career. Assign jobs that your subordinate believes he can just barely do. If the task is too easy or too difficult, motivation and effort plunge. Studies have indicated that motivation and effort are greatest when the worker has a 50 percent chance of success. Resist the temptation to assign tasks to the best-qualified person on your staff. You may get better results as far as the task is concerned, but a person who is overqualified for the task may interpret the assignment as a sign that your expectations of him are low.

2. Before assigning certain tasks, especially if there is a possibility that you may have overestimated your subordinate's ability, have the subordinate role-play the task. Explain the task and ask how he would handle it. Offer verbal imaginary obstacles to see how he responds. If after this dry-run approach you are satisfied that the subordinate can handle the task, assign the task. But if you are convinced it is a task too advanced for the subordinate at this time, you can gracefully back off and assign the task to another person.

3. Give your subordinate positive strokes on his capabilities, not on how well he does the task. Most subordinates measure success in terms of praise or criticism from their superiors. Provide each subordinate with a balance of positive and negative feedback.

4. Break down large tasks into a series of smaller assignments. Review each small assignment when it is completed. If problems arise on a small assignment, corrective action can be taken before going on to the next assignment and the whole task is not adversely affected.

5. After a subordinate has completed a task, go over it with him. Ask him to evaluate his own work—which parts of the assignment did he handle better than other parts, for example. Give your own estimation of the work, but avoid talking in terms of "good" or "bad." Talk in terms of "stronger" and "weaker." Have the subordinate tell you what he would do differently if he were given a similar assignment in the future. This encourages the subordinate to make objective evaluations of his own work.

6. There are six responsibility levels. As you work at developing a subordinate, start at the level he is on and help him to progress upward to the sixth level.

Level 1: Your subordinate works only on your orders. When routine work is finished, he waits for your instructions.

Level 2: Instead of waiting for "orders" your subordinate accepts suggestions from you. You may suggest more than one possible course of action. Your subordinate weighs them and chooses the course to take.

Level 3: Your subordinate plans what he thinks should be done and gets your approval before going ahead. He may gather data for a report, draft a reply to a letter, or plan a project and get your approval before taking action.

Level 4: Your subordinate goes ahead with action on minor problems: he gets work started. He keeps you informed at all times.

Level 5: Your subordinate acts on any problem he feels secure about and notifies you later. Even if he errs occasionally, he gains confidence and is on his way to becoming a valuable assistant. Give him credit publicly and in private for what he does right. A brief complimentary note from you is something your subordinate can proudly show his family and friends and will help build his self-confidence.

Level 6: Your subordinate acts entirely on his own in carrying out his responsibilities with the possible exception of major projects. You give him complete authority to carry out his responsibilities. He reports to you only when there is an exceptional problem he cannot handle.

7. Delegate parts of your work to your subordinate. (See Chapter 14 on delegation.)

8. Create action learning teams. Some large organizations utilize project teams to train middle managers. The team consists of from four to six career-minded managers that the organization is interested in training for top-level management positions. An advisor from either within or without the organization is assigned to the team. The team is then given a project to tackle which will require the use of all the leadership skills, such as fact finding, diagnosis, creativity, decision making, and learning how to communicate and create motivation in others. The project may take from six months to a year to complete. The projects are usually aimed at future action by the organization.[2]

9. Enter into a learning contract with your subordinate. For example, during a performance evaluation conference your subordinate tells you about his career goals. In order for your subordinate to make progress toward his career goals, he needs further education or training. This is a stumbling block to many people and they procrastinate getting started on a training program. Suggest that your subordinate construct a plan which will become a contract between you and him. The contract should include:

- Description of learning objectives
- Learning resource for each objective
- Target date for accomplishing each objective
- Evidence that demonstrates accomplishment of each objective (You will give him a real or imaginary assignment that he will use to demonstrate new knowledge.)
- Validation of evidence (course certificate, diploma, etc.)

10. Play management games with your subordinate. Recall situations from your past experience that required you to use

[2]Nancy Foy, "Action Learning Comes to Industry," *Harvard Business Review*, September/October 1977, pp. 158-68.

management expertise. Ask your subordinate how he would have solved that kind of a situation. Then engage in a discussion of the pros and cons of how you handled it and how he would have handled it. Keep the discussion on an impersonal basis. Discuss what happened with what result—not who did what.

11. Encourage your subordinate to attend seminars and workshops in management and related subjects. Allocate money in your departmental or organizational budget for in-service training. When an employee attends a seminar at organizational expense, require an oral or written report on the subject matter. Perhaps the subject matter would lend itself to your subordinate presenting the information in a mini-workshop to other employees. He would not only benefit from attendance at the seminar, but would also gain practice in presenting information to a group.

Outside seminars offer a very practical way to bring new ideas into an organization. They are advertised in university extension brochures and management publications. Available seminars can also be located by contacting speakers listed in the *Speakers Bureau Directory* mentioned in item 12 below.

12. Arrange in-house training programs. You can do this through a college or university or through a private consultant firm. The Training Resources Center of the American Society for Training and Development publishes a *Speakers Bureau Directory* that makes it easy to locate speakers for in-house meetings and workshops. Their address is P.O. Box 5307, Madison, Wisconsin 53705.

13. Self-administered regimens permit developing leaders to give themselves feedback and positive reinforcement in skill areas where they are weak. For example, as a leader you observe that your subordinate manager needs to be more forceful. Help this manager develop a regimen and feedback mechanism to overcome this fault. Have him keep a tally of the times he publicly acknowledges his differences of opinion with peers and superiors. One manager related to us that his boss told him he was perceived as a grouch and suggested that every day he tell at least three people something nice about themselves or their work and *keep score.*

A LOOK AT INDIVIDUALS

There are a number of types of employees who deserve special comment.

First-line Supervisors

The first-line supervisor (a person who supervises people who do not supervise other people) is often referred to as a part of the management team, but is seldom allowed to participate in that role. If anyone is entitled to a "belonging" crisis, it's the first-line supervisor. By the nature of his position he is separated from his workers. If he is to supervise effectively, he cannot be "one of the boys (or girls)." They consider him a representative of management. Yet, in reality, he is not management because he does not participate or contribute to the management function. His organizational identity is often vague in his own mind and his potential contribution to management of the organization is virtually untapped.

First-line supervisors are key elements in any organization. They supervise the people who produce for the organization. And yet they are often placed in their positions with little or no prior training in how to supervise.

If the morale of the first-line supervisor is low because of an identity crisis or any other reason, it follows that the morale of his department will be low. Low morale always results in low productivity. High morale among the workforce is built upon a high degree of respect, trust, and confidence in the boss. A first-line supervisor can be leavening for this respect, trust, and confidence if he is properly trained and motivated and if he has the same respect, trust, and confidence in his superior.

A special effort should be made by middle and top management to include first-line supervisors in the management process. This can be accomplished in several ways:

- They can be represented on the leadership team.
- They can be included in training and development programs.
- There can be more interaction and feedback between the supervisor and his immediate superior.

With regard to the last point, too often distinct lines of demarcation are drawn between the supervisor's function and management's function, with a minimum amount of interaction between the two. This middle ground of interaction should be enlarged to include the supervisor's participation in the establishment of goals, policies, etc. for his workers. He should have some degree of authority in the evaluation, hiring, and firing of workers. In other words, the supervisory staff should participate in the management of the work force.

Your Administrative Assistant

Your administrative assistant is a staff person who may or may not be part of your leadership team. If you are interested in developing your assistant for a leadership role, consider making him or her a part of your leadership team. Participation in your leadership team would be a good learning experience for your assistant.

If you are considering employing your first administrative assistant, consider the type of person you need. Since an assistant's first function is to make your work easier so you can work more effectively, choose one who has a lively interest in what is going on in the department. He should be a person who does not merely report problems to you or pitch in to help when the work piles up (although these are desirable traits), but one who also can come up with constructive suggestions for improvement. You need an assistant who is a creative person with initiative. Your assistant should be a person whose personality and temperament does not duplicate yours. It is difficult, for example, for two people who are dynamic and aggressive to work together. If your assistant often has to suppress his own natural responses to defer to you, sooner or later there will be conflict. Or you will suppress your natural tendencies and be less effective than you can be. However, your assistant's strengths teamed with your weaknesses can result in an effective working relationship.

Your administrative assistant should be a person who gets along well with others, including peers, customers, salespeople, subordinates, superiors (his and yours). Ask yourself, "Is this person's friendliness genuine, or might it turn into bossiness when I'm not around?"

You can help your assistant develop into an invaluable aide if you take time to train him. Here are some suggestions for training your administrative assistant. You may think of others that relate more specifically to your situation.

1. Have your assistant work along with you for the first few weeks. This way he will get a manager's point of view. Explain the contribution-to-organizational-goals concept of management (mentioned in Chapter 5). Help your assistant to see why certain

policies and procedures are helpful to the achievement of organizational goals.

2. As you assign functions of your department to your assistant, assign corresponding authority to carry out the responsibilities of the function. When you assign a specific responsibility and authority to your assistant, introduce him to the people in the department who are involved in that function. Stress the fact that your assistant is taking your place and has your authority and responsibility for that function. This is especially important if the persons engaged in the assignment are former peers of your assistant.

3. Your new assistant may make mistakes. Help him to learn from mistakes. Discuss mistakes privately. Don't cast blame. Help your assistant to figure out better ways the task could have been handled. If it is necessary to change what your assistant has done or even to reverse a decision your assistant made, guide him privately and then allow him to make the necessary changes. Never lower your assistant's status in the eyes of his subordinates.

4. Share information with your assistant, even when it does not relate to his function. If you are working on a project, share information and your plans concerning the project and any problems you anticipate. Your assistant will be better able to answer questions or handle emergency situations concerning the project in your absence. Be sure your assistant knows the extent to which you would want him to act in your absence.

5. Have a definite period, at least weekly, to have an informal discussion with your assistant concerning the work of the department. At this time, information can be exchanged and constructive criticism and praise given.

Your Secretary

There are two kinds of secretaries—the career secretary and the secretary who uses her secretarial position as a stepping-stone into other kinds of work.

A career secretary is one who enjoys being a secretary. She or he finds it exciting and challenging work. She may be career-minded and choose to move laterally across division and department lines in order to learn as much about the organization as she can and eventually reach the "top," which would be secretary to the top executive. Or she may transfer laterally to find the department where her talents and interests fit best. For example, she may be particularly interested in personnel work and so she may want to work her way up in her secretarial career until she is secretary to the personnel manager. A career secretary will always be someone's secretary. If she is your secretary, if she has good rapport with you, and if she finds the work of your department interesting, she may be content to stay in that position indefinitely. She is more interested in the furtherance of your career than her own.

The other kind of secretary, the one who uses her secretarial training as a stepping-stone to move up in the organization in non-secretarial positions, has a different viewpoint than the career secretary. Although she may have good rapport with her "chief," she has no feelings of being "tied" to him. If you have this kind of secretary, you will find her to be more interested in her own career than in yours. This does not mean she will not be an effective secretary for you. She may try harder than a career secretary because when she does move out of secretarial work, she will value your goodwill and your assistance up the corporate ladder.

Your secretary, regardless of how she views her position, is a very important member of your staff team, perhaps the most important because of the uniqueness of her position. She is certainly a person whose needs must be met if you want her to develop into an achieving employee who is loyal to the organization for which you both work. Here are some ideas for developing your secretary:

1. If she is a career-minded secretary, be aware that great changes are taking place in office work. With the advent of word processing many large organizations set up centralized word-processing departments. Many secretaries were moved into supervisory positions in these word-processing centers. Some people thought that secretaries would soon be obsolete. Nothing could have been further from the truth. Now, as technological advances are refined, computer-type equipment is being brought into individual offices rather than being centralized in one large department. This means that your career secretary will have to learn how to operate these computers. You should help your secretary to look at the new technology as a tool to help her do her work—not as a threat to her position.

Your career secretary can become your unofficial office manager and relieve you of many details of managing the office. But to function this way, she needs to be given the responsibility and authority to do so. Train her to function in this capacity and give her the authority to do so. Remember, your career secretary wants you to succeed because your success is her success. She is eager to relieve you of routine tasks, such as answering correspondence, compiling reports, representing you by speaking for you or acting for you in matters where she has the necessary knowledge to do so. Training and allowing your secretary to do these kinds of tasks will help to satisfy her self-actualization needs because by doing these things she is realizing her greatest potential as she sees it.

2. If your secretary is using secretarial work as a stepping-stone to higher ground, allow her to be open about it. Discuss her career goals with her and help her to achieve them. Instead of hiring someone else, train your secretary to be your administrative assistant. When she is able to function in this capacity, give her the title and, if possible, the salary. Sing her praises to your peers, if you think she is deserving. Be a fan of hers and she will be a fan of yours.

Your Technician

The office of the future will consist of such things as advanced word-processing systems, centralized and distributed data-processing systems, electronic mail and correspondence systems, standalone minicomputers, reprographics, micrographics, teleconferencing, and the telecommunications-based interconnection of these technologies in integrated networks.[3]

One of the goals of organizational leadership in the next 10 years will be to organize and direct the introduction of new technologies. To succeed in this complex task, the leader must have a thorough understanding of the applications of technology and information needs and how these affect employee performance. He will have to be a very versatile person, with a broad understanding of human as well as technical issues.

Just as managers must learn how to use the new technologies, technicians must learn how to manage people. If you have a technician on your staff who is interested in career advancement into organizational leadership, you should encourage him to engage in leadership training. Include your technical people in as much of the nontechnical aspects of management as you can. Give them opportunities to interrelate with other leadership team members and staff people. Encourage your leadership team members to have a recipro-

---

[3] Jeffrey S. Prince, "What It Will Take to Manage in the 80s," *Administrative Management*, January 1980, pp. 34-35, 54.

cal attitude toward your technical people. Your managers can help your technicians understand the human elements of change, while your technicians can help your managers understand the applications of technology.

9

Staffing for Productivity

The bottom line in any organization is productivity. How many pieces produced, how many sales completed, how many clients serviced, and how many new customers gained in a given period depends on the productivity of the people of the organization. You can invest more capital, spend more on research and development, update your equipment, and use better methods; but these resources will have little effect on productivity unless you give paramount attention to the management of human resources. The greatest undeveloped resource in most organizations is its people. The leader who can develop people can build a productive team.

CHANGES IN THE WORK FORCE

Three major changes have taken place in the work force in the last decade. They are changes in age of workers, sex of workers, and attitude of workers.

Age

The median age of Americans increased in the last decade from 28 to 37.4; and it is predicted that by the year 2000 the median work force age in the United States will be 40.8.[1]

A study conducted by Benson Rosen and Thomas H. Jerdee, professors of business administration at the Graduate School of Business, University of North Carolina, concluded that many times managers base their decisions about employees' qualifications on stereotyped views of age.[2] Some of the stereotyped views have to do with resistance to change, obsolescence, lack of creativity and innovativeness, and declining mental alertness. Ironically, many stereotypes of older workers (over 50) are formed by organizationally created self-fulfilling prophecy. Managers who expect a decline in motivation among older workers are often inclined to make decisions that lead to decreased motivation for those employees. For example, managers are likely to view older employees as less motivated to keep up with the latest technology in their field and therefore provide less opportunity for older workers to receive training. When a request for such training comes from an older employee, instead of attributing it to a desire to keep up to date, a manager will often attribute the request to some other motive. For example, Jim Adams, age 59, and Tom Garcia, age 36, both production supervisors, applied to their division head for funds to attend a production seminar in Atlanta. The division head evaluated the two requests and concluded that the younger man was more concerned with keeping up with the latest production technology and the older man was more concerned with receiving a fair share of the training budget. Sometimes leaders select a younger employee for training on the assumption that the younger employee has more productive years to give to the organization. This might seem to be a reasonable assumption; however, leaders might also consider the problem of turnover among younger employees. Another aspect to keep in mind concerning older employees is that they tend to be more dependable. Often, simply because they feel competition with younger employees, they will put forth more effort and be more punctual and steady than younger employees. Also, it

---

[1] "The Productivity Crunch," *Training World*, May/June 1979, p. 25.

[2] Benson Rosen and Thomas H. Jerdee, "Too Old or Not Too Old," *Harvard Business Review*, November/December 1977, pp. 97-106.

can be argued that older employees often have more ability due to experience than younger employees.

We can only generalize on the age factor. A managerial leader looking for high productivity should evaluate all employees on an individual basis, being careful not to allow personal bias or preconceived ideas to influence his evaluation of any employee.

Sex

Equal rights legislation has changed the role of women in business and industry in recent years, and now more women are being promoted to higher levels of responsibility than a few years ago. Unfortunately, this is a source of frustration to some male leaders. It need not be. As we said in Chapter 2, sexuality, whether male or female, is a power tool that can be used to advantage. The leader who recognizes this will have more freedom in placing subordinates where they will be most productive. Sex, like age, is a factor that can be considered only generally. To repeat: a leader looking for high productivity should evaluate all employees on an individual basis, being careful not to allow personal bias or preconceived ideas to influence his evaluation.

Attitude of Workers

Changing values and life styles of recent years are reflected in the attitude of workers at nearly all levels of employment. A worker's priorities used to be "the job, then me." Whatever it took to do a good job and win the approval of one's superiors had precedence over one's personal and family life. The "boss" *was* the boss, and his decisions and orders were seldom questioned. Now the prevailing attitude is "me first, then the job." We live in an era when old standards are being challenged. The rights of minorities of all kinds are championed, and most individuals and groups tend to think defensively in relation to their jobs and the workplace. Thus, there are more demands made on management for better working conditions, more fringe benefits, shorter hours, and more pay—and now, viewed by many workers as more important than all of these, an opportunity to participate in making decisions that affect them.

These are changes that have taken place in the work force in general and they are changes that leaders must be aware of and deal with. But in dealing with these changes, leaders should never lose sight of the fact that their staffs are made up of individuals. The treatment of the individual is still the most consequential aspect of leadership. Employees want and should be recognized as individual persons, not as individual cogs in a large wheel. An employee wants to be called by name, not by a number on a payroll nor a title on an organizational chart.

It is on a personal, individual basis that effective leaders approach the task of placing their workers where they can be most productive.

INTERVIEWING FOR JOB PLACEMENT

Just as the employee puts "me" before the job, leaders should put the employee before the job when they are placing employees. The strength of any organization lies in the combined strengths of its employees—not in the functions of jobs on the organizational chart. Whenever a leader makes the job fit the employee (instead of the employee fit the job) he staffs for productivity. When the employee is made to fit the job, mediocrity or failure is the result. When the job fits the employee, success at some degree above mediocrity for both the employee and the organization is the result.

Suppose on your staff you have a number of employees. Each one fills a certain position on your organization chart. You have placed each one in his job according to his strengths. Suppose one of these employees leaves and you have a vacancy to fill. Consider your staff as a strong productive unit made up of the combined strengths of x number of employees. It has been weakened by the loss of the strength of one employee. Conduct your interviews with the idea of at least replacing that lost strength and, if possible, exceeding it.

Before your first interview, revaluate all the jobs and all the strengths of the remaining employees. Employees change as they become more experienced in their work. Some outgrow their jobs and develop strengths that could be used to better advantage in other positions. Some may have grown stale in their present jobs. Others, because of changes in personal life style, might do a better job in a different position. If you have kept up with each employee as we will suggest in Chapter 10, you will know whether or not each one is still in the position where his greatest strength can be utilized.

After revaluating your staff in this manner, you may see where you can make some reassignments of job tasks so that the jobs better fit the strengths of the employees. On the other hand, you may find that each employee is in the job where he can be most productive, in which case you would not need to make any reassignments.

With a fresh overall view of your employees and their individual strengths and functions in mind, you are ready to interview applicants. As you interview, look for someone who not only can perform the duties that have been vacated, but who also has strengths that will complement the present strengths of your staff.

Look for achievers. It is not enough to have talent or ability, one must be able to use his talent or ability to achieve objectives. Most achieving leaders select achieving team members because they know that if their team members achieve or surpass their objectives, their own achievements are reasonably assured. While nonachieving employees can be encouraged to develop into achievers on the job, it is easier and quicker to build an achieving team by hiring new employees who are already achievers.

Achievers are difficult to recruit. They don't as a rule answer help-wanted ads, because they are generally already in positions where they are achieving. They usually have job satisfaction because achievement is the root of job satisfaction. Achievers are generally compensated in proportion to their above-average contributions to organization goals. Achievers who are looking for work are scarce. A leader who is looking for achievers to add to his team will have to actively search for them. They seldom come looking for employment unless they have been the victims of a merger, a lost company contract, or some other situation beyond their control.

Here are questions a leader should seek answers for when considering applicants:

To determine strengths:
1. What has this person done well?
2. What is the person likely to be able to do well because of education, training, experience, and personality?
3. Would this person need additional education or training in order to perform the duties of the vacant position?
4. In what way would this person complement my present staff?
5. Does this person have any knowledge, talent, or characteristic that would open up a new opportunity for my department to contribute to organizational goals?
6. If this person were put in a supervisory position, how would he affect

those working under him? Employees tend to fashion themselves after a forceful boss. Is this the kind of person that I would want other employees to emulate? Would his style be constructive or destructive?

To determine past achievements:
7. Does the applicant stress past or present responsibilities and duties, but say very little about accomplishments?
8. What is the depth of the applicant's accomplishments and how consistent has it been?

The ability to interview people to gain information and make decisions is an essential part of leadership. Here are some techniques or guidelines productive leaders follow when interviewing applicants:

1. Avoid creating stress for the interviewee. In all probability the interviewee is already under some stress. Grilling the applicant with a series of difficult, unexpected, anxiety-producing questions will put him on edge and he will likely respond with yes and no answers which give little information. Such grilling breaks down any rapport there may have been between you and the interviewee and puts the applicant on the defensive.

2. Avoid asking leading questions. A leading question is one that suggests the correct answer and puts words in the other person's mouth. "Do you think . . .?" and "You enjoy . . ., don't you?" are examples of leading questions. The applicant will usually agree with you in order not to jeopardize himself.

3. Avoid loaded questions, like "When are you going to settle down with one company?" This question suggests that you think the applicant has been unstable. If the applicant answers the question, "When . . .," he admits to this fault. The only other answer he can give is to disagree with your premise, which puts a barrier between you and him.

4. Avoid questions that have the possibility of yes or no answers. Asking questions that require more than yes or no will help the applicant reveal himself more openly, and you will derive more insight into the applicant's ability to express himself.

5. Accept clarifying questions in response to your questions, and be prepared to give examples in order to explain your question.

6. Invite the interviewee to ask questions about the job. Few questions on the part of the applicant may indicate he would be submissive, unimaginative, or even unthinking on the job.

7. Be an active listener. The purpose of the interview is for you to gain information. The applicant should do most of the talking. Your job is to lead the conversation to the subjects about which you want information. Then listen attentively. The applicant will be encouraged to speak frankly and freely if he feels you are genuinely interested in what he is saying.

8. Have notepaper on the desk and pen in hand from the start of the interview. Make frequent notes and invite the applicant to do likewise. If you take out a notepad and begin making notes during the course of the interview, the applicant will become uneasy, wondering what he said that you are noting and whether it pleased or displeased you. But if you explain at the start that you are going to be making notes, and invite him to make notes, your notetaking should not disturb him.

9. Read cues. Messages are sent by voice inflections, gestures, mannerisms, posture, and dress. Sometimes cues and words disagree. When they do, the nonverbal cues are more likely to be the truth. For example, if an applicant says, "I'm excited about the prospect of working here" and says it in a monotone, slumped over in a chair with elbow on desk and chin resting in the palm of the hand, you would be wise to believe the nonverbal message.

Where to Find Applicants

There are various hunting grounds you can explore when looking for a person to fill a specific job. For example:

- You can advertise in newspapers and trade journals. Some managers keep a looseleaf notebook tab-indexed by classification. Each time they place a help-wanted ad, they put a copy of it in the appropriate section of the binder. They also place in their binders copies of eye-catching help-wanted ads that others have placed. These can be helpful when devising future ads.
- Colleges have placement offices that keep a register of graduates looking for positions.
- Government employment services.
- Private employment agencies: if you have given a private employment agency your job specifications, the agency can do the preliminary screening for you.
- Professional journals often carry ads of applicants who are looking for positions, or you can place an ad in a professional journal.
- Your own organization's data bank on current employees, especially

if it is the policy of your organization to promote from within. We recommend that you keep a staff audit for your own staff.[3] If you do this, you will always have current information on the qualifications of each staff member.

ASSIGNING EMPLOYEES

If the job fits the employee, as mentioned earlier in this chapter, you are well on the way to creating job satisfaction for the new employee or the employee in a new position. There are some other things to consider, too.

The structuring of relationships among all staff members is an important aspect of job satisfaction. Each staff member must know his responsibility and authority. Responsibility is the obligation to do an assigned job. An employee needs to be clear on what his job encompasses and what is expected of him. Authority is the right given the employee by his superior to (1) make decisions in regard to his work assignment; (2) assign tasks to his subordinates in accordance with these decisions; and (3) seek and receive information relating to his assignment laterally from other employees of the organization.

It is a great mistake for a leader to assign responsibility without sufficient authority to carry out the responsibility. But often this is done; or if authority is given with responsibility, it is sometimes not made known to other staff members. Consequently, an employee may fail in an assignment because he cannot gain the support he needs from others.

Employees gain job satisfaction by feeling worthwhile. They feel worthwhile when they understand how their work contributes to the achievement of the goals of their department and the organization. They want to be recognized as a necessary part of the team. Their ego needs must be satisfied and they must have an opportunity to work toward the fulfillment of their self-actualization needs.

ORIENTING THE NEW EMPLOYEE

All new employees should have an opportunity to attend an orientation program, whether it is on a one-to-one instruction basis or a formal group program. Most large organizations plan orientation

---

[3] See Helen Reynolds and Mary E. Tramel, *Executive Time Management: Getting Twelve Hours Work Out of an Eight-hour Day*, Englewood Cliffs, N.J., Prentice-Hall, 1979, p. 141.

programs for new employees on a regular basis. These are held monthly, quarterly, semiannually, or yearly depending on the size of the organization and the number of new employees. Sometimes the programs are planned for all new employees and sometimes they are for certain classifications of employees. For example, most school districts have teacher orientation programs before school starts in the fall. Some school districts follow the teacher orientation program with programs for various classified services such as clerical, custodial, maintenance, and transportation. As a rule, school districts require all employees, both new and those who have been on the job for years, to attend. This is a way to update the experienced employees at the same time the new employees are being oriented.

The purpose of having orientation programs is twofold. From the organization's point of view it is beneficial to have employees who are informed, motivated, and productive in their jobs. From the employees' viewpoint, they want and need clarification in many areas relating to their employment. The Corning Glass Company conducted a study a few years ago to learn what new employees expect from an orientation. The study revealed that employees deemed the following information to be essential: review of duties; introduction to fellow workers; a physical view of the plant or department; an explanation of hours, pay, and security; how the job relates to organizational goals; a cordial welcome; and a discussion of performance reviews. Other areas considered desirable but not essential included such things as an opportunity to ask questions; information on pensions, benefits, and insurance; locations of necessary facilities; and encouragement to offer suggestions and ideas. The Corning study showed that new employees considered to be unimportant information on cultural activities in the community and being introduced to others with similar recreational interests.[4]

Group Orientation Programs

Inasmuch as group orientation programs are planned by the organization, they are often planned solely from the organization's viewpoint. They are aimed at instilling in the employee the information the organization deems the employee needs to make management's job easier. Often very detailed information on policies, procedures, history of the organization, who's who in the manage-

[4]"Orientation Program: Meeting the Real Needs," *Management World*, February 1977, p. 4.

ment, and so forth is given—and quickly forgotten by most employees. It is the wrong kind of information and in too much detail for most people to remember. It is information they will absorb in time, as they need it, on the job. For a group orientation program to be successful, it must be aimed at filling the needs of employees. A carefully planned group orientation should include:

1. Basic information about the job, how it is to be performed, and how performance will be evaluated, as well as how the job fits into the total plan of the organization and how it contributes to the achievement of organizational goals. If organizational goals are not known to new employees, some time should be given to an explanation of goals, but not in too much detail at this time.
2. Information new employees should have regarding organizational policies, procedures, and benefits. This kind of information should be mentioned briefly and provided in writing so employees can take it with them for later reading and to keep for reference.
3. A time for new employees to ask questions and receive clarification on any job-related subject.

The largest part of any orientation program for new employees should deal with work-related functions. In some situations, for example, ample time should be provided for preparation on the part of the employee. Workers may need time to furnish their desks with needed supplies, to get acquainted with their office staff, to learn where the various offices with which they will have frequent contact are situated, and to learn how to use the telephone system if it is a complicated system in a large organization. Teachers need time to arrange their classrooms, to study the cumulative folders of pupils, and to prepare the first day's lessons. This time of preparation will help the new employee to feel comfortable the first day on the job rather than starting cold. Most new employees want to begin achieving from Day One; but if most of Day One is spent in preparing to work, not much achievement is possible.

On-the-Job Orientation
of New Employees

The task of orienting a new employee is not completed at the conclusion of the formal orientation program. Plan an ongoing learning program very carefully for each new employee. Here are some guidelines that achieving leaders use to train new employees:

1. If there has been no formal group orientation program, meet with the new employee on his first workday and provide him with the information that is ordinarily provided in a group orientation, as listed above.

2. Assign a trainer for the new employee. In doing this, select one who will likely be compatible with the new employee. Avoid personality clashes if you can foresee them. The trainer should be one who:

> Knows the job well and has all the answers about the job. To assure that this will always be the case, prepare a job analysis for each job in your department.
>
> The trainer should be a person who generally gets along well with people and has empathy and patience. He should be a booster of the organization, enthusiastic and optimistic.

3. Have a definite procedure for the trainer to follow. The procedure should include the following:

- Prepare the trainee. Help him to relax and feel at home. A few minutes at the start to talk about the trainee's interests, ambitions, and hopes will help the trainee to relax and gain confidence in the trainer as a person who is interested in the trainee's success.
- The trainer determines how much the trainee already knows about doing the tasks that make up the job. Training should always begin at the point of the trainee's need. If the job consists of more than one task, train the new employee on one task at a time.
- The trainer explains the task. Why is it necessary? How does it fit into the scheme of things? Who will see his work when he finishes it?
- The trainer tells the trainee how the task is done.
- The trainer demonstrates how the task is done.
- The trainer lets the trainee do the task.
- After each of the above points, encourage questions and feedback from the trainee.
- Once the trainee demonstrates that he can perform the job correctly, leave him to do it. Check back frequently to see if he is doing the task properly.
- Take a personal interest in the new employee. Encourage him, solicit questions, and correct errors.
- As the new employee improves, taper off your training and coaching until he can work well under normal supervision.

10

Upgrading Achievement

Upgrading achievement is not a one-time, shot-in-the-arm kind of operation. It is an ongoing, day-in-day-out task. This chapter will deal with how to upgrade the achievement of employees and keep achievement on a high level.

ACHIEVEMENT MOTIVATION

Pouring more fuel into the tank will not make an automobile perform better if there is no life in its battery. Neither will putting more dollars in the pay envelope make an employee perform better if he has no motivation to do a better job. More pay is an employee satisfier but it is not an employee motivator. In Chapter 1 we discussed Maslow's Needs Hierarchy. The lower needs on the Needs Hierarchy (physical, safety, and social) do not motivate except temporarily. It is the higher needs (ego and self-actualization needs) that motivate and continue to motivate as long as they are being satisfied. Physical, safety, and social needs must be fulfilled, however, because if they are not satisfied, they can become employee dissatisfiers. These needs translated into work language are salary, fringe benefits such as insurance, good work environment, job tenure, pension plan, parking facilities, coffee breaks, and so forth. Most of these are regarded as "rights" by today's workers, and seldom influence achievement. What does influence achievement is satisfaction of the higher needs, represented by pleasing work, recognition of good work, responsibility, advancement, growth possibilities, and in general the way employees are allowed to participate in the success or failure of organizational goals.

OBSTACLES TO ACHIEVEMENT

When employee dissatisfiers are coupled with a drop in performance, look for an obstacle to achievement. There are two kinds of obstacles to achievement: performance obstacles and work gratification obstacles.

Performance Obstacles

A performance obstacle is not the same as a demotivator, but a continuing obstacle can become a demotivator if no attempt is made to eliminate it. Obstacles to performance are those things that make work difficult. Examples of performance obstacles are: red tape; bottlenecks in work flow; inadequate facilities or equipment; unrealistic schedules; lack of skill, ability, or training; lack of communication; conflicting orders; rapidly fluctuating goals; too much work; heavy demands on noncontributing elements of the job; and responsibility without authority.

If a leader ignores an obstacle or shrugs it off as unimportant, or tells the employee to go ahead in spite of it, the obstacle will block the employee's motivation to perform. But if the leader and employee attack the obstacle in a spirit of "How can we overcome this obstacle?" the obstacle will become a challenge and the employee will be motivated to perform even though the obstacle remains.

Some performance obstacles cannot be removed. However, employees can be motivated even with one or two major obstacles if they know their leader has earnestly attempted to remove them.

Work Gratification Obstacles

Obstacles to employees gaining gratification from their work are more abstruse than obstacles to performance, but they can be every bit as damaging to achievement. Work gratification obstacles are such things as lack of recognition for work that is done well, non-constructive criticism of poor work, purpose of the work not under-stood by the employee, no sense of closure or completion of a specific task, under- or oversupervision, work below employee's capabilities, and work too far beyond employee's capabilities.

As an achieving leader, do not rely on employees to tell you when they are affronted by an obstacle. They probably will not volunteer that they feel over- or undersupervised or unappreciated, or that they don't understand the work or that the job is too diffi-cult for them. Walk through your department once a day and make daily checks on the status of work flow and workload. Frequent questioning of the staff will often bring to light obstacles to achieve-ment. Make periodic reviews of equipment and facilities.

The chart in Figure 10–1 illustrates the points at which work gratification and performance motivation affect the level of achievement. Boxes 1, 2, and 3 in the center of the chart indicate the natural progression from the contribution to be made to achievement of the goal.

Figure 10-1 *Leader-Employee Agreement*

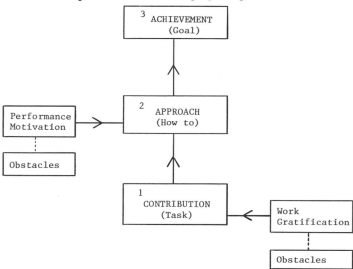

LEADER-EMPLOYEE AGREEMENT

Blocks 1, 2, and 3 in Figure 10–1 can be considered a three-part contract between the leader and the employee. As with all contracts, each part must be thoroughly understood by both parties and both parties must agree with the content of each part.

Contribution

As an inspector, Bill doesn't inspect a sufficient amount of work in a day and throws off the inspection schedules. He feels that he can make a greater contribution to his organization by tracing the causes for the errors he finds and making recommendations to the production department.

Sue spends so much time keeping a file on information she thinks might be needed by her employer that she is unable to keep up with her assigned duties.

Both Bill and Sue are working hard to achieve, but they are failing because they are attempting to achieve the wrong goals. What they think their contribution to the organization should be is different from what their employers think it should be. If they continue on this route, Bill and Sue will not only fail in what they are supposed to be doing, but they will become demotivated because their efforts will be neither recognized nor appreciated.

Written job descriptions are important and should be very carefully thought through before being put down on paper. However, even with the best possible job description a leader and employee should converse from time to time to be certain the employee understands what contribution is expected of him. Job descriptions can be amended and should be when an employee and the supervisor sees where the amendment can benefit the organization or department.

When writing a job description:

1. Be on guard against the impossible job. Sometimes a job was originally designed for a person with unusual talent or ability and does not fit anyone else. If several people with a history of success fail in the job, the job is not performable and the job description should be rewritten.
2. Make every job challenging to the doer. The job should be big enough so that the employee can grow in it—but not so big that he is overwhelmed by it.

3. Focus on results to be achieved, not on the work itself. For example, instead of saying, "Publish an employees' newsletter," say, "Keep employees informed on company activities and objectives." This latter statement allows more creativity in achieving the result.
4. The job description should indicate priorities of the job. If the job encompasses several tasks, state a priority order for the tasks.
5. Delegate responsibility and state limits of authority. To delegate a task without giving authority to do the task is a sure way to demotivate an employee. It is like giving an employee the nails but no hammer.
6. Make the job description as complete as possible. However, from time to time there will be unforeseen tasks you will want to assign to an employee. To take care of those include a phrase such as "and to do other work as assigned."
7. If you write a new job description for an old job, do it in cooperation with the employee on the job. Or have the employee write the job description for your editing and/or approval. If there are points of disagreement between what the employee thinks the job includes and what you think it includes, work with the employee toward agreement.

Approach

Approach is the second part of the three-part agreement between leader and employee. Approach is the procedure the employee is to follow to do the job. How detailed this part of the agreement is depends on the level of job. If it is a managerial job, the procedure would not be spelled out in detail although there could be some guidelines for the managerial employee to follow. The lower the level of position, the more detail of procedure should be understood and agreed upon by leader and employee.

Any job that consists of narrowly defined tasks should have written instructions for each task.

Some people like to put everything in writing while others would rather tell an employee how to do a piece of work. Here are some guidelines that some achieving leaders follow when deciding this question:

Use verbal orders when:
- The task is a simple one or a repetitive one.
- The task and the task doer are nearby.
- The task is to be demonstrated.

- The task is part of a confidential project and written instructions might fall into wrong hands.
- When the worker is reliable, experienced, and intelligent.

Use written orders when:
- The task is difficult.
- A sizable amount of time is involved in doing the task.
- The task is to be done in another office of department.
- Complicated details or exact figures are involved.
- Instructions must be followed exactly.
- A record of action is required.
- The worker is slow to understand or forgetful.
- It is desirable to hold the worker strictly accountable for the task.

Giving orders or instructions involves three parts: what you say, what you think you said, and what the other person thinks you said. As with all informing, your message should be concise, complete, and understood. To get your message across do it this way:

Orally:
1. Find out how much of the process the worker already knows and begin your instruction with the step where his knowledge seems to be incomplete. To do this have the worker tell you the procedure as far as he can.
2. Start your instruction at the worker's point of need.
3. Explain one step at a time, demonstrating if possible, and being certain the worker understands the "why" of each step.
4. Answer questions the worker has about the instruction.
5. Have the worker repeat to you the instructions you have given him.
6. Allow the worker to do the task.

In writing:
1. Begin with very first step. When writing instructions, don't assume the worker knows any part of the task.
2. Write the objective of each step and how to accomplish it. Use clear, concise language.
3. Anticipate any problem the worker might have doing the task and answer in writing any question you imagine the worker might have.

Achievement

The third part of the leader-employee agreement relates to achievement. What the leader expects the employee to achieve should be thoroughly understood by both leader and employee. Achievement relates to the first part of the agreement, contribution, but spells out in more detail not only what is to be contributed by the employee, but also how much and by when. Achieving leaders and employees should be able to write effective long-range goals and short-range objectives.

A *long-range goal* is the end result that is desired. A short-range objective describes desired mini-achievements along the way that contribute to the maxi-achievement of the long-range goal. This is called the MBO (management by objective) approach to achievement planning and achievement appraisal used by many organizations. The MBO approach can be initiated at any level of management in an organization. It works best if started at the top.

The clearer the goal, the greater the possibility that it will be accomplished. The clearer the objective, the more easily can progress toward achievement be measured.

A well-written goal or objective contains:

- An action verb
- A single result
- A date when result will be achieved
- Cost, in terms of money and/or effort

An example of a poorly written goal or objective is "Continue to provide employee orientation programs." A better stated goal is "Provide orientation programs for all new employees within three months of employment at a cost of one workday per new employee."

To be effective, goals and objectives should include as much detail as needed to answer any question an employee might have. There may be conditions that should be spelled out—for example, restrictions or limitations if any, tools, equipment, clothing to be used if applicable, list of references or job aids to be used, and so forth.

Goals and objectives should cause the employees to stretch their talents and skills because this will help them to grow and upgrade their performance. However, goals should not be set out of reach of employees. Impossible goals discourage most employees and hinder achievement.

Goals should be attainable within a reasonable time and dependent upon resources of time, money, personnel, and materials involved.

Here are some leadership maxims to keep in mind relative to goals:

1. The leader should clarify common objectives for his whole staff. When each individual is interested in only his own work goals and doesn't have a picture of what the staff as a whole is attempting to accomplish, staff members may use approaches that thwart one another's efforts.
2. The leader should shape his staff objectives to fit the organization's goals. Otherwise he will lead his staff down a noncontributing road and arrive far afield of organizational goals. Continuing on such a route, he and his staff may be considered unnecessary to the organization.
3. The leader should not make two or more individuals responsible for the same task. One responsible person is better. When more than one person is made responsible for a task, neither one will assume responsibility or both will assume responsibility and conflict may result.
4. A leader should not stress approach (method) without clarifying task (contribution).
5. Leaders should not leave the impression with employees that "pleasing the boss" is what counts more than achieving objectives.
6. A successful leader works with employees in establishing their goals and the plan of action for achievement of each goal. Sometimes a too casual leader will permit subordinates to work out their own goals which the leader then accepts uncritically, even without a plan for achievement.
7. A successful leader never ignores obstacles to goal achievement. That is like driving at night with no headlights. Allow time for regular duties and emergency situations that interfere with goal achievement.
8. Successful leaders are flexible. They are open to new ideas and new goals, even when they originate with subordinates. Sometimes previously established goals prove to be unfeasible, irrelevant, or impossible. Occasionally unexpected opportunities arise that should take precedence over established goals.

ACHIEVEMENT EVALUATION

Achievement (performance) evaluation is an important step in upgrading achievement. An employee may be aware of what his contribution (task) is and the proper approach (method for doing the task), but unless he is aware of how well he is achieving the goal, he will be unable to improve his performance.

Achievement Standards

Evaluation of achievement, to be realistic, must be based on achievement standards. Achievement standards are the result of achievement planning. They are the goals the employee is working toward—the third part of the leader-employee agreement. When goals are written they become the standards against which the employee's achievement or performance can be measured.

Evaluation for upgrading achievement focuses on how the employee uses his skills to achieve his goals. Evaluation for the purpose of upgrading achievement concentrates on positive development of skills, abilities, and behavior, which encourages the employee to reach his potential in personal growth and achievement.

Appraisal Basis

There are three appraisal bases for evaluating employees: comparison with others, comparison with standards, and comparison with objectives.

Comparison with others measures the employee's performance in relation to that of others within a specific classification. This is the base usually used to rank employees and to determine "average" productivity.

Comparison with standards requires the establishment of minimum acceptable standards, such as typing speed, shorthand rate, pieces processed, or units produced.

Comparison with objectives is evaluation for upgrading achievement, which this chapter deals with.

Appraisal Techniques

In an article by Marion G. Haynes, employee relations associate with the Shell Oil Company, nine appraisal techniques are listed. They are:

- *Objective measures.* Usually used to appraise production workers by using units produced as the base.
- *Graphic scales.* Judgment of appraiser is recorded on a continuum from low to high degree of the factor being appraised.

- *Critical incident report.* Appraiser records examples of outstandingly good or poor performance. Ignores day-to-day performance.
- *Free-written statement.* Appraiser writes a narrative report on employee's performance.
- *Forced choice report.* Appraiser describes without evaluation the person being evaluated by selecting one or more descriptive terms from a set. The terms in each set are matched so they appear equally favorable or unfavorable to the appraiser. The appraiser is forced to choose the most descriptive terms.
- *Weighted random checklist.* Brief descriptive phrases which have been assigned weights are listed and the appraiser checks the descriptive phrases that best describe the employee. The appraiser doesn't know the weights. After the forms are completed by the appraiser they are evaluated by a staff specialist.
- *Ranking.* Appraiser lists people in order from high to low.
- *Nomination.* Appraiser identifies exceptionally good and exceptionally poor performers who are then singled out for special treatment.
- *Work sample tests.* Employees are given work-related tests which are then evaluated. These tests are usually limited to mechanical and clerical tasks.[1]

Achieving leaders who are interested in upgrading achievement of their employees select the evaluation techniques that will enhance performance. Sometimes this will prove to be a combination of techniques. Achievement evaluation should be both oral and written.

The Achievement Interview

Oral evaluation that upgrades achievement is continuous and not restricted to a once-a-year formal type of interview. If evaluation is limited to a formal interview with the signing of forms, it usually results in one-way communication. The employee and often the leader are self-conscious. The leader tends to play a parent role and the employee becomes a defensive child. This is not to say that the formal evaluation interview should not take place. It is necessary for a number of reasons:

- It provides a written record of the employee's performance and achievement.

[1] Marion G. Haynes, "Developing an Appraisal Program," p. 18. Permission to reprint by *Personnel Journal*, Costa Mesa, CA., copyright January 1978.

- It is often needed for purposes of promotion, demotion, or firing.
- It is usually required by top management in large organizations.
- Unions may require it, and if they do, be certain you have observed all the legal requirements pertaining to it.

For the formal evaluation interview to be effective, it must be preceded by day-to-day evaluation. Here are some precepts to keep in mind:

1. Effective evaluation is a two-way process. It is a joint effort of leader and employee in defining goals (desired achievement), establishing priorities (what contribution is to be), and defining strategies (approach to be used).

2. Effective evaluation is positive. It stresses the strengths of the employee. It does not ignore employee weaknesses, but helps employee to see how he can use his strengths to overcome or minimize his weaknesses.

3. Effective evaluation allows feedback from the employee. For the leader to help an employee he must know how the employee sees himself.

4. Effective evaluation allows feedback from the leader to the employee.

This feedback from leader to employee should be:

- *Timely*. If correction is needed, it should be given immediately, not saved for a formal interview. Likewise, if commendation is in order, it should be immediate. Remember to criticize in private and praise in public.
- *Descriptive*. Describe the action, behavior, etc. You are feeding back the behavior to the employee, rather than evaluating it. If you can help the employee see himself, he can make his own evaluation.
- *Specific*. Don't talk in generalities. Name the specific action, work, behavior, etc.
- *Directed toward behavior the employee can do something about*. If undesirable behavior is the result of obstacles beyond the employee's control, he should not be evaluated on that behavior. For example, if a report the employee is resonsible for is always late because necessary information for the report is late getting to him, his tardiness should not be a factor—unless it is within his power to get the information sooner.
- *Problem-directed rather than employee-directed*. If you focus on the problem instead of the employee, you will be less apt to put him on the defensive and he will be more receptive to change.
- *Tested for validity with the employee*. Rather than making a state-

ment, ask a question. There may be something about the situation you are not aware of.

- *Solicited rather than imposed*. Sometimes it is necessary for the leader to initiate the feedback; but if the leader can by appropriate means (questioning, etc.) get the employee to ask for feedback, the employee will be more receptive to it.
- *Sometimes reversed* (from employee to leader). A leader needs feedback from those he leads in order to get some understanding of the effect of his own behavior on them. Peter Drucker says that effective executives have learned to ask, "What do I do that wastes your time without contributing to your effectiveness?"[2]

Achievement Evaluation Forms

Most organizations have employee evaluation forms that are tailored to the specific needs of the organization. An effective form allows for employee input as well as leader input. Sometimes leader and employee fill out their respective sections prior to the achievement interview and then any discrepancies are discussed and agreement reached during the interview.

Figure 10-2 is a suggested achievement report based on the three-part leader-employee agreement. Here is how to use the achievement report:

1. The first part is self-explanatory. The employee's name, position title, supervisor's name, etc. are filled in prior to distribution.

2. A copy is given to the employee one week or more prior to the achievement interview.

3. The employee fills in sections 1 through 4 in the left-hand column prior to the achievement interview.

4. During the achievement interview the employee and leader discuss the employee's answers in sections 1, 2, and 3. If the leader's concepts of these sections are the same as the employee's, he can write the word *agree* in the right-hand column. However, if the leader disagrees with what the employee has written, or wishes to add or delete an item, he indicates this in the right-hand column—after a two-way discussion with the employee on each change.

If the employee has indicated obstacles in section 2, they should be discussed and solutions or actions to be taken to overcome the obstacles recorded in the left-hand column.

[2] Peter F. Drucker, *The Effective Executive*, New York, Harper & Row, pp. 38-39.

```
XYZ COMPANY                                    Date: _____
                    EMPLOYEE ACHIEVEMENT REPORT

Employee Name: _____  Employee No.:_____

Employee's Position Title: _____  Dept.: _____

Supervisor's Name: _____  Supvr. Title: _____
```

Employee fills in this side.	Supervisor fills in this side.
Sec. 1: The specific contribution to department and/or organization goals this position requires.	
Sec. 2: The best approach to achieve the above-stated contribution.	
Sec. 3: Noteworthy achievements since last Achievement Report.	
Sec. 4: Development needs	Action to be taken re Development Needs
Sec. 5: Additional information	Sec. 6: Supvr's Achievement Appraisal of employee.
My supervisor has discussed the above information with me. _____ Signature of Employee Date	This employee has been under my supervision for _____years,_____months. _____ Signature of Supervisor Date

```
When completed, this form is placed in the employee's Personnel File.
Copies are retained by the employee and the supervisor.
```

Figure 10-2

5. The leader and employee will next discuss the development needs of the employee. This is an opportunity to do something concrete to upgrade performance. Perhaps the employee would like

to have time off to take some classes or attend a seminar. Perhaps the leader can offer partial or full expenses to enable the employee to do so. Maybe the employee is ready to take on additional responsibility and the leader can delegate more responsibility to the employee.

Development needs that come to light through discussion are recorded in the left-hand column of section 4; the solution(s) to development needs are recorded in the right-hand column of section 4.

6. If the employee wants to make a written statement regarding his achievement interview, he does so in section 5. For example, if the achievement report turns out to be negative to the employee, he may want to reiterate a statement he has made during the interview so it will be in writing and a part of his personnel records.

7. The leader writes his appraisal in narrative form in section 6. This is the leader's overall estimation of the employee's achievement. Some leaders prefer to fill in this section before the interview takes place. They feel they can take enough time to think through what they want to say. This usually works out well. However, if the leader has given some thought to what he wants to say prior to the interview, it should not be difficult to complete section 6 during the interview. Through the interview discussion you might gain more insight that causes you to want to change what you originally intended to write. Section 6 should be completed before section 5 in fairness to the employee.

8. As the form states, when it is completed the original is placed in the employee's personnel file and copies are retained by the leader and the employee.

ACHIEVEMENT INCENTIVES

As we said at the beginning of this chapter, upgrading achievement is an ongoing, day-in-day-out task. There are a number of incentives a leader can use from time to time, as the situation directs, that will help the employee create motivation within himself to achieve. Motivation is anything that moves a person to action of some kind. All motivation is self-created. Regardless of the stimulus or its source, the employee alone decides how he will respond and to what degree. There are three responses an employee can have to an incentive.

One response is desire or "want to." But a desire or a "want to" does not necessarily create motivation within the employee.

For example, Jane wants to create a procedures handbook for the clerical staff. To do so would require making a time-consuming methods analysis. Jane has received the incentive and has the desire to do this. She even feels guilty that she has not yet started on the project. However, she spends all of her time on routine tasks which are of first priority, in order to keep a backlog of work from piling up. It cannot be said that Jane is motivated to create a procedures handbook because she has not actually done anything toward achieving such a goal. To quote an old cliché: Where there is a will there is a way.

Another response to incentive is protective motivation. Protective motivation causes one to perform just well enough to protect one's own interests. For example, John was criticized by his employer for being late and making too many mistakes in his work. He has been threatened with dismissal if he doesn't improve. John has received an incentive (he doesn't want to be fired) and is moved or motivated to do better in order to protect his own interests. He will perform, at least for a while, at a safe level, but he is not motivated to do any better than necessary to keep from being fired.

The third response a person can have to an incentive is to become achievement-motivated. Achievement motivation causes one to attempt to achieve beyond merely safe levels over a long period. One who is achievement-motivated will "stretch" to reach goals. For example, Pete's last achievement report indicates that management thinks highly of Pete and his ability and is willing to invest time and dollars to help him rise in the organization. Pete has received the incentive and has within himself a very strong desire to achieve success. He is moved to achieve even though he may have to overcome many obstacles along the way to do so.

Obviously, the kind of motivation a leader wants his employees to have is achievement motivation. Here is a list of incentives that can help bring about achievement motivation within an employee:

1. *Being "in" on what is going on.* Employees want to be kept informed about their organization's plans, policies, and so forth. It is extremely demotivating to an employee to be told something that his organization is doing or plans to do by an "outsider." Employees can be kept up to date on organization happenings by various means, including employee newsletters, meetings, and conversation with superiors.

2. *Prizes.* This is not an incentive that we recommend in all situations. It has been used with success in dealing with salespeople or other types of employees where achievement can be measured concretely by number of sales closed, pieces produced, etc. The motivation that occurs when prizes are offered usually lasts only until someone wins the prize.

3. *Meaningful work*. When the employee can readily discern the contribution his work makes toward the achievement of organization goals, he is apt to be achievement-motivated. If he thinks his work does not make any difference one way or the other—that company goals will be achieved whether or not he does his work or regardless of how well or how poorly he does it—he is not likely to be achievement-motivated.

4. *Frequent feedback on performance*. When an employee does not know how well he is doing—when the leader neither commends nor criticizes his work—he loses interest in the work.

5. *Recognition for good work*. Recognition reinforces feelings of worth, especially when recognition comes from the "boss" or someone who can influence the employee's future. Some ways that organizations have of recognizing achieving employees are: Employee-of-the-Month award, Hall of Achievement, special parking privileges, having outstanding employees train new employees, permitting a productive employee to explain the function of his office or position to honored visitors.

6. *Fairness from the leader*. The leader who shows partiality by commending the good work of one employee and ignoring the good work of another employee doesn't cause motivation in either employee. The same applies to criticizing poor work of one employee and overlooking equally poor work of another employee. This type of leader creates within workers the belief that good work is less important than being "on the right side of the boss."

7. *Tangible accomplishment*. When a worker can actually complete an assignment and have a sense of closure, he feels that he has achieved a tangible result and is achievement-motivated to tackle the next assignment. Some work is of a continuous nature. It is ongoing and there never seems to be a point where it is completed—for example, the billing clerk who performs a routine task day in and day out. These types of jobs are necessary, but an achievement motivation-minded leader can create closure points for the employee. He can encourage the employee to set daily, weekly, or monthly goals of so many pieces of work accomplished. He can encourage the employee to look for new and better ways of doing the work. The installation of a new system by an employee, no matter how small the

change, can be a tangible result of effort put forth by the employee. The leader should let the employee know that he recognizes this accomplishment.

8. *The right amount of supervision.* Too much or too little supervision can demotivate an employee. Too little supervision can cause the employee to feel his work is unimportant. Too much supervision not only frustrates the employee, but causes him to feel that the work is not really his responsibility but the supervisor's responsibility. Feeling lack of responsibility for work does not motivate an employee to achieve.

9. *Consistent rewards.* Rewards for good work (whether they be in salary, bonus, or boss recognition) should be the same for all employees. Reward should be given only for contributing elements of the job. A good worker can be discouraged by a lack of recognition when other employees receive recognition for the same work that he does when he does it as well as the others. A good worker can be discouraged also when noncontributing elements of the job are compensated more than contributing elements. For example, employee A receives a bonus for doing extra work that does not contribute to the achievement of the department's goals, while employee B who does outstanding work that does contribute to the achievement of the department's goals receives no bonus.

10. *Challenging work.* Work should not be so easy for an employee that he becomes bored with it. Work should be difficult enough to make the employee put forth effort to accomplish it. When a worker has held the same position for many years, the work can become second nature to him. When this happens, or before, it is time to assign more difficult tasks to this worker. An employee who is constantly being challenged to stretch his ability in order to achieve is more achievement-motivated than one who knows his work so well that he does not have to put forth any exceptional effort to accomplish it.

11. *Acceptance by peers.* A person's social needs, that is, his need to belong and be accepted by others, must be met before he can strive to meet higher needs, including his need to achieve. Some people who satisfy their social needs outside the workplace can still be achievement-motivated on the job. However, in such cases the work itself is the incentive for achievement motivation. The employee who finds himself in this position can be influenced to leave the organization and accept identical work in more congenial surroundings.

This might be the best outcome for all concerned. However, if the employee is an outstanding achiever and the leader wishes to hold him in the organization, some action should be taken to make him acceptable to his peers. (See Chapter 11 on building team loyalty.)

12. *Confidence*. When an employee struggles with a job for which he is not qualified a lack of confidence builds up in him. Lack of confidence leads to frustration and frustration can lead to blaming others for one's own incompetence. Before the problem reaches this point the leader should consider additional training for the employee or a reassignment of the employee to a job where he can have confidence in his own ability to achieve.

13. *Personal involvement*. An employee who has responsibility for making some of the decisions involved in his work will likely be more achievement-motivated than one who simply follows instructions. Bear in mind, however, that some people do not like responsibility and are happier in a position where they can "go by the book" and not have to make decisions. Achievement-minded leaders are careful to make work assignments in accordance with employees' personalities in this respect.

14. *Career interest*. Some employees are career-minded while others are job-minded. An employee who is interested in advancing in his or her career is more achievement-motivated than one who is only interested in having a job. It used to be that leaders could assume that most women were job-minded—wanting to work only temporarily until the baby came or until the summer cabin was paid for—and that most men were career-minded because they were the long-term breadwinners for their families. This is an assumption that is no longer valid. Many working women now are as interested in having a career as men are. And there are both men and women who are interested only in having a job doing whatever it is they are capable of doing Both career-minded and job-minded people are needed in organizations. Achievement-minded leaders recognize which type their employees are and make work assignments accordingly. If an employee has career interest, his leader should encourage him by providing opportunities for him to grow and advance in his career.

15. *Leader's behavior*. A leader's personal behavior is a very important incentive for achievement motivation. He can show personal appreciation and approval, or he can show neglect, apathy, or disapproval. He can increase motivation through personal attention and sometimes through social contact. He can decrease it by

separating himself from certain members of the organization. In a large organization, a leader cannot personally pay attention to all employees, but he can assign a complementary role to a subordinate who can supply the necessary recognition, appreciation, and encouragement. If a leader is of a reserved nature, he can hire an assistant whose personal style complements, rather than coincides with, his own. This will relieve the leader of trying to play an out-of-character role.

16. *Flexible work schedule.* Some people, with home and family responsibilities, need time during normal working hours to take care of these responsibilities. A worker who is preoccupied with nonjob problems has less achievement motivation on the job. He may have an incentive to achieve, but the desire to get the job done so as to take care of these other responsibilities conflicts with the desire to excel on the job. Sometimes this problem can be overcome by flexible work schedules. Some employees might start work at an early hour and finish before the close of the business day. Or they might start work late, allowing time in the morning for off-job chores, and finish work late. Another possibility is job sharing. This is when two people share the same job, one working mornings and the other afternoons, or one working three days a week and the other two days a week. It might be possible for two people sharing a job to work out their own schedules from week to week as they see fit. Flexible scheduling and job sharing might not be possible in every situation, but it is an idea a leader might consider when faced with an achievement motivation problem like this one.

11

Building Team Loyalty

A high rate of turnover among employees is costly to the organization because it reduces productivity, lowers morale among remaining employees, and consumes valuable time. Robert E. Kushell, founder of Dunhill Personnel Systems, says that the answer to the problem of high turnover faced by many organizations is complex, but the key lies in the quality of the working environment. He goes on to say:

> One of the most pressing tasks facing corporate leadership today is to develop and maintain a working climate that will stimulate rather than stifle employees. They [top management] must learn to assign the same priority and prominence to human resource development as they do to manufacturing, finance and marketing.[1]

Kushell suggests the following guidelines to reduce turnover:

- Always keep employees informed on company matters.
- Set up clear channels of communication between employees and top management.

[1] Robert E. Kushell, "How to Reduce Turnover by Creating a Positive Work Climate," *Personnel Journal*, August 1979, p. 551.

- Always define a person's job and the expected results.
- Encourage employee creativity, and try to keep jobs as challenging as possible.
- Encourage self-improvement and point out opportunities for advancement.
- Finally, never oversell a candidate in the employment interview.[2]

While top management can do many things at the organizational level to reduce turnover, the core of the problem lies with the front-line or immediate supervisors of individual employees.

The Edwards Personal Preference Schedule, a psychological measurement instrument, was administered to a group of forty-three pro-union employees who were hostile and negative and had voiced strong dissent against the company and to a group of nineteen pro-company employees.[3] The result was a description of some of the essential differences in needs between pro-union and pro-company employees, as seen by the employees themselves.

These differences pointed to the fact that pro-union employees either were not getting enough personal attention and nurture from their supervisors or they had a stronger need for nurture than pro-company employees had. When people have needs that are not being met they will usually look elsewhere to get their needs met, whether it be to a union, a new employer, or some other source outside their workplace. Others will react in an aggressive or vindictive way in an attempt to force attention to themselves, much like "problem" schoolchildren when their teachers fail to understand their particular needs.

Achievement-minded leaders will recognize employees who have wavering loyalty as persons who probably have high need for nurture. When such employees are recognized it is imperative that their immediate supervisors take the initiative to work with them in a positive manner. Unless they do, such employees will turn their loyalty to a union if one is available, they will seek employment elsewhere, or they will become a hindrance to the morale of other employees.

[1] Robert E. Kushell, "How to Reduce Turnover by Creating a Positive Work Climate," p. 551. Permission to reprint by *Personnel Journal*, Costa Mesa, CA., copyright August 1979.

[3] Joseph P. Cangemi, Lynn Clark, and M. Eugene Harryman, "Differences between Pro-Union and Pro-Company Employees," *Personnel Journal*, September 1976, pp. 451-52.

WHAT FRONT-LINE LEADERS CAN DO

Front-line leaders can do much to fill the nurture needs of employees. Here are a few of the things they can do:

1. Be genuinely concerned about each employee. Concern cannot be a pretense. Leaders must be willing to listen to whatever an employee wishes to talk about.

2. Leaders should periodically discuss career plans with employees who are career-minded. Recommending an achieving employee for advancement outside one's own department might seem to be self-penalizing, but the advantages outweigh the disadvantages. The supervisor who does so may lose a good employee, but he would probably lose this employee anyway, and more than likely, to another organization. Keeping in mind that the worth of all employees including supervisors is measured in how much they contribute to organizational goals, it would be more of a contributing act for this leader to make the recommendation and keep an achieving employee within the organization.

3. Leaders must be willing to, and know how to, delegate responsibility. (See Chapter 14 on delegating.)

4. Supervising leaders should think of themselves as problem preventers rather than problem solvers. However, when an employee needs help in solving a problem, the supervisor should be willing to help the employee solve the problem. If the supervisor were to take the problem out of the hands of the employee and solve it himself, there would be no growth for the employee and other employees would soon learn that they could redelegate problems to the leader.

5. Leaders are models that their employees emulate. Subordinates consciously and unconsciously imitate their leaders' attitudes and actions. Leaders should therefore strive to be models of the kind of employees they want their subordinates to be.

6. When hiring, leaders should choose the best people they can—even people who may initially threaten them. Leaders should be confident enough to think of new employees with new and better ways of doing things as assets rather than being intimidated by them.

7. Leaders should organize their departments so that there is no doubt about who does what. Whenever there are four or more people there should be an organization chart to indicate who is responsible for what. Once responsibility lines have been established, preferably with the help of employees concerned, the leader should see that these lines are observed. No one should be permitted to

come directly to the leader with a problem if the lines of responsibility show that he should go through someone else.

8. Employees with personal problems should be listened to, but a wise leader will not attempt to solve personal problems. He might, however, suggest several alternative solutions for the employee to consider.

9. Employees need prompt feedback from their leaders, whether positive or negative. Leaders should be quick to offer both praise and constructive criticism. Workers have a need to know how they are doing in the eyes of their leader.

10. Leaders should be able to accept negative feedback from their employees. It is a rare person who does not feel that they would like to direct some steam at their supervisor occasionally. When this happens, the leader should be able to take it without fighting back and without holding a grudge. The leader should be magnanimous enough to take the initiative to restore harmony between employee and leader. This is not to say that insubordination is acceptable conduct by employees or that it should be condoned by the leader. But an outburst by an otherwise achieving employee could be the result of pressures that the leader knows nothing about and might better be overlooked than built out of proportion to the situation by a reprimand or other punitive measure.

WHAT TOP MANAGEMENT
LEADERS CAN DO

Principles of management begin with top management and filter down through the various management and supervisory levels to employees. Top management can set the tone for employee relations. Here are some activities that organizational leaders can promote to build loyalty in employees:

1. An employee-oriented newsletter can be distributed. People like to see their names in print and even more their pictures. No message from management that could be construed as threatening should be included in the employees' newsletter.

2. Workers should be informed about planned changes as far in advance as possible.

3. As much as possible, workers should be allowed to participate in planning and decision making that affect them and their jobs.

4. Our humanity unites us. Managers on all levels should show their humanness by admitting their mistakes quickly and openly.

5. There should be a systematic effort to inform employees of promotional vacancies and to give them a chance to apply for those in which they are interested. This would not only pay off in improved attitudes among workers, but in greater acceptance of the individuals chosen to fill the vacancies.

6. Meetings between employees and management should be held regularly. These should be informative meetings where employees can have their questions (any job- or organization-related question) answered. If the answer is not immediately available, the inquirer should be told when and where the answer will be available. Above all, management must not drop the ball by failing to follow through with answers. Honest, unbiased praise should be a part of such meetings. If one person is singled out for praise when another is equally deserving but receives no recognition, employees can become alienated instead of aligned with the organization.

7. It is important for corporate management to be visible to workers. Management should visit employees on the job imparting information and praise.

8. There could be a designated person within the organization to whom employees could go for help with personal or job-related problems.

9. Front-line supervisory positions should be filled with people who have sound interpersonal skills. These are crucial management positions. Cold, arrogant, insensitive persons should not be placed as front-line supervisors. Supervisors should have been trained in supervisory techniques before they become supervisors. This is one area where basic techniques ought not to be learned by trial and error on the job.

10. Pro-organization employees should be encouraged to go out of their way to show a friendly, accepting attitude to all employees. Some organizations assign a peer sponsor to each new employee. People selected as sponsors should be pro-organization employees who are friendly and outgoing.

11. Organization-sponsored athletic and recreation programs and outings tend to bring together employees and their supervisors. Supervisors and other management personnel should be encouraged to take part and mingle with employees on such occasions.

12. Very large organizations can know the condition of morale among employees by means of periodic surveys. The Bank of

America uses employee opinion surveys for suggesting needs and in showing management how they are doing with a new program. A. W. Clausen, president and chief executive officer of the Bank of America, in an interview for the *Harvard Business Review* stated that employee opinion surveys

> tell us the mood and attitude of our employees toward supervisory treatment, benefits, salaries, what they feel about their jobs, their image of the bank, and so forth. We poll a cross section of employees every six months—a fourth of them at a time. Every employee is surveyed at least once every two years. We ask the same questions perhaps 95 percent of the time so that we can spot changes in employee opinions. We compare the results we get in April with the results we get in October to see if the trend is up or down. We chart long-range trends as well. Then we try to react, to address the situation.[4]

13. Wherever employees are separated from top management by several levels of management personnel, there should be a well-planned procedure by which employee grievances can be heard. The Bank of America has a program they call "Let's Talk It Over." According to Clausen, in 1978 about six to seven thousand employees used it, and he feels that is a good measure of its acceptance. In grievance procedures, the employee should start with his or her immediate superior. If the grievance cannot be settled between the employee and immediate superior, there should be a very definite procedure and path for the employee to follow upward to top management.

In organizations governed by a board there is usually a grievance officer who is neutral as far as the grievance is concerned. If an employee wants to file a grievance, he notifies the grievance officer who guides the employee through each step of the grievance procedure. This system can work well where the grievance officer is truly neutral—where he or she is answerable only to the board. However, where the grievance officer is part of top management and a grievance is against top management, it would be difficult for this grievance officer to remain neutral without jeopardizing his own position. In such situations it would be unlikely that the employee could be convinced that he will receive a fair and unbiased hearing.

[4] "Listening and Responding to Employees' Concerns" (interview with A. W. Clausen), *Harvard Business Review*, January/February 1980, pp. 101-14.

14. Some organizations recognize employees for their years of loyal service by giving five-year, ten-year, and twenty-five-year pins or other types of award.

LEADER AND LOYAL ASSISTANT

Achieving leaders give lots of thought to the selection and training of their professional assistants or secretaries. A leader's secretary is in a key position to either help or hinder the "esprit de corps" of the department or office. A loyal secretary can enhance the image of her leader in the eyes of other employees at all levels, both subordinates and superiors. If she displays consistent loyalty to her leader, others will tend to believe in him, too.

Loyalty, however, is not an ingredient of a secretary that can be taken for granted. Loyalty must be earned by the leader. It is true that students in secretarial training learn that loyalty to their employer is a "must" for success. They learn that they should not divulge confidential information or criticize their leader in the presence of others. This is functional loyalty—loyalty that goes with the job. Most secretaries will have a portion of functional loyalty. This is not the type of loyalty we are dealing with in this chapter.

We are dealing with the kind of loyalty that is the result of true respect and admiration for a leader—the kind the leader must earn in order to have it. It is this kind of loyalty that is a leavening agent in the department and organization.

The role of the secretary has changed in the last few years and will continue to change. Three things contribute to this change: women's liberation, management's motivation, and office automation. The women's liberation movement has raised women's consciousness of their own value as individuals. They want personal fulfillment in their work, and more of them are becoming career-minded rather than job-minded. The increased emphasis that management now puts on job enrichment as a means of motivating employees has had an effect on secretaries. They, too, want their share of job enrichment. Technical advances in office operations, such as computers and word-processing equipment, have freed many secretaries from such time-consuming tasks as taking dictation, posting, and filing. The leader who is aware of these changes and actively attempts to fill his secretary's needs created by these changes is one who is loyal to his secretary and will earn her loyalty in return.

Some secretaries are still content with the old secretarial functions of typing letters, making coffee, running errands, and playing the mother role to their bosses. It is also true that some leaders need this kind of secretary. Sometimes a leader who moves from one position to another in the organization, or to another organization, will take his secretary with him. He has trained her to function just the way he wants her to and he feels he cannot do without her. This may not always be a good posture for a leader. Some organizations protect their employees who are serving well and are unwilling to move a secretary to make room for a new manager's secretary. From the secretary's viewpoint also it is not a wise posture, unless she has little desire to advance in a separate career of her own.

An achievement-minded leader will confer with his secretary to determine what her feelings are toward her job and her career. Here are some pointers a leader can use to adjust his relationship with his secretary to allow her to meet the challenges of this new era:

1. Delegate assignments to her. Give her authority to draft letters, reports, and so forth in areas with which she is familiar.
2. Outline the boundaries of her authority and make them clear, not only to the secretary, but to your superiors, peers, and subordinates. Back her up when she is acting within the boundaries of her authority.
3. If the secretary is a woman, treat her the same as you would treat any other staff member. Make the best use of her talents, whatever they may be. Don't talk down to her or give her "office boy" assignments. If she makes an error, give constructive criticism rather than venting anger upon her.
4. Respect the secretary's opinion. From her viewpoint she may command more insight concerning a specific problem and be able to come up with a solution you may never think of.
5. Introduce her to others who come to your office. She is a person, not a piece of office furniture.
6. Do not expect your secretary to do personal chores for you unless you are willing to return the favor. One happy secretary describes her relationship with her leader in these words, "If he's busy, I get him coffee. If I'm busy, he gets me coffee."
7. Keep your secretary's career goals in mind. Promote pay increases when warranted and recommend her for promotion if you think she deserves the promotion—even if it means losing her.

four

LEADERSHIP METHODS

12
Managing Creativity

Many of the usual leadership techniques used in ongoing situations can be used in temporary situations where a group of people come together for one purpose, and when that purpose or task is finished there is a definite closure. Creative projects such as the development of a new product or a new program and the solving of a problem such as increasing production or cutting down on absenteesim are examples of tasks that a temporary group might tackle. When the product is designed or the problem is solved, the group's task is finished.

For such temporary creative tasks a group of present staff members may be assigned to perform the task, or outsiders may be brought in on a temporary basis for this one purpose. Sometimes consultants in special areas of expertise are brought in to help solve a problem. Often an administrative staff will divorce itself from day-to-day administration of an organization (leaving others in charge) in order to become a task force on one specific project.

Leadership of such temporary creative groups requires more personal skills than day-to-day leadership of a regular staff.

While these same personal skills are important in dealing with a permanent staff and routine matters, they take on additional significance when dealing with a temporary staff and a creative assignment.

RECRUITING GROUP MEMBERS

When it comes to high-pressure creative tasks, the success of the group's work will depend almost as much on compatibility and interpersonal skills as it will on creative or technical skills. With this in mind, a leader, when choosing group members, places high priority on rapport and finesse. If the prospective group members are well known to the leader (perhaps chosen from his existing staff), he will already know their personalities. But if the prospective group members are unknown to the leader, he will have to depend on how other supervisors of these people answer questions about them. Questions that might be asked are:

- Is this person short-tempered? How does he behave when he loses his temper?
- Is this person sensitive and responsive to the feelings of others?
- Is this person easily frustrated when given an "impossible" task or conflicting instructions? How does he react?
- Can this person work under pressure without sacrificing quality of work?
- Does this person have a sense of humor?
- Can this person see another's point of view?
- Can this person disagree without being disagreeable?

On short-term projects a leader may not have time to help people go through a period of change. So it is important that the leader closely watch critical members of a group during the early stages and replace them if they don't measure up.

It is also important that the leader acknowledge the contributions of the more effective group members early so they feel valued and become committed to the task.

DEVELOPING WORKING CONDITIONS

Isolation of the group from other persons and other activity concentrates effort on the task and increases the intensity of personal interaction among group members. Away from all disturbances, including telephones, a great deal of work can be accomplished in a relatively short time.

If the members of the group are unknown to each other, a time at the beginning of the project spent in getting acquainted with one another is valuable. A shooting-the-breeze session is a good way for the people to develop relationships and a unifying feeling of "family" or "team." Members need to have an opportunity to discuss the task with the leader in order to learn the leader's expectations and concept of the project and his way of working.

When the work of the group is to be kept confidential or is unlikely to be easily understood by lay people, special effort should be made to involve family members of the group—especially if the group is to work in isolation for any length of time. Personal family problems arising out of a feeling of rejection or misunderstanding of what is going on can have a devastating effect on the contribution of individual group members.

MOTIVATION AND THE GROUP

When a group has a complex, technical task to perform, many group members may be indispensable. For this reason alone it is important that group members be highly motivated. To accomplish any kind of task, to accomplish it to the best of the group's ability, requires that the group be motivated. Here are some ways a leader can help keep a special task force motivated:

1. Maintain a high sense of professionalism. If the leader is committed to the standards he and the group have set, he can be a pacesetter for the rest of the group.

2. Fulfill each group member's need to exercise competence. This can be done best by being sure each group member's assignment fits his qualifications. People quickly lose their motivation when they struggle with a task for which they are not qualified. Likewise, they lose motivation when they are overqualified for the task and become bored.

When a person is overworked so that he does not have time to do his best work, even though qualified, he loses motivation. People are motivated when there is generally an even work flow and their task exceeds their capabilities just enough to be challenging.

3. The need for approval and appreciation is one of the human needs commonly recognized by leading psychologists. One

who does not get approval and feels unappreciated will not stay motivated for long. Effective leaders never take for granted the contributions of group members, but actively look for ways to provide realistic, positive feedback. Even unsuccessful efforts should receive the respect of the leader. This encourages risk taking in creative work.

4. If a temporary assignment on a task force fits in with the career plans of an individual, he will likely be a motivated group member. Effective leaders listen to employees and take an interest in their career plans. When assigning work to an employee within a task force, they strive to make a fit between the personal aspirations of the employee and the task needs.

CLOSURE OF THE TASK

When the group has completed its assignment, some leaders express appreciation by arranging some kind of informal get-together for the group to celebrate the completion of the task. It gives the group members a sense of closure on the task and they feel psychologically ready for another assignment.

13

Using
Executive Time

Have you ever flown into Los Angeles International Airport in the daylight? First you get a panoramic view of Los Angeles as it seems to sprawl unendingly in all directions. The buildings look like an architect's models placed on a plot plan for the local Chamber of Commerce. As you descend a little more you can see only part of the city, but you see that part in greater detail. You see what look like toy cars and buses on the streets, then tiny people moving about. The more you descend, the more your view narrows and focuses on one small area of the great city. The more you focus on one area, the more details of life you can see. Eventually your plane lands and now you are one of those people and can see only those other people who are around you and the part of the airport you are in at that moment.

From high up on the executive ladder, you have a magnificent view of your whole organization—its purpose, its relationship to other organizations. From the top rung of the executive ladder you can see the big picture. From here your attention is on the organization as a whole. You are well aware that within the organization there are divisions, departments, factories perhaps, sales regions, and so forth, but from your viewpoint they look like small parts of the big picture. Important as you know these parts are, your attention is primarily on the whole organization.

If you stand on a lower rung of the executive ladder—say, about where middle management would be—you get a different view entirely. You may be aware that there is the large picture, but your attention is focused on what you can see around you—your division, your department, your staff, your job.

What has this to do with time? Everything! In the Bible the psalmist sang of God, "A thousand years are as yesterday to you! They are like a single hour!"[1] Executive leaders' concepts of time differ depending on which rung of the executive ladder they are on.

Generally speaking, long-range whole-organization planning is done at the top of the executive ladder, while the day-to-day department minutiae are handled by the junior executives.

Top executives make plans for five, ten, or fifteen years hence, while junior executives usually plan from day to day, week to week, or month to month, but seldom for more than one year in advance. There are exceptions, and work assignments differ somewhat from organization to organization, from person to person, and from time to time.

No leader ever outgrows entirely some of the routine tasks. He will always have a letter to dictate, an occasional report to write, a meeting to attend, or an appointment to keep. But higher up in the organization, he is more likely to be able to delegate these kinds of tasks to other people. The more he delegates to other people, the more time is freed for that part of his job that has to do with leading.

To lead is to:

> *L*egislate (make decisions)
> *E*ducate (create a "want to")
> *A*ccelerate (get action)
> *D*elegate (guide action)

THE IMPORTANCE OF INNOVATION

Innovating is getting ideas, developing ideas, and bringing ideas to fruition. A leader must innovate before he can legislate, because decisions are based on ideas. He must continue to innovate in order to educate (What is the best way to present this idea and create

[1] Psalms 90:4.

a "want to?"); accelerate (How can I get people moving on this idea?); and delegate (Who would be the best person to handle this idea or this part of the idea?).

THINKING TIME

If to lead is to legislate, educate, accelerate, and delegate—and all of this requires innovating—and if innovating requires thinking, then leader time has to be used for thinking. However, one of the most difficult problems leaders have is finding time for uninterrupted thinking.

How to Create Uninterrupted Thinking Time

Here are some ideas for solving this problem that many successful leaders use.

1. *Avoid fragmentation.* You are fragmented when you have to spread your attention thinly over many projects. It is very easy for managerial leaders to get into this kind of a situation because generally they are creative people. Ideas come easily and are hurriedly followed by enthusiasm to see the idea take root and grow. Writers are often faced with the danger of fragmenting themselves with more writing projects at one time than they can possibly give their attention to. Consequently, concentration is divided and no one project gets the in-depth concentration it needs for the writer to do the best job that he can do. The result is frustration, which in turn has still more negative effect on concentration.

The same thing can happen to managerial leaders who see an anxiety-producing pile of work growing on the corner of their desks. Valuable executive time is lost by the leader who constantly shifts from one project to another.

If you find yourself in this situation, list all your projects in column A on a project priority rating chart such as the one shown in Figure 13-1.

- Check each project in column B and/or C. "Organizational Want" means that this project was assigned to you by someone within the organization, probably your superior. If it is an assignment you are glad you got, check both columns B and C. "Personal Want" means that this project originated with you.

PROJECT PRIORITY RATING CHART

A Project	B Organizational Want	C Personal Want	BOTTOM LINE D Organization Gain	E Personal Gain	F Total Gain	TIME ELEMENT G Approx. Time To Complete	H Estab. Com.Date	I Priority
I	✓	✓	5	5	10	4 mos.	3 mos.	1
II		✓	1	5	6	1 wk.	(2 wks)	2
III	✓	✓	1	5	6	1 mo.		4
IV		✓	3	1	4	1 mo.		7 3
V	✓	✓	1	3	4	2 mos.		7
VI	✓	✓	2	1	3	1 mo.		3 4 5
VII		✓	1	2	3	1 day	1 mo.	6

Figure 13-1

- Under "Bottom Line" rate each project on a scale of 1 to 5 in columns D and E, and show the total in column F. "Organizational Gain" can be in dollars, public relations, or some other measurable profit. If the organization will make a good profit or benefit highly in some other way by the completion of this project, put 5 in column D.
- In column E rate your "Personal Gain" in dollars or career advancement. (Will completion of this project help you get a raise? Will it give you experience you need?)
- Column F is the total of columns D and E for this project.
- Under "Time Element" in column G put the approximate amount of time it will take to complete the project and, if a definite deadline for completion has been established for the project, indicate it in column H. If there is not a definite deadline, but there is a date beyond which completion of the project will lessen in value, show that date in parentheses.
- When you have completed the above steps, study the chart and arrive at a priority rating for each project and enter the priorities in column I, 1 being highest priority.

Sample projects have been listed on the chart in Figure 13-1. There are seven projects listed, Projects I, IV, and VI are organizational wants, so we will look at them first. Project I has the highest total bottom-line rating. It will take about four months to complete. The deadline for completion is only three months away. Project I is already running behind, so project I gets priority "1" rating. Projects IV and VI appear to be of equal importance except that project IV has a slightly higher total bottom-line rating. So *for now* we will assign priority "2" to project IV and priority "3" to project VI.

Looking at project II, we find that if it is not completed in two weeks, we might as well forget it (indicated by "two weeks" in parentheses in column H). But it has a high personal gain rating (column E) and it will take only one week to complete (column G), so we will give project II priority 2 and move project IV to priority 3 and project VI to priority 4.

Project III and project VI will both take one month to complete. But project III has a higher total bottom-line gain than project VI. On the other hand, project III shows very little organizational gain, while project VI shows more organizational gain than project III although not a great deal more. Here we have a great temptation to do project III before project VI.

Now we have to decide between project III and project VI. The chart cannot help us make that decision. It is a decision we will have to make based on our best judgment and our relationship with our superior. In our example we decided to put project III ahead of project VI. So we gave project III priority 4 and project VI priority 5.

Now we have left project V and project VII. Project V has a slightly higher total bottom-line rating. But project VII could be completed in only one day, whereas it will take two months to complete project V. So we chose to get project VII out of the way before starting project V. Therefore, we gave project VII priority 6 and project V priority 7.

2. *Calendaring uninterrupted time*. Calendaring time is simply making appointments with yourself. Most executive tasks require large blocks of time. They cannot be accomplished in 15- or 30-minute periods scattered throughout the day. When you have put everything else out of your thoughts and are able to begin concentrating on one particular problem, your next appointment arrives or your secretary reminds you of a meeting that is ready to begin. The only way you can get blocks of executive time to accomplish executive leader tasks is by making firm commitments to yourself on your calendar.

A weekly master calendar will help you accomplish this (see Figure 13-2). Keep a supply of these on hand and keep them filled out for your secretary one month in advance. Your secretary should have at least four weekly master calendars ahead at all times, because she probably will be making appointments for you that far in advance.

Note the following about the weekly master calendar: There is a time reserved at the beginning of the week and at the end of the week for you and your secretary to plan: one hour early Monday morning for your secretary and you to go over plans for the week and an hour late Friday afternoon for you and your secretary to evaluate the week that is closing. If your secretary is to serve you efficiently, she must have regular planning time and recapping time scheduled with you weekly. Your secretary needs to be able to know that these times are firm on your calendar and that they will not be shoved aside except in dire emergency.

This does not mean that you and your secretary will not communicate at any other time. But it does mean that on these two specific occasions your secretary can count on having your undivided attention. She is the staff member who has the closest working relationship with you. She must be informed so that she can ably speak for you or represent you in your absence. Many times during the week your secretary can guide other staff members concerning your expectations in certain areas of work, and your staff should know they can rely on her to do so.

In Figure 13-2, "A/S" means available time for staff members. In our example (Figure 13-2), we have put those times on Mondays and Fridays. These are times when your assistants can schedule appointments with you through your secretary. They should be made aware that this time is available to them and that, except in an emergency, those are the only times you will schedule appointments with staff members.

Our sample calendar has a regular staff meeting scheduled in the middle of the week on Wednesday. This is when you will meet

Figure 13-2

WEEKLY MASTER CALENDAR

Week of: _____

Time	MON.	TUES.	WED.	THURS.	FRI.
8:00 a.m.	PLAN w/ SEC'y		A		A
9:00	A/S	/S	STAFF. MEETING	/S.	A
10:00	A/S	HRS		HRS	A/S
11:00	A/S				A/S
12 NOON		SERVICE CLUB			
1:00 p.m.	A		A	A	A
2:00 p.m.	A		A	A	A
3:00 p.m.	2 HRS	A	2 HRS	MGMT. MEETg.	RECAP TIME SEC'y
4:00 p.m.		A			A
5:00 p.m.					

formally with your staff. The A/S times are for informal appointments with individual staff members.

"A" on the sample calendar means available time for your secretary to schedule other appointments—people from other departments and outside the organization. These times should be scheduled in such a way that there will be time available every day of the week and at various times of the day. In our example, "A" time has been scheduled for early morning on Wednesday and Friday, early afternoon every day except Tuesday, and late afternoon on Tuesday.

The "X" times are very important times on your schedule. These are the blocked, uninterrupted times for you to accomplish your executive tasks. When scheduling appointments for you, your secretary should never use these times without your consent, which you should give only reluctantly and in case of extreme emergency.

It is very easy to let other people work their way into those times, but you must stand firm that this time is yours. It would help if there is a secluded place away from your office where you could work during those times—perhaps a vacant office in your building or an office in your home.

It is not likely that you would be able to plan a weekly master calendar exactly as in our example. But the ideas expressed in the example should be considered as you tailor your weekly master calendar to fit your needs.

3. *Cut down on staff meetings.* If you ordinarily hold staff meetings once a week, consider holding them every two weeks or even monthly. This may not be possible in your situation, but it is worth considering. A great deal of time is spent in staff meetings when the payoff is not worth the time so spent. Some leaders don't have regular staff meetings at all. They call a staff meeting only when there is a specific problem to discuss. They cancel a regular meeting now and then to test the need for it. If you cancel a regular staff meeting and you do not receive negative feedback from staff members because of the cancellation, it is possible that they, too, can use the time to better advantage. You can keep a folder of agenda items and, instead of having regularly scheduled meetings, call a meeting only when your folder has sufficient items for a meeting. You will find that some of the items will take care of themselves without a meeting.

If you meet at different times with different groups of staff members, consider scheduling the meetings in such a way that they follow one another in sequence on the same day. Schedule group A for 9:00 A.M., group B for 10:00 A.M., and group C for 11:15 A.M. This will limit the time for each group, and you will usually find that just as much can be accomplished in the shorter period of time.

4. *Put daily things on a weekly basis* and put weekly things on a monthly basis. For example, don't answer mail every day. Train your secretary or professional assistant to take care of all routine mail and to hold for your attention once a week only that mail that requires your personal attention. If she needs instruction from you in order to answer some mail, she can get that needed information when you have your Monday morning planning session with your secretary.

5. *Plan effectively.* Priority planning is perhaps the most effective way to use leader time. (See Chapter 15 on planning.)

6. *Take care of minor problems as they come up.* They will use up less leader time if you do what has to be done while the problem is minor, rather than letting the problem ride until it becomes a major issue.

7. *Develop patience.* A car that idles too fast wastes fuel. A leader who is impatient for things to happen wastes energy. All things take time to happen. The leader who unduly nags a subordinate to finish a report may get the report sooner, but chances are it will be an inferior report, and more leader time will be used going back to the subordinate for more information. On days when the wheels of progress seem to stand still, even though you have planned well, remember this quotation of Jeremy Taylor: "Enjoy the blessings of this day, if God sends them; and the evils of it bear patiently and sweetly: for this day only is ours, we are dead to yesterday, and we are not yet born to the morrow."

8. *Learn how to procrastinate effectively.* Some problems, if left alone, will take care of themselves. To some people one of the most comforting phrases in the Bible is "It came to pass." That is exactly what some problems do—they come to pass. And it is a wise leader who can distinguish the problem that came merely to pass from the problem that must be solved. A good way to test problems is by using the Procrastination Record found in Executive Time

Management.[2] Items for procrastination are listed on the Procrastination Record and the date they are listed. A review date is also listed for each item and a note of future action to be taken on that date. Very often when the review date arrives, the item will no longer need anyone's attention. If it does, the action to take is recorded on the Procrastination Record and you can dispense with it at that time.

9. *Use a bring-up file.* Free your mind of trying to remember many things to do, many dates, and so forth, by using a bring-up file. With your mind free of minutiae you can concentrate on current leader tasks. A bring-up file is a set of manila folders, one for each month and one for each day of the month (1 to 31). The set of daily folders are placed in front of the set of monthly folders. Keep the current day's daily folder in front of the set of daily folders and the next month's folder in front of the set of monthly folders.

If you want to remember to write a letter, make a phone call, or contact someone some day during the current month—say, on the tenth—put a note concerning it in the daily folder labeled "10." If it is now October and you want to remember something in November, put a note about it in the folder labeled "November." At the beginning of each month transfer the items in that month's folder to the appropriate daily folders. Be certain to look in the daily folder each morning for items that need your attention that day.

10. *Learn to delegate effectively.* See Chapter 14 on delegation.

11. *Use time management tools.* Our book *Executive Time Management* contains many time management tools for executives. A leader needs to use good judgment in choosing the time management tools he will use. Use only those tools that you find effective in saving *your* or *your subordinate's* time. As you become a more expert planner you will need fewer tools. However, it is doubtful that you would ever reach the point where you can lead effectively without the use of some leadership and time management tools. However, we recommend that you select and use the tools with discretion. It would not be practical to attempt to use every time management idea in the book.

12. *Become aware of your high-energy and low-energy periods*, your moods and inclinations, and when your power to pro-

[2] Helen Reynolds and Mary E. Tramel, *Executive Time Management: Getting Twelve Hours out of an Eight-hour Day*, Englewood Cliffs, N.J., Prentice-Hall, 1979, p. 30.

duce is high and when it is low. To do this, record your energy, mood, and efficacy fluctuations over several weeks. Figure 13-3 will help you do this.

For each period of each day record your energy, mood, and efficacy levels as being high, medium, or low.

Energy: How good did you feel physically? How much horsepower did you feel like you had?

Mood: What was your mood? Were you optimistic (high), pessimistic (low), or somewhere in between (medium)?

Efficacy: How much were you able to accomplish? Was your productivity high, medium, or low?

In the "Activity" column, note the activity or task you were engaged in at the time. In the "Remarks" column note any

Figure 13-3

RECORD OF ENERGY, MOOD, AND EFFICACY LEVELS

Week of: _____

MONDAY	ENERGY	MOOD	EFFICACY	ACTIVITY
Early A.M.				
Mid A.M.				
Early P.M.				
Mid P.M.				
Late Day				
Evening				
TUESDAY Early A.M.				
Mid A.M.				
Early P.M.				
Mid P.M.				
Late Day				
Evening				
WEDNESDAY				

usual thing that may have affected your energy, mood, or efficacy, such as a cold, a personal problem, good or bad news, and so forth.

Once you have an appreciation of your energy, mood, and efficacy variations, and how they seem to relate to one another, you can work them into your schedule to your most productive advantage.

Use the times when your energy, mood, and efficacy are at their peaks for difficult work, overpowering assignments, starting on new projects and challenges, and meeting deadlines.

Schedule influencing tasks (presenting ideas, persuading others, generating enthusiasm) for when your energy and mood levels are apt to be high.

Use the times when your efficacy level is apt to be low for less pressing tasks and for socializing. This would be the best time to leave your door open for drop-in visitors.

14

Delegating
for Achievement

Effective delegation does not mean simply assigning work to someone else. It is a complex skill requiring planning, organizing, and controlling. It is basically the passing on of a responsibility from one person to another, but it is a great deal more than that. Delegation administered properly is the key to increased productivity and the attainment of goals.

WHY SOME LEADERS
DON'T DELEGATE

The idea of delegating is a roadblock to some people. Some managers have failed to achieve personal goals and have failed in their contribution toward organizational goals because the idea of delegating parts of their function to others looms as a threat to their status as "the problem solver and decision maker" for their staffs.

Some reasons that nondelegating managers give for not delegating and disproofs of these reasons are:

Reasons	*Look at it this way*
My subordinates lack experience and I don't have time to train them.	If your subordinates lack experience, that is all the more reason to give them experience. Delegating will release time for you.
There are some duties I can't delegate. I must do them myself.	This is true—but probably does not apply to all your duties.
I can do the task better myself.	Maybe—but your way may not be the only way. Give yourself a chance to gain confidence in your employees.
Mistakes are too costly.	You can establish checkpoints and controls to prevent mistakes.
I enjoy the work and I like to keep busy.	Your success as a leader depends on your contribution to the achievement of organizational goals. You cannot contribute at the executive level if you keep busy on minor details. Free yourself of the minor tasks so you can tackle the major ones.
The task will take only a few minutes.	If it is a one-time task, this is a legitimate reason. But if the task will be repeated, consider delegating it.
Decision making is my job.	Delegating *is* a decision.
I want credit for myself. I'm afraid if I delegate responsibilities to a subordinate, he may do better than I and eventually take over my job.	If your subordinate can do a better job, that is to your credit. You trained him. He cannot take over your job responsibility. That is your responsibility and it is nondelegatable.
There is no part of my work I can delegate.	Looking at your overall responsibilities it may seem so. But break down your work into small units and you will probably find tasks you can delegate.
I'm not sure of the boundaries of my responsibility and authority.	You must have a clear understanding of your function, responsibility and the limits of your authority. If you don't, you

I don't like taking risks.	should arrive at a clear understanding with your superior.
	Leadership involves risk taking.
If I'm not in control of a project, something could go wrong.	You can lessen the risk by giving clear instruction and establishing controls, such as checkpoints and reports.

ADVANTAGES OF DELEGATION

The achievement leader multiplies his own effectiveness when he delegates. He creates thinking and planning time for himself. He is not as likely to suffer from overwork and fatigue. He develops his staff and tests the potential of possible successors. He boosts his own success and advancement possibility by *not* being indispensable.

The employee receives recognition and job gratification. He becomes aware of his superior's respect. His morale is boosted. He has an opportunity to grow and achieve. He sharpens his decision-making skills. He gains in initiative, self-confidence, and imaginative reasoning. He becomes a more productive employee.

WHAT TO DELEGATE

Any leader can find delegatable tasks if he will look for them. Here are a few that generally apply to any executive position—you may find other more specific ones pertaining to your position.

1. Analysis of problems and development of alternative solutions.
2. Securing data for a report or some other purpose.
3. Preparation of rough drafts of written material such as formulation of policies, programs, plans, and letters—from which you can develop the final draft.
4. Most recurring tasks—jobs that you do daily, weekly, or monthly.
5. Assignments that will help develop your subordinates.
6. Consider delegating those duties you do best and retaining those you do poorly. This will benefit your own development. You are not likely to learn any more from the duties you do best; and repetition of the tasks you do poorly will help you build expertise in those areas.

HOW TO DELEGATE

Delegating should be done with foresight and planning for the most benefit to be derived from it.

- Begin with a review of your responsibilities. List them in writing. Then keep a record of your daily activities for a month. You may be surprised at the number of small assignments that show up on your record that you don't have on your original list. Sometimes routine, repetitive tasks become so routine that we tend to forget about them.

- After you have a list of all your duties, divide the large ones into small units of delegatable work.

- Think about each of your subordinates and determine which ones could handle the delegatable work on your list. Think about them in terms of:

  How much work they already have.

  The relationship of the work they do to the delegatable work on your list (You may find a natural fit).

  The individual interests, talents, experience, and adaptability of your subordinates.

- Delegate work assignments. Provide the employee you have chosen for an assignment with complete information:

  Organizational policy and procedure as they relate to the assignment.

  The goal or result you expect when the assignment is completed.

  How the assignment fits into other work in the department or organization, particularly how it contributes to organizational goals.

  Define the limits of the subordinate's responsibility in relation to the assignment. Make certain he understands his authority within these limits, and also make certain that others know your subordinate's authority. This will make it easier for your subordinate to get the cooperation he needs.

  Define the assignment clearly and be sure the subordinate understands it. Encourage questions and feedback to you regarding the assignment.

  Set a realistic date for completion of the assignment if it is the kind of assignment that would have a definite completion date. If it is an ongoing assignment, set one, two, or three checkpoint dates when the subordinate will report to you how the assignment is working out. After one or two reports, if you find the subordinate is handling the assignment satisfactorily, no further routine reports would be necessary.

Other points to remember when you have delegated an assignment are:

1. If you have given a subordinate the responsibility for a decision, don't make the decision for him. If he asks for help, help *him* to make the decision.

2. If a subordinate asks a question or is having a problem with a task, don't answer the question or solve the problem for him. Rather, help the employee to think through the question or problem and arrive at his own solution.

3. Except in a critical situation, don't reverse a subordinate's decision or order. If a decision must be reversed, permit the person who made it to reverse it.

4. Stand behind your subordinates in their relations with their staffs.

5. If a subordinate fails in one assignment, realize that you are partly to blame. After all, you made the assignment and you selected the wrong person for it. Unless the failure was deliberate on the part of the subordinate, try him on a number of less responsible assignments until you find where he is capable of performing well. Most employees can grow into assets for the organization when they are given opportunities compatible with their strengths. Except in extreme cases, it is often more economically prudent to develop an employee already on the job than to train a new employee. This practice builds employee morale.

6. Remember that it is easier to have hindsight than foresight. Don't be quick to criticize mistakes made in an emergency or unusual situation. Back up your subordinates in crises to whatever extent you conscientiously can. Ask yourself, "In the same circumstances might I have done the same thing?"

7. Final responsibility for your staff is yours. Your subordinates are accountable to you, but you are accountable to your chief or board of directors. You can delegate assignments you are responsible for—but you cannot delegate your responsibility.

8. See our book *Executive Time Management* for use of a form titled Delegation Planning Guide.[1] This form will help you keep track of tasks you have delegated, to whom delegated, and completion dates. Another form, Time Norms, will help you in setting realistic completion dates.[2]

---

[1] Helen Reynolds and Mary E. Tramel, *Executive Time Management: Getting Twelve Hours Work out of an Eight-hour Day*, Englewood Cliffs, N.J., Prentice-Hall, 1979, p. 31.
[2] Reynolds and Tramel, *Executive Time Management*, p. 29.

SOME CAUTIONS
REGARDING DELEGATING

Because effective delegating is a complex skill, some cautions are in order:

1. Avoid delegating busy work—work that is unnecessary and whose only purpose is to keep someone busy. Neither should you delegate only boring tasks solely because you don't want to do them. Delegate meaningful tasks that carry some responsibility and tasks that are challenging to the subordinate.

2. Be careful to delegate only those tasks that are *your* responsibility. Know the boundaries of your responsibility and do not duplicate the delegation of a task someone else has delegated.

3. Delegate assignment to *your* subordinates only.

4. Resist the temptation to delegate an assignment to more than one person in order to see who does the best work on the assignment. Delegate a specific assignment to only one capable person.

5. If possible, delegate a complete project or function to an individual, rather than separate parts of a project to several individuals. Giving an employee full responsibility increases initiative and eliminates time-consuming coordination with others. The individual may reassign parts of the project to others within his organizational unit and coordinate efforts, but the ultimate responsibility belongs to the individual to whom you delegated the project.

6. Make delegatees responsible for results, rather than activities. Spell out the results you expect and permit the delegatee to choose the method to accomplish the results.

7. Certain functions should not be delegated at all. For example, the top executive leader should retain responsibility for strategic planning and board of directors issues. Personnel actions—hiring, firing, promoting, evaluating—cannot be delegated.

8. You cannot delegate accountability. You may hold your subordinates accountable to *you* for delegated tasks—but you are accountable to your superior for your performance and the performance of your employees.

ARE YOU DELEGATING EFFECTIVELY?

Here is a quiz to determine if you are delegating effectively. The more yes answers you give, the more likely you are delegating effectively.

1. Do you seldom work overtime?
2. Do you usually finish each day's work?
3. Do you have enough "thinking time" for planning and innovating?
4. Do you usually meet your objectives on time?
5. Do you have confidence in your subordinates?
6. Do you have a clear understanding of your responsibilities and the extent of your authority?
7. Do high morale and "esprit de corps" characterize your staff?
8. Is your staff results-oriented, rather than activities-oriented?
9. Do your staff members show a high degree of initiative?
10. Have you established clear policies to guide your subordinates in making decisions?
11. Do your subordinates bring their ideas to you?
12. Do the operations of your department progress as usual when you are away from the office?

15

Planning for Achievement

The success of a touring vacation in the family car depends on the plans that are made before the trip is started. The route is mapped out and interesting sites to see on the way are noted. Then the family car is prepared in relation to the expected road conditions along the way to the destination. Perhaps a tune-up is needed, new tires or at least a new spare might be a good idea, the radiator may need additional antifreeze. How much luggage will fit in the trunk of the car is another consideration. The more planning that is done, the more successful the trip will be.

Some vacationers like to start with no particular destination in mind and just go as their daily whims suggest. However, if a vacationer has a destination in mind, he must have a plan for reaching it.

It is the same with achievement leadership. Achievement depends on planning. First a goal is determined and then plans are made for reaching it.

WHY PLAN?

Planning increases the probability of success because it focuses on results rather than activities. Achievement leaders put more emphasis on "what to do" than on "how to do it." They are results-oriented, rather than activities-oriented.

Planning establishes a framework for making decisions. If you don't know where you want to go, any road will take you there. If you know the goal you want to reach, you can make decisions that will take you there.

Planning can eliminate peaks in workload and pressures to meet schedules and unrealistic deadlines.

Planning helps to avoid crisis situations.

Planning is an effective way of managing employees. It provides a basis for measuring performance. It increases employee involvement and improves communication.

Planning improves decision making because it forces analytical thinking.

Planning lessens anxiety brought on by rapidly accelerating change.

SETTING GOALS

Planning begins with determining a goal or end result. In order to achieve a goal it must be broken down into manageable and measurable components. We shall call these components "steps."

Both goals and steps, to be achieved, must be translated into action. Therefore, the way a goal or step is stated must suggest action. The action suggested must be specific, and the goal statement must include a definite date when the action is to be completed.

A poorly stated goal would be: "To improve the efficiency of the telephone system." A well-stated goal would be: "To improve the efficiency of telephone service by 5 percent by January 1."

A well-stated goal answers specifically the questions "what?" and "when?" A well-stated step answers the questions "what?" "when?" "by whom?" and sometimes "how?"

A poorly stated step would be: "Improve telephone service by 5 percent by Nov. 1."

A well-stated step would be: "Assign employee A to survey number of incoming calls per day handled by each operator, and determine number of calls going unanswered by operators during period September 1 to September 15."

The Significance of Dates

Dates written into a goal or step to reach a goal should be, first, realistic based on the leader's best judgment of when the task could most likely be accomplished, then flexible enough to provide a cushion for unexpected delays.

Remember, setting a date or a deadline is not developing a plan. A plan consists of a goal and steps to reach the goal. Dates and deadlines are merely checkpoints along the way of the plan to ensure that the plan continues along a time line to completion.

A leader who is an effective planner is results-oriented. He develops a plan to use as a tool to attain results. Therefore, he is more committed to results than to the plan. He is never so tied to a plan or a date that he cannot adjust it or even scrap it for a better one if conditions indicate such action is necessary to attain desired results. An effective leader does not get so involved in the details of planning that he never gets around to implementing the plan.

FORECASTING

Forecasting is estimating future significant things that may occur. Forecasting is a task that most leaders are faced with. Whether your organization deals in products or services, top-level executives need to be able to foresee the future 5, 10, or even 20 years hence. Forecasting a few years ago was not as difficult as it is now. With the flood of data coming off computers, it would seem that accurate forecasting could be more easily accomplished. However, we live in an era of rapid change. Recognizing this instability, forecasters predict several different environments and develop strategies for each of several most likely ones. Leaders can no longer rely wholly on trends, although a trend must be considered when forecasting. But there are too many variables to depend wholly on trends today.

RISK TAKING

A leader who takes risks is one who tempers logic (known facts) with intuition (a gut feeling that may or may not jibe with the known facts).

Instinct, intuition, hunch, and judgment are all part of a sixth sense used by executives to "see" ways to solve problems that often defy logic. John Fetzer, owner of the Detroit Tigers and chairman of Fetzer Broadcast, says, "Intuition helps you read between the lines. Or walk through an office and intuition tells you if things are going well."[1]

A hunch is a peculiar feeling of almost knowing but not being quite certain. It is based on facts stored just below the conscious level of the mind.

Cautions Regarding Hunches

Here are some cautions to observe when dealing with hunches:

1. Maintain some degree of pessimism. If you have an odd little hunch that is trying to tell you what you don't want to hear, don't disregard it.
2. Don't confuse hope with a hunch. Wishful thinking is just wishing and no more.
3. Don't act on a hunch without acquiring all the data you can. Unknowledgeable hunches don't usually turn out well; however, in managerial leadership it may be necessary to act with insufficient information when timing is important.
4. Don't act too quickly on a hunch. Remember your staff members can have intuition, too. Listen to their intuitive feelings and weigh them against your own.
5. Don't spend an unreasonable time gathering data. There is a right time to move on anything and your intuition will tell you when the time is ripe.
6. Don't accept past experience alone as intuition. Just because an idea failed once before doesn't mean that it would fail again.
7. Don't ignore your hunches. When one comes your way, treat it like you would a fish nibbling at your bait. Feed it a little line and play with it until you can land it. If it gets away before you can land it, it probably was not a good idea after all.

[1] Quoted in Roy Rowan, "Those Business Hunches Are More than Blind Faith," *Fortune*, April 23, 1979, p. 111.

16

Leading in Problem Solving and Decision Making

When something goes wrong with the family car and you take it to a garage for repair, the first thing the automobile repairman will ask you to do is define the problem or tell him the car's symptoms so he can define the problem. Automobiles, like people and organizations, are complex, and defining what the problem is when something goes wrong is not always easy to do. When something goes wrong a leader must be able to define the problem.

Someone has said that the time between the first reactions to a situation and the moment of final decision is the safety zone of decision making. The more experience a leader has had in making decisions the more he is tempted to make snap judgments on the basis of past experience and intuition. The leader who attempts to solve managerial problems by depending entirely on experience, general information, memory, intuition, or a superficial survey of the problem risks making ineffectual decisions. A definite scheme for problem solving and decision making is necessary to arrive at a clear understanding of the problem and to cover all aspects of it.

SCHEMATIC PROBLEM SOLVING/
DECISION MAKING

In order to ensure that all aspects of the problem will be covered, begin with a master checklist (see Figure 16-1). You can use this checklist whether you are going to solve the problem yourself or assign a subordinate to solve it.

Step 1: Define the problem. This is an important first step in problem solving. Unless you can define the problem briefly, you don't have a clear understanding of what the problem is or you may have several problems rather than one.

Step 2: Classify the problem as either *uncommon* or *symptomatic*. An uncommon problem is one that is very unusual and that can be solved only by you or with your personal involvement and leadership at all stages of problem solving. For example, top management might be faced with the problem of deciding whether the organization should merge with another firm that has asked for a merger.

A symptomatic problem is the kind most executives must deal with. A symptomatic problem is one whose cause or causes are likely to be found in other subproblems. The symptomatic problem is the symptom of other underlying problems not readily seen.

Step 3: If the problem is uncommon, proceed to step 5.

Step 4: If the problem is symptomatic, classify it as a *deviation, alternative*, or *rank-order* problem.

- A deviation problem is one where there is a deviation between what is supposed to happen and what is now happening.
- An alternative problem is one that offers alternative actions and a choice must be made between them.
- A rank-order problem is one where a number of possibilities exist and they must be ranked according to some criterion or criteria.

Step 5: Determine limits within which the solution to the problem must fall. For example, if money is involved, one limit might be the amount of money you are willing to have the organization spend to solve the problem. The solution might turn out to be additional training for a certain classification of employee. How much would you be willing to see spent on additional training? There may be other limits you want to establish depending on the nature of the

```
Master Checklist for:

         SCHEMATIC PROBLEM-SOLVING/DECISION-MAKING

 1.  Define the problem:

 2.  Classify the problem:  Symptomatic: _____ Uncommon: _____

 3.  If "uncommon," proceed to No. 5

 4.  If "symptomatic problem," classify as:  Deviation:    _____
                                             Alternative: _____
                                             Rank Order:   _____

 5.  Determine limits for problem:

 6.  Select procedure for solving problem:

 7.  Determine who is to solve the problem:

     7A.  Delegate:

 8.  Receive problem solutions:  Accept: _____
                                 Return: _____

 9.  Determine who is to put decision into action and when:

     9A.  Delegate:

10.  Determine who is to follow up to see if solution is working and
     when:

     10A.  Delegate:

11.  Receive follow-up report:

12.  If solution is not working out as expected, put next best solution

     into effect and proceed from Step 9.
```

Figure 16-1

problem. If limits do not seem to apply to the problem, indicate this by "NA" (for "not applicable") on the checklist.

    Step 6: Select the appropriate procedure for solving the problem.[1]

[1] Helen Reynolds and Mary E. Tramel, *Executive Time Management: Getting Twelve Hours our of an Eight-hour Day*, Englewood Cliffs, N.J., Prentice-Hall, 1979, Chapter 5.

If it is a deviation problem, use:

1. Problem Analysis form
2. Problem Cause Analysis form
3. Problem Solution Analysis form

If it is an alternative problem, use the Best Possible Solution Matrix.

If it is a rank-order problem, use the Decision Matrix.

Step 7: Determine who is to solve the problem. You may want to assign the problem to one person or to a group. If you assign the problem to a group, name one person to chair the group and be responsible for seeing that the group functions. See that all persons who are involved in a problem or affected by it are included either directly or indirectly in its solution. Be sure your assistant to whom you delegate the problem knows the procedure you selected in Step 6 above.

Assign the problem to the person who will solve the problem and ask for two solutions—a "best solution" and a "next best solution." If solving the problem will extend over several months, establish progress report dates. In this way you will be assured that work is being done on the problem. Establish a date for completion of the assignment.

Use a Project Progress Schedule, Figure 16-2, to keep yourself informed on the current status of each project.

Column 1: Describe the project.
Column 2: Name the person who is responsible for the project.
Column 3: Enter the date on which you delegated the project.
Column 4: Enter the date on which you expect the project to be completed.
Column 5, 6, and 7: Enter progress checkpoints. In these columns enter one of the following:

A date when you expect to receive a progress report from the person named in column 2.
A date when you will check on the progress being made on the project.
A point (event) in the progress of the project. You may have told the person in column 2 to report back to you when he has reached a certain point in the progress of the project.

Step 8: Receive problem solutions and accept them or return them to the problem solver. Enter this action in column 8. If

PROJECT PROGRESS SCHEDULE							
1 Project Description	2 Delegated to	3 Date Delegated	4 Anticipated Completion	5 PCP	6 PCP	7 PCP	8 Project Completed

Figure 16-2

the solution seems feasible to you, accept it. If the solution seems to you not to be feasible or incomplete, discuss it with the problem solver. The solution may need only a little adapting in order to be feasible and the two of you will be able to make the necessary change or changes. Or your discussion might bring out a whole new and better approach in which case you can return the problem to the problem solver to work out another solution using the new approach.

Step 9: Determine who is to put the decision into action and when. The solution itself might indicate this. If not, you as leader would make these decisions. Someone must be responsible for carrying out the solution (or decision), and a definite date when you expect it to be done should be known to the person who is responsible for the task. Assign the person you choose to put the decision into action.

Step 10: Determine who is to follow up to see if the solution is working and when. Make this assignment.

Step 11: Receive a follow-up report. It may be that you will want several periodic evaluations of the solution until the solution is well established.

Step 12: If the solution is not working out as expected, discuss it with the problem solver. It may be that one slight amendment is needed to make it work. Or you may decide to scrap the solution and institute the next best solution; in which case you would then proceed from step 9—after notifying all concerned that the first solution is no longer in effect.

How closely it is possible for you to follow each step on the checklist for schematic problem solving and decision making depends on the nature of the problem. But even if some steps have to be skipped, having the checklist before you will ensure that no necessary step for any given problem will be overlooked.

REMINDERS FOR MAKING WISE DECISIONS

Several reminders for making wise decisions deserve emphasis.

1. Don't give in to the temptation to make snap judgments on the basis of past experience or intuition. The longer one is in a leadership position, the stronger is the temptation to make snap judgments.

2. Analyze the problem. Think it through. Usually in a problem situation the apparent problem is only a symptom of other, not-so-apparent problems. Answer the question "Why?" at all stages

of problem solving. For example, suppose production is behind schedule. Why? Because absenteeism is high. Why? Because employee morale is low. If these are correct answers to "Why?" it is obvious that the problem to be solved is not how to speed up production, but how to raise employee morale.

3. Group problem solving is only possible when there is a mutual interest in goals. Individual and personal goals must be set aside in favor of the common goal. For example, our nation, although divided politically, has always united in time of national emergency.

4. When there are differing opinions on how to reach a goal, write down on a chalkboard or flipchart the conflicting solutions and encourage the group to think of others. Seeking additional solutions together tends to unify the group.

5. In a problem-solving group leaders should attempt to separate idea getting from idea evaluation. If possible, two group sessions—one for generating ideas and one for evaluating ideas—would be valuable. When a person presents an idea that immediately gets a negative response, he is discouraged from presenting other ideas.

6. Do not hurry the process of generating possible solutions. Write down all solutions suggested by others or that occur to you. The more possibilities you have, the less likely it is that you will settle for a merely workable solution rather than the best solution. Keep studying the data as long as additional solutions, ideas, patterns, or explanations are being derived from it. Sometimes it is a good idea to lay the problem aside and give your attention to other matters. Let the problem "jell" in your subconscious mind. When you return to it, you will have fresh insight.

7. Gather as much data as possible. Don't make assumptions when it is possible to obtain facts and figures. Don't look merely for data that support your preconceived ideas. Be open-minded and objective in your search for facts.

Evaluate each piece of information. Ask: Is the source reliable? Is it a fact or an opinion? If it is an opinion, is it an expert's opinion? Remember that an opinion of your superior is not necessarily infallible. If your superior is relying on you to solve a problem, you owe it to him to evaluate his information for validity as thoroughly as you do all other information.

8. Test each possible solution, measuring it against a common yardstick. Will it remedy the problem completely, or partially? Is it a permanent solution, or an emergency measure? Will it work in

actual practice? How much will it cost in money, time, and so forth? Would the solution be acceptable to all concerned? to the organization? to the employees? to the customers? To determine the best solution, evaluate one solution against the other by using a form similar to Figure 16-3.

- Across the top list the specific criteria that an acceptable solution must meet. Start at the left with most desirable and most essential criterion and end at the right with the desirable but least essential criterion.
- In the right-hand column list each solution.
- Evaluate each solution against each criterion, placing a checkmark if the solution meets that criterion.
- If one solution appears to have more checks in the criteria columns to the left of the chart, that solution is probably the best solution.

However, often it is not that simple. Two or more solutions may appear to be equally desirable. Or one may be very desirable in relation to one or two essential criteria, but totally undesirable when measured against all criteria. Sometimes the best solution will turn out to be a combination of solutions. If you can combine the strong points of one solution with different strong points of another solution, you may arrive at a solution that is better than any others. This is an area of executive decision making requiring imagination and foresight.

9. Don't put emphasis on placing blame for a problem. Don't look for who caused the problem—look for what caused the problem. Emphasis on blame will result in a decline of innovation among staff members.

GROUP PROBLEM SOLVING AND DECISION MAKING

Milton Berle once said that a committee is a group that keeps minutes and loses hours. Someone else said that a camel is a horse put together by a committee. There are certainly occasions when a problem can be solved or a decision made better and more quickly by one person than by a group. The danger of group decision making lies in the fact that group members, while wanting agreement, also want their own ideas heard and accepted. So they

SOLUTION EVALUATION				
Solution	Criterion	Criterion	Criterion	Criterion

Figure 16-3

often bargain and compromise until the final decision is a mixture that no group member wholeheartedly supports.

But this need not be the case. Dr. Jay Hall, president of Teleometrics International, tells of research developed that shows a group's final decision when compared with the independent points of view held by members of the group before entering the group is almost always better than the average and often better than the best individual contribution. Dr. Hall says that when individuals decide on their own and then meet with three to seven other persons to produce a consensus, the group's decision stands a good chance of being better than any of the individual decisions.[2]

Group decisions are best under the following circumstances:

1. When every member is involved. When points of disagreement are actively sought and worked out. As a group leader, encourage conflicting ideas. Conflict brings opposing viewpoints to the surface where they can be dealt with. Avoid assigning persons to a committee because they tend to agree with your point of view.
2. When every member is committed to arriving at a decision the group can agree on. Ineffective groups use such techniques as majority rule, averaging, and bargaining.
3. When every member can accept the group's decision on the basis of logic and feasibility. This does not mean that complete agreement is necessary, but that every member can accept the consensus of the group as being logical and workable.
4. When members avoid arguing for their own viewpoints. Members should present their viewpoints as clearly as possible and be willing to listen to other members' viewpoints before pressing for their own.
5. When members don't assume that someone must win and someone must lose.
6. When members don't change their positions merely for the sake of group harmony. Leaders should be suspicious of agreement that comes too quickly and too easily.

In Dr. Hall's research it was discovered that groups who were previously instructed in group decision making scored higher in quality of decisions reached than those who were not previously instructed in group decision making. This indicates that leaders would do well to train their staffs in the techniques of group decision making.

---

[2] Jay Hall, "Synergism in Group Decision Making (How to Make the Whole Greater than the Sum of the Parts)," *Personnel Journal*, January 1979, pp. 12, 13.

17

Communicating for Achievement

Each person has four areas of relationship between himself and other people: (1) that part which is known to both the individual and others; (2) that part that is hidden from both the individual and others; (3) that part that is known to the individual, but hidden from others; and (4) that part that is known to others, but hidden from the individual.

You can visualize your four areas of relationship to others by imagining yourself seated in your automobile.

Area 1: The windshield is there for you to see out and others to see in. The windshield represents your behavior and motivation that is open and honest. In this area there is a free flow of information. The larger and cleaner the windshield, the more easily others can know you and accept you and the fewer communication problems you will experience.

Area 2: Picture luggage stacked high in the back seat completely covering the rear window. You cannot see out; neither can others see in. This represents your behavior and motivation that is not known to you nor to others. All of us have unknown and untapped resources—resources that are hidden to both ourselves and others. Sometimes these hidden resources come to light unexpectedly. For example, Jo was not a quick thinker. He always reacted slowly to new situations. He even spoke slowly. Others would wait impatiently for him to get to the point. Jo never thought of himself as one who could react quickly and effectively in an emergency. But while driving on the freeway one day, his quick and precise action avoided what could have been a disastrous accident. That day Jo discovered a part of himself he never knew existed.

Area 3: Extending out from both sides of the automobile are rear-view mirrors. You can see others through these mirrors, but others cannot see you. The rear-view mirrors represent that part of you that is known to you, but not known to others. It represents your "hidden agenda." It is that secret incentive that causes you to act or speak in a certain way. For example, Jo resented his boss's criticism of his work, but he kept his resentment to himself because he didn't want to lose his job. On the surface Jo was polite, and his boss was not aware of Jo's resentment and that Jo was being polite in order to keep his job (Jo's hidden agenda).

Area 4: Suppose that on a hot day last summer you placed foil on the side windows, but you made a mistake and put the wrong side of the foil to the glass. This resulted in your outward vision being obscured, but others could see you clearly. The side windows with the foil represent that part of you that is hidden to you but apparent to others. This part consists of your mannerisms in speech and gestures, such as the habitual use of a word, or the failure to look at the person you are speaking to, or any of the various positions that are called body language if you are unaware that you are using them.

Leadership in communicating is achieved by paying attention to these four personal areas of relationship between people and encouraging others to do the same. Achievement leaders have wide, wraparound, squeaky-clean windshields; they remove as much luggage from the rear window as they can; they prefer not to use their rear-view mirrors much, but they recognize that others may have to and do; and they remove the foil from the side windows.

All of this takes honest effort. The tendency to be self-protective and distrustful of others is a natural instinct such as animals have. But man has a will that does not have to rely on the lower instincts. Man has the power within to decide the kind of person he wants to be and the kind of relationships he wants to have. If he wants to be a leader in the communicating process, he will decide to have a very clean windshield so others can see him as he really is and he can be accepting and understanding of others.

INTERPERSONAL COMMUNICATIONS

The question is not whether to communicate with others. Everyone does that. The question is how to communicate to achieve results. Robert Frost once said, "Half the world is composed of people who have something to say and can't, and the other half who have nothing to say and keep on saying it." You can change those percentages by joining the ranks of people who have something to say and know how to say it effectively.

Influential Self-expression

People who have little influence on others are people who have no specific position on any question or who have a specific position but make no effort to express their position or feelings. They are also people who may express an opinion, but are easily discouraged by any expression of disagreement from another person.

People who have a negative influence on others are those who are overly opinionated. They attack others with their opinions. They use words, tones, and body language that "put down" or humiliate the other person.

Those people who have a positive influence on others are those who have an opinion, but are flexible. They are not timid about taking a position and letting their position be known—but they are willing to listen to opposing viewpoints. They encourage dialogue. They are not above admitting they may be wrong or conceding that there may be two "right" positions depending on viewpoint. People who have a positive influence on others are leaders in the communicating process.

We can exert a positive influence on others by observing the following areas of communicating:

1. Use "I" messages. There are five types of "I" messages: appreciative, disclosing, informative, declarative, and responsive.

Influential leaders express their appreciation. Their sentences often start like these:

> I appreciate . . .
> I am pleased . . .
> I am glad . . .
> I like . . .

Influential leaders tell others how they feel with sentences that begin like these:

> I value . . .
> I feel . . .
> I think . . .
> I believe . . .

Leaders who influence others tell why in sentences like these:

> I would like you to . . . because . . .
> I want . . . because . . .
> I need . . . because . . .

Leaders who are influential let others know where they stand:

> I can . . .
> I am . . .
> I will . . .

Influential leaders respond to questions of others (spoken or unspoken) with more than yes and no:

> Yes, because . . .
> I'd like to because . . .
> No, because . . .
> I would rather . . . because . . .
> I choose to . . . because . . .
> I have decided to . . . because . . .

2. Be clear. Clarity can be accomplished if you think before you speak. Know the person or group you will speak to, know

what you want to say and why you want to say it. Arrange your points in logical order. *And come to the point quickly.* Others will lose interest and you will lose influence if you talk all around the point you want to make, never arriving at the point or arriving at it after you have lost the attention of your audience.

Practice using precise words. If the other person can "picture" your message by the words you use, he will have a clearer understanding of the point you are making.

Avoid hedging on the truth with phrases like "It would appear that . . ." and "The report seems to indicate that. . . ." You will be judged truthful, trustworthy, and intelligent if you speak forthrightly without hedging or hesitation.

3. Know your communicating style and, as much as possible, the other person's communicating style. We tend to communicate with others as if their communicating styles were identical to ours. But many times that is not the case. For example, Hazel, sales representative of a large women's wear wholesaler, is a very vivacious, warm, and outgoing person. True to her own communicating style, she approached a prospective buyer for a leading department store exuberantly. "I have several wonderful ideas I want to tell you about," she exclaimed.

The prospective client, being a well-organized, businesslike, conservative type, asked, "How many is 'several'? And please, just give me the facts."

Realizing the error she had made, Hazel switched her communicating style to match that of her prospective client. She proceeded in a precise, businesslike manner to relate just the bare facts that she wanted to convey to him. He was impressed and Hazel gained an important new account. If she had not changed her communicating style to match his, she would probably have not roused his interest in her ideas and she would have lost the sale.

Nonverbal Self-expression

For our words to be influential, our nonverbal expressions, such as gestures, body postures, and voice qualities, must match the words we use. If our words and nonverbal signals do not match, the nonverbal cues will be believed rather than our words. If you express displeasure with a smile, your words will have little effect because you will be sending an unclear message. The other person has no idea whether or not you are really displeased. He may rationalize, "Maybe you think you should be displeased and so you verbalized displeasure, but you are not really displeased because you are smiling." It is the nonverbal signal that is usually believed.

We express ourselves nonverbally through gestures, facial expressions, eye contact or lack of it, body posture, and the tone, inflection, and volume of our voice.

Gestures should be open and graceful. Avoid clenching hands and fingers and shaking a fist or finger at another person. Facial expressions should match your inner feelings. The voice should be clear, firm, and well modulated. A low, whispering, or whiny voice denotes submissiveness, which is not a leadership characteristic. Too loud a voice, loud to the point of hurting the eardrums, conveys the impression that you think the other person should feel guilty, stupid, or intimidated.

Other nonverbal factors that affect self-expression are timing, distance, environment, and clothing.

When you speak to another your speech should be spontaneous and the timing appropriate to the situation. Criticism and appreciation ought to be spontaneous. What you say will seem more important and be more readily accepted if it is "on the spot" and not something you have obviously rehearsed several times before saying it. On the other hand, your speech should be appropriate to the situation. You should not spontaneously criticize another publicly. If others are present, plan your criticism for a time and place when you and the other person can be alone.

Maintain a comfortable and relaxed space between you and the person with whom you are speaking. What is a comfortable and relaxed space is sometimes a cultural matter. In some cultures people naturally stand closer together than people of other cultures. If the other person seems to back away from you, you are probably standing too close to him for his comfort.

Arrange your office surroundings in such a way as to allow people to relax and converse easily. Don't place a barrier, such as a desk, between you and your conversant.

Your clothing should be clean, neat, and in good taste. Review Chapter 2, which discusses appropriate dress for leadership.

LIVELY LISTENING

For centuries people took the ability to listen to be more natural for a normal child than the ability to talk. A child has to learn to say words and then put words into sentences that make sense. But anyone who could hear—it was assumed—could listen. The problem was that many people confused hearing with listening. Now, one can take a university course in how to listen. Such courses are offered because misunderstandings abound in daily life—misunderstandings between friends, wives and husbands, parents and children, employer and employee. Many people are poor listeners or do not listen at all, causing personal, professional, and diplomatic problems. Achieving leaders are expert listeners because they use a technique which we call *lively listening*.

Lively listening is letting the other person know what you understood his message to be and what you understand his feelings are. People who are considered good conversationalists are those who engage in lively listening.

Lively listening clarifies potential misunderstanding and reduces defensiveness. You give the other person recognition and understanding. Lively listening gives you time to reflect on what the other person has said and to consider your response. Your response will more likely be direct and appropriate because you have really comprehended the other person. When the other person recognizes that you are making an attempt to understand him, he will work harder to understand you.

You can engage in lively listening by paraphrasing, reflecting, acknowledging, encouraging, and by asking open-ended questions.

Paraphrasing

Paraphrasing means repeating *in your own words* what the other person has said. For example, suppose an employee says to you, "Do I really have to work this Saturday?" You might reply, "Yes, so be here early and you'll get through early." Or you might say, "Are you complaining about overtime again?"

If you used either of these replies, you would not be showing that you understood what the employee said. You would appear cold, uncaring, and uninterested in the employee's predicament.

190

The following imaginary conversation is an example of how paraphrasing would work in this situation.

> *Employee:* Do I really have to work this Saturday?
>
> *You:* You would rather not work this Saturday.
>
> *Employee:* Well, I really wanted to stay home with the family this Saturday.
>
> *You:* You feel you don't spend enough time with your family and so you wanted to stay home with them this Saturday.
>
> *Employee:* It's not that I don't spend enough time with them. It's just that I sort of promised we might go to the mountains this weekend.
>
> *You:* You promised to take your family to the mountains and you feel it's important to keep your promise.
>
> *Employee:* Yes. But I didn't promise when we'd go. I guess we could go next weekend.
>
> *You:* Then you would be able to work this weekend?
>
> *Employee:* Yes.

Even though you could not reverse your decision that this employee had to work this Saturday, by using lively listening you have won his support because he now feels that you have "heard" him and you understand his viewpoint.

Reflecting

Reflecting is guessing what the feelings of the other person are and expressing them verbally to check out their accuracy. In the above conversation when you said, "You feel you don't spend enough time with your family . . . ," you were guessing that this is how your employee felt although he had not actually said that. Your guess was incorrect and he was able to correct your misunderstanding in his reply, "It's not that I don't spend enough time with them. . . ." When you said, "You feel it is important to keep your promise," you guessed correctly and the employee let you know that in his reply.

Reflecting can nip misunderstandings in the bud and keep them from blooming into real communication problems.

Acknowledging

When a person speaks, he likes to know if he is getting through to his listener. Some ministers enjoy hearing a hearty "Amen" to their affirmations. It encourages them to go on. The same is true in conversation. An occasional "hmmmm," "right," or "that's so" will let the speaker know that you are listening. Be sure that you *are* listening, however, so you will not respond with a wrong acknowledgment.

Encouraging

You can support the speaker by saying, "Tell me more," or "Please continue." Supporting the other person in this way will tell him that you are interested in what he has to say and encourage him to go on.

Open-ended Questions

Questions that ask what, how, when, and where will also encourage the speaker to go on and will let him know that you are engaging in lively listening. Be wary of asking, "Why?" The other person might take "Why?" as a challenge to what he has said. This would put a barrier between you and hinder conversation.

Barriers to Lively Listening

Described below are ten poor listening habits that have been described as the most common barriers to effective listening and the remedy for each.[1]

Barrier	Remedy
1. Many people are uninterested in the speaker's subject and set their minds in another direction. direction.	Take the attitude that, if you are going to use valuable time to hear a speaker, you want to collect any new ideas he might have. You can add these to your storehouse of knowledge.

[1] Institute of Government, Georgia Center for Continuing Education, University of Georgia, *Interpersonal Communication: A Guide to Staff Development*, 2nd edition, Athens, p. 79.

Barrier	Remedy
2. Some people mentally criticize the speaker's delivery or his appearance. Their minds are so preoccupied with the speaker that they do not tune in on the subject of the speaker's talk.	By concentrating on the speaker's words, you can soon forget your first impression of the speaker.
3. In a discussion, sometimes a person will feel so strongly about the subject that, instead of listening, he plans his rebuttal and misses or fails to grasp the the full message the speaker is sending.	When differences of opinion develop, institute this rule: Each person may speak up with his own thoughts only after he has first stated the ideas and feelings of the previous speaker. Any distortion can be corrected immediately by the original speaker.
4. Some people listen for the facts and want to be spared the details.	Sometimes facts make sense only when supported by the details. Facts and details together usually make up the point of what is being said.
5. Some people try to write down everything a speaker says. Or they try to fit the speech into their own outline. Being so busy making notes, they miss much of what the speaker says.	Adapt your notetaking system to the speaker's organization of his talk. Leave plenty of space between points to fill in his afterthoughts.
6. Some people, while appearing to be attentive, actually tune the speaker in and out at will.	Lively listening requires constant attention and effort.
7. Sometimes a speaker cannot be heard distinctly or he gives only fragmentary information.	If it is a one-to-one conversation, or a small-group discussion, tell the speaker you cannot hear or ask questions to complete the information the speaker has omitted. You might say, "I am interested in your viewpoint and I am anxious to know more. Tell me . . ." If you are listening to a platform speaker whom you cannot hear, move closer to the speaker even if you have to carry your chair with you. If the

Barrier	*Remedy*
	speaker is giving fragmentary information, write down your questions. If there is a question-and-answer period at the end of the presentation, you may get your answers then; if not, make a point of talking to the speaker on an individual basis after the meeting. (See the Audience Participation form in our book *Executive Time Management*.)[2]
8. People who are not technically minded sometimes tune out any message that borders on the technical.	Technology is becoming more and more a part of daily life. Absorb as much of the message as you can. You can at least pick up some new technical terminology. (If you are the speaker, remember to speak in terms your audience can understand.)
9. Some people are distracted by certain words, phrases, grammatical errors.	If you let these get in your way, you will miss an important point. Listen to the speaker on his terms and not yours.
10. Sometimes a person's mind will wander from the message the speaker is sending.	This happens because one can think so much faster than one can speak. Most people think about four times as fast as they can talk. Use the extra time to summarize what the other person has said and determine what point he has made. Mentally question what the speaker has said. Do you agree? Weigh the speaker's evidence. Are his facts accurate? Is he an authority on the subject? Is he prejudiced? Am I getting the full picture? Read between the lines. But while you're doing all this, remember to listen.

[2]Helen Reynolds and Mary E. Tramel, *Executive Time Management: Getting Twelve Hours out of an Eight-hour Day*, Englewood Cliffs, N.J., Prentice-Hall, 1979, p. 93.

CORPORATE COMMUNICATIONS

So far in this chapter we have dealt with mainly one-to-one or group-to-one communication. Now we will deal with corporate communication. By corporate communication we mean how an achieving leader, representing an organization, communicates with employees as a group.

People vs. Paper

Most formal corporate communicating is done on paper because the same message can reach all employees, or all groups of employees, on paper faster than by word of mouth. Paper communication is also used when it is necessary for a policy, procedure, or announcement to be in writing for verification or future reference. It is sometimes used to prevent misunderstanding. However, paper communication does not always prevent misunderstanding. Clarity in written communication is as important as it is in verbal communication, and it takes constant vigilance on the part of the message sender. A big disadvantage of paper communication is that it doesn't allow much feedback. Even when feedback is invited in the message, the sender receives only a small percentage of the feedback he would have received if he had verbally communicated the same message. He may get some written feedback, but he will not be able to read facial expressions, gestures, voice tones and inflections. The point is that whenever it is feasible, verbal corporate communicating is better than written corporate communicating. No means of communicating is more effective than when people can converse orally face to face. If a record is needed, oral communication can be followed by written confirmation of what was said.

VERBAL CORPORATE COMMUNICATION

Verbal corporate communication can take place in various settings, such as the grapevine, lunch and coffee breaks, in the office or shop, and at the company picnic.

The Grapevine

While the grapevine is looked upon by leaders of some organizations as a pesty, uncontrollable rumor mill grinding trouble for management, achieving leaders of successful organizations consider the grapevine an effective communication system.

Psychologists have learned that rumors emerge to explain confusing situations that are important to people and to relieve the tension of uncertainty. Highly anxious people spread rumors more frequently than calm ones do. Research indicates that rumors persist until the condition that gave rise to the uncertainty is alleviated or until the anxiety abates.

Achieving leaders make no attempt to restrict the grapevine. To do so would be to distort and amplify the grapevine messages. Achieving leaders nourish the grapevine by injecting themselves into the informal communication system. One way they do this is through what has been called the "open-floor" policy. The grapevine then serves the needs of both management and employees because it is spontaneous, natural, and unscreened.

Open-floor Policy

In the open-floor policy executives at all levels of the corporate ladder leave their plush surroundings and mingle with the troops during coffee and lunch breaks and other casual and natural encounters. At these times management can feed the grapevine with factual rumors, or they can produce facts that will alleviate anxiety caused by nonfactual or partial information. By simply listening during these encounters management can receive feedback from employees on organizational policies, practices, goals, and so forth. It helps spontaneous, two-way flow of information if there are no rank-oriented status symbols. A leader may take off his tie and his suit coat before visiting the shop. A woman leader might consider removing any costly jewelry that can put a social distance between her and the employees. Leaders can leave instructions with their assistants that they are not to be called from the "floor" except in case of emergency.

The open-door policy, which enables people from any organizational level to walk through any door, should not be substituted for the open-floor policy. There are aspects of the open-door policy that lessen its effectiveness. Many employees feel uncomfortable about walking on carpeted floors, dressed in work clothes, to strike up a conversation with management in formal surroundings. Moreover, their intent could be misconstrued by their supervisors.

Employees are not encouraged to go "over the head" of their immediate supervisors.

More genuine communication occurs when management, supervisor, and employee talk informally in the employee's home territory.

✗ The Importance of Feedback

Many people think of communicating in terms of instructing, informing, selling, influencing, persuading, and so forth. Because of this way of defining communication, management often communicates in parent-to-child fashion. Effective corporate communication is almost always adult-to-adult and always allows for feedback. There is no evidence that communication has taken place unless the communication process has provided for feedback.

For example, information compiled by management and dispensed by management at a department meeting with no opportunity for discussion does not provide for feedback. But if the information was derived from a survey of employee opinion and the results brought before the employees at a department meeting, and the employees were then given an opportunity to analyze the results and make recommendations, then the opportunity for feedback has been provided.

Suppose management-originated information is to be disseminated to employees. How can feedback be provided? First of all, if the management-originated information is a decision affecting employees, employees should have been involved either directly or indirectly in making the decision. The fact that this involvement occurred and how it occurred should be reviewed with the employees before the information is disseminated. Following the presentation of the information, there should be time for questions to be answered.

Some decisions must be made by management without the input of employees. How can feedback be provided when these decisions are presented to employees? Feedback that is needed by management in this type of situation is the knowledge that the employees understand, accept, and will support management's decisions. Most employees recognize that there are decisions management must make without their input. If the rapport between management and employees has been kept at a high level by effective communication processes in the past, and if questions are answered candidly and openly, employees will be likely to accept decisions management must make alone and will show their support.

The key to the extent of employee acceptance of management's decisions is the degree of mutual trust that exists between management and employees. A high degree of trust can be maintained only by day-in-day-out openness, respect, and consideration and two-way communication.

Announcing Bad News

Suppose a plant or department must be shut down or an expected raise in salary is not forthcoming. How can management present bad news properly? Avoid the tendency to sugarcoat bad news. People can usually detect when information is being screened and they are not receiving the whole story. When management sugarcoats bad news, they activate the grapevine and through it employees learn the bad news. Often the bad news that employees learn via the grapevine is inaccurate. It can be distorted and incomplete. Employees also learn that management has not leveled with them and therefore cannot be trusted in the future.

When management presents bad news candidly and openly, it is more likely to be accepted, though not welcomed, than if the bad news was received by employees via the grapevine.

While there are occasions when management can feed the grapevine to disseminate truthful information to employees, it is risky to use it as a means to spread bad news.

Another problem associated with bad news is that often first-line supervisors are required to tell the bad news. This would be more acceptable to them if they were also given the glory of disseminating favorable news. But too often top management makes the favorable announcements and expects first-line supervisors to make the unfavorable announcements. This can create a barrier between employee and supervisor—the worst place for communication to break down because here is where it affects productivity.

ATTITUDE SURVEYS

An attitude survey is one of the most effective methods for facilitating organizational development, if it is done correctly. Organizational development is the process of improving the organization's effectiveness in achieving goals and meeting needs of employees.

An engineering firm involved all twelve hundred of its employees in the development of an attitude survey. Employees helped in compiling the questionnaire and in administering it. All employees answered the questionnaire. Employees participated in task forces for interpreting the survey results and translating them into organization action. When the survey was completed, all employees had the same information, were thinking like managers, and were united in the pursuit of organizational goals. Strategies of this sort are essential for leaders of today's enlightened workforce.

SAME DATA BASE FOR EMPLOYEES AND MANAGEMENT

We said that employees should be included in decision making that affects them. In order for employees to participate fully in decision making they must have access to the same information management has. They must learn to think like managers, and they must be committed to organizational goals.

One way this can be accomplished is by putting all employees, including top management, on overlapping problem-solving teams. Firms that do this find that problem-centered teamwork enables all members of the organization to understand organizational goals and how to collaborate in pursuit of these goals.

Another way is to give all employees the same opportunities for training and development. Employees of all levels and functions should become informed and skilled in the same managerial and communication processes.

THE SUGGESTION BOX

While the suggestion box works well in some organizations, it has fallen into disrepute in others. The dangers inherent in a suggestion box plan are many, especially if reward of some kind is offered for best suggestions. It encourages employees to conceal their creativity from others and creates distrust among employees. There is always dissatisfaction with the evaluation of suggestions. There is the danger of killing initiative in those employees whose suggestions are routinely passed over.

Better than a formal suggestion system is an informal, spontaneous communication system operating between workers and management. When employees and management are united on a common data base, when they are pursuing common goals, they generate innovations and implement them through their normal, everyday relationships.

NONVERBAL CORPORATE COMMUNICATION

Company newspapers, letters to the home, public-address systems, and closed-circuit television are all means by which management communicates with groups of employees. Very often these types of communication are incomplete because they often do not allow for feedback from employees. There are methods for incorporating feedback into these types of corporate communications, such as special employee-written columns in newsletters and employee interviews on closed-circuit television. These types of corporate communication and feedback are not spontaneous and therefore not as effective as the verbal types of communication we have been discussing in this chapter. However, there is a place for nonverbal corporate communications, especially in large organizations where employees are scattered geographically and not in daily or weekly contact with one another.

Perhaps the most common nonverbal corporate communication with employees is the employee newsletter. Bulletin board notices and displays are another type of nonverbal communication. Needless to say, careful planning should preface any nonverbal corporate communication.

18

Coaching and Counseling Employees

Achieving leaders do not overlook the importance of coaching and counseling employees. There are four kinds of counseling problems that leaders need to recognize and deal with.

First is job-related coaching and counseling, which is two-fold: (1) informal daily contact with employees when praise and/or criticism is given on the spot; and (2) the more formal periodic performance evaluation conference. Both of these were covered in Chapter 10, "Upgrading Achievement." However, there are other job-related problems that employees may bring to you.

Second, leaders are sometimes called on to counsel employees who are having personal problems that affect their productivity.

Third, there are the employees with a health and/or emotional problem such as alcohol and drug problems.

Fourth, leaders may have to counsel difficult employees—those who have human relations problems or cause disturbances among other employees.

JOB-RELATED PROBLEMS

Probably the most frequent employee problems that confront leaders are job-related. Here are some pointers to keep in mind when counseling an employee with a job-related problem:

1. Show courtesy, attention, patience, and sincerity when you discuss an employee's on-the-job problems. Discuss on-the-job problems privately.

2. Allow the employee to talk out his problem in whatever amount of time it takes. Ask questions. Look at the problem from the employee's viewpoint.

3. Attempt to find out what the real problem is. It is usually hidden beneath the surface and often is not the problem that the employee relates to you. The problem the employee relates may be only a small part or a result of a deeper problem. Ask questions to determine what the deeper problem is.

4. Help the employee to see what the real problem is. Don't be satisfied until he agrees that you have fairly and accurately stated the problem.

5. The problem may turn out to be a misunderstanding which you can explain. Often the employee will solve the problem himself as he talks about it. If the solution to the problem requires positive action on your part, handle it promptly to the best of your ability. Tell the employee how you will handle it.

6. If the problem is beyond your authority to settle, you can discuss it with others higher up in management. Let the employee know this is what you intend to do and keep him informed concerning the answer or decision you get.

7. Some problems may have to do with matters that another manager should deal with, such as a garnishee on wages. If so, refer the employee to the manager that handles that particular kind of problem. Before doing so, however, alert the other manager and secure his approval of the referral.

8. If the problem is one that might develop into a grievance against you or someone else in the organization, be careful to follow all organizational policies and procedures which govern the handling of employee complaints.

PERSONAL PROBLEMS

Most leaders know when an employee is troubled. A change in a person's usual appearance, work quality, or behavior usually indicates a problem of some sort. It could be a work-related problem or an off-the-job personal problem. Either way, it becomes his leader's problem too when it begins to affect the way the employee does his work, his attitude, or his relationships with co-workers.

Most people like to have someone to turn to for counsel or to share a burden. Off the job, this might be a close friend or a relative. On the job it will be someone for whom the employee has respect, someone who will take a sincere interest in his problem with warm understanding and sympathy.

Achieving leaders are people employees feel they can go to with a problem. They are approachable, but not busybodies or snoopers. They do not "take over" the problem and make it their own, but they are good listeners. Here are some guidelines on counseling employees with personal problems:

1. Listen to the employee in private. Even if the employee brings up the problem in the presence of others, don't discuss it with him when others are present. Suggest that the two of you discuss it privately.

2. Even though he yearns to discuss his problem, he may feel ill at ease, hesitant, or timid, especially if the problem is a very personal one. Help him feel comfortable. Be friendly. Show genuine interest in him.

3. Give the employee an attentive audience. The problem may seem trivial, humorous, or even ridiculous to you—but remember it looms large and serious in his eyes. So give him the floor and let him talk while you listen in a sincere and sympathetic manner.

4. Don't rush him. Let him take enough time to tell it in his own way, even retelling parts of it. Don't interrupt him or remind him that he has told you something before. By being a patient listener you allow the employee to think things through for himself. The odds are good that he will solve his own problem as he tells it, or that he will realize it is not as serious as he thought before he began talking about it.

5. You may need to ask some questions to get more facts about the problem. But don't question in a probing manner. If the problem involves a sensitive personal matter, such as marital troubles, it is usually best not to do any questioning whatsoever.

6. Approach personal problems of an intimate nature as though they were explosive—which they are. Rarely give any advice that calls for action on the employee's part. If it is a marital problem, it is better not to suggest any action. Just by listening you will have done a great deal. You can restate the problem, being careful not to add anything to the employee's own analysis of the problem. Don't add your own assumptions or reactions to the problem. If the employee has suggested some alternative actions he might take, you can restate them. Sometimes hearing his own alternatives from another will help him make a choice. You can preface your restatements with words like these: "As you stated, your problem is . . ." and "The possible solutions you see are . . ." All of this helps the employee think the problem through, arrive at solutions on his own, and get it off his chest.

7. If the problem is a serious one, you can suggest that he talk to someone outside the organization, such as a clergyman, family doctor, lawyer, or social worker.

8. Above all, don't suggest any specific action to solve a personal matter. If it doesn't work out, you will be blamed for the failure.

9. After the discussion, be extremely careful to respect the employee's confidence. Keep the decision confidential. Even if at a later date someone else appears to know all about the employee's problem, continue to keep your discussion with the employee confidential.

ALCOHOL AND DRUG
ABUSE PROBLEMS

The estimated annual cost to all employers in the United States of untreated alcoholic cases varies from $2 billion to over $4 billion annually.[1] Staggering as the monetary cost is, it is not the

---

[1] Paul W. Cummings, "Handling the Alcoholic Employee," *Supervisory Training*, February 1975, p. 43.

total cost of alcoholism. We must consider the loss of human potential in individual lives devastated by this disease.

Today many organizations have a written statement of policy concerning alcoholism and drug addiction of employees which says, in effect, that the organization regards alcoholism and drug abuse as illnesses which are treatable. Alcoholism and drug abuse are defined and the purpose of the statement explained.

Leaders of organizations of all sizes need to be on the alert for possible alcoholic cases and encourage employees who are possible alcoholics to seek treatment. Supervisors should be alert to employee work performance that fails to meet established work standards, when absenteeism increases, and when increased accidents, insubordination, and disruptive personal relations show up. They should document employee behavior in all of these instances where standards are not met. Documentation could become very important if the employee refuses to get help and the situation worsens to where termination is unavoidable.

It is wise not to write a diagnosis or supposition of alcoholism or drug abuse on any organizational or company forms. Such written diagnosis could place the organization in an embarrassing position if it were later proven that the substandard work performance was not due to either of these causes.

The supervisor should conduct corrective interviews when substandard performance warrants it. If alcoholism or drug abuse is suspected, the employee can be told that the organization is willing to offer counseling and diagnostic services to assist him, if this is the case. If the employee accepts this help, he can then be referred to professional resources, such as Alcoholics Anonymous, Narcotics Anonymous, the clergy, social workers, or community agencies. If the employee refuses help, he should be given a firm choice between accepting professional help or accepting existing disciplinary procedures exercised for all cases of unsatisfactory job performance.

A previously satisfactory employee should not be terminated for unsatisfactory performance when alcoholism or drug abuse is suspected without first giving the employee opportunities to seek assistance.

Under no circumstances should a leader attempt to diagnose the cause of the alcoholism or drug abuse problem or even discuss such problems with the employee other than to offer the counseling and diagnostic services of the organization.

DEALING WITH DIFFICULT PEOPLE

People are as complex and varied as snowflakes. All snowflakes appear to be similar. But scientists who have studied them under a microscope agree that there are probably no two snowflakes shaped exactly alike. The shape of snowflakes depends on the environment in which they were formed.

Psychologists who study the processes by which people respond and adjust to the world about them agree that there are no two people exactly alike. The mental attitudes of people depend in large measure on the environment in which they have been nurtured, or not nurtured, up to the present moment.

Because the mental attitudes of people are different, no one can predict with certainty how another will react in any given situation. The best anyone can do is to accept another person as he is and deal with him in a way that will help him become what he is capable of being.

The Overly Aggressive, Inconsiderate Person

The best way to deal with a person who is being inconsiderate of your feelings is to confront the person with your feelings. Use "I" statements, such as "I'm uncomfortable with . . ." and "I feel like I'm under attack and therefore I cannot give you an effective answer." Avoid such statements as "You're being unreasonable" and "You're attacking me."

If you express your own feelings, rather than describing the other person's actions, you will help avoid creating a defensive attitude in the other person which could result in more aggressiveness on his part.

The Hostile, Violent Person

People can lose their tempers and become hostile and even violent. If someone in this frame of mind approaches you, the best action you can take is to listen. If possible, establish a basis of mutual trust. If appropriate, you might say, "I'm impressed with your argument." Be careful not to talk patronizingly. Keep your remarks on the adult level.

Give him room to vent his feelings. Don't insist that he sit down if he wants to walk around the room. Don't say, "Sit down and cool off." Let him walk and let him talk.

Remove physical barriers. For example, don't sit behind your desk, and don't stand if the other person is sitting.

Have your assistant hold all phone calls and other distractions. Having to wait on you will cause even more anger in the hostile person.

Be calm and encourage him to relax—but don't *tell* him to relax. If he smokes and there are cigarettes available, offer him a cigarette. Face him and give him your full attention. Use lively listening to the degree that it seems appropriate.

If the person is too hostile, or if you find yourself becoming angry, terminate the interview and schedule another time for it. Admit that you can't handle the situation now and need time to regain your calm.

The Passive, Depressed Person

Depression can be brought on by a crisis in a person's personal life, such as the death of a loved one, physical illness, and so forth. Depression may be temporary or chronic. If it is chronic, it is best to suggest that the person get professional help.

Usually a depressed person needs positive stroking. Give the depressed person listening time, warmth, and intimacy. He needs to feel that someone cares about him. Avoid confronting the depressed person by attempting to explain his depression or by insisting that he follow a certain course of action. Stroke him by showing genuine appreciation for the good things he has going for him.

However, if the depressed person is trying to gain your support by playing "hero" or "martyr" or by putting down someone else, withhold your positive strokes for these actions because they should not be encouraged.

COUNSELING HABITS
THAT HINDER HELPING

Negative expressions can creep into our conversation with those whom we are attempting to help through coaching and counseling.

1. Telling the other person what to do—for example:

   "You must . . ."
   "I expect you to . . ."
   "You cannot . . ."

2. Threatening with "or else" implied:

   "You had better . . ."
   "If you don't . . ."

3. Telling the other person what he ought to do:

   "You should . . ."
   "It's your duty to . . ."
   "It's your responsibility to . . ."

4. Making unasked-for suggestions:

   "Let me suggest . . ."
   "It would be best if you . . ."

5. Attempting to educate the other person:

   "Let me give you the facts."
   "Experience tells us that . . ."

6. Judging the other person negatively:

   "You're not thinking straight."
   "You're wrong."

7. Giving insincere praise:

   "You are an intelligent person."
   "You have so much potential."

8. Putting labels on people:

   "You're a sloppy worker."
   "You really goofed on this one!"

9. Psychoanalyzing the other person:

   "You're jealous."
   "You have problems with authority."

10. Making light of the other person's problems by generalizing:

    "Things will get better."
    "Behind every cloud there's a silver lining."

11. Giving the third degree:

"Why did you do that?"

"Who has influenced you?"

12. Making light of the problem by kidding:

"Think about the positive side."

"You think *you've* got problems!"

Employees can be quick to sense insincerity, lack of interest, or lack of human warmth in a leader. When they do, they stop taking their problems to their leader. Word about a supervisor's ineptness in handling problems spreads fast. But so does praise for the supervisor who earns the employees' respect. Knowing that employees respect and seek your advice is one of the true rewards of leadership.

19

Change Leadership

As long ago as the fifth century B.C., Heraclitus said, "There is nothing permanent except change." In the nineteenth century, A.D., Benjamin Disraeli said, "Change is inevitable—change is constant." Today one need only to look about to see change in personal life styles; technology at home and in the workplace; politics, both domestic and foreign; foods; medicine; education—nothing of this world remains the same as it was a mere 10 years ago!

THE DIRECTION OF CHANGE

If everything changes, then nothing remains the same. It either gets better or it gets worse. It grows or it diminishes. It lives or it dies. Neither a leader nor his organization can stand still.

But many people and organizations resist change. Many people fear and resist new and unknown things. When this attitude pervades top leadership it can permeate the entire organization.

If you always drive your car in the same direction the wind blows, you will use less fuel but you may not arrive where you wanted to go. If a leader allows the direction of unplanned changes to dictate his actions, it may seem easier to lead, but he and his followers are not likely to reach their goals. Unless he confidently takes hold of change and plans the direction of change he wants, change will take hold of him like a strong wind and buffet him about. He will become the victim of change, rather than the victor.

An achieving leader is a maverick when it comes to choosing the direction of changes for himself and his organization. He keeps his organization alive and growing by directing change. One reason an achieving leader does not conform to the direction every change blows is because he knows that, left alone, change can carry his organization backwards. The achieving leader steers change in the direction he wants his organization to go. He initiates changes, not for the sake of change, but for the sake of improvement. The improvement of anything is usually a *planned* change process.

BLOCKS TO INNOVATIVENESS

To improve anything, whether it be a situation, a procedure, or character, one must use a certain amount of innovativeness. Most people have sufficient innovativeness, but many do not use the innovative potential they have. The six most powerful blocks to innovation, according to behavioral psychologists, are:

1. *Excessive need for order.* Planning is useful. The automobile industry plans what each year's model will be like before building it. However, planning is only a tool, not the craftsman. For years the auto manufacturers planned on the premise "the bigger, the better." Now small cars are in demand and the auto industry has had to change what they did for years and build small cars. A leader needs to be flexible enough to innovate new plans when it is desirable to do so. Just because something has been done a certain way for 10 years is no reason to continue doing it that way.

2. *Too little childlikeness.* Children have lively imaginations. They like to play "just pretend" and "what if" games. They daydream about the wonderful things they will do when they grow up. An achieving leader is like a child in this respect. He likes to take

present situations and play "what if." He enjoys imagining what utopia would be like.

3. *Nearsightedness*. It is judicious to see things as they are. But achieving leaders go a step further and see things as they could be. A book is a book is a book. But might it not also be a prop to hold open a window, or a lift on Junior's chair so he can reach the dining table?

4. *Too much carefulness*. To make progress a turtle has to stick his neck out. So do leaders. "Nothing ventured, nothing gained" is their motto.

5. *Too little assertiveness*. Many people have convictions but because the majority does not agree, or because they are afraid of being considered pushy, they often keep their convictions to themselves. When achieving leaders conceive good ideas, they have enough assertiveness to give them birth.

6. *Closed mind*. The more strongly one feels that he really knows something, the less open he is to new ideas in that area. Strong conviction, housed in an open mind, is one mark of an achieving leader.

HOW TO ACQUIRE INNOVATIVENESS

If you are short on innovation, there are certain ways you can induce it:

1. Concentrate on the unique. Notice the thing that is different from all other things. Notice how a situation, although similar to other situations, is different from all other situations. Look for the unique quality in things, situations, and people.

2. Realize that there are gaps in your knowledge and be aware of what they are. Avoid making assumptions to fill in the gaps. Assumptions can be erroneous and they can get so firmly embedded in your thinking that you can't distinguish them from fact.

3. Practice making connections between diverse factors in situations. Try to find a link between opposite factors.

4. Someone once said that a little information can be dangerous; but too much information can be just as dangerous. Too much detail can obliterate the simple truth you need to spark your innovation.

5. Provocative thinking is another way to induce innovation. Logical thinking brings to mind what is right and reasonable. Provocative thinking does the opposite. It brings to mind what is not right and not reasonable. It begins with the thinker attempting to answer the question "What if?"

For example, suppose you are a sales manager and your salespeople turn in weekly reports that are often incomplete and erroneous. You want to issue written instructions that will cut down on errors. It would seem illogical to ask the salesperson who is the worst offender to help you decide what the instructions should include. So begin provocative thinking by asking yourself, "What if I ask Joe [worst offender] to write the instructions for me?" This thought leads to the next thought, "I would find out what Joe doesn't know about the weekly report. I would find out what Joe thinks is important and what he thinks is unimportant about the report. I could find out why Joe's reports are incomplete. I might learn that parts of the report place an undue burden on the salespeople. I could think about revising the report form. I could assign Joe to work with another salesperson to revise the report form."

Provocative thinking does not necessarily lead you back to your original solution for the problem, which in this example was that you would issue written instructions. Although it could reinforce the original solution, it often leads to a better solution.

HOW TO CREATE READINESS
FOR A CHANGE IN OTHERS

The definite steps that a leader takes to promote improvement are not nearly as important as his underlying attitude toward improvement. Employees can catch their leader's zeal for achievement and they can get satisfaction from the challenge to excel.

However, an achieving leader does more than hold a supportive attitude toward improvement. He backs up his attitude with specific steps to encourage innovativeness in his employees. Here are some specific steps you can take to create readiness for change in your employees:

1. Be an example. Periodically think about your own work. Have you collected some noncontributing routine tasks like

corrosion collects on your car battery? Do you have tasks that don't contribute to achievement of goals? If you are engaging in these kinds of tasks, eliminate them from your schedule.

2. Review the tasks you have imposed on your staff. Are they contributing tasks? For example, are you requiring a report that is nice for your personal information but not really necessary to achieve an objective? Periodically review with each employee his specific work to determine what parts are contributing to achievement and which parts should be eliminated and perhaps replaced with more productive work.

3. Consider your work team as a whole. Which members are achieving objectives and moving on to higher objectives? Are any members resting on past achievements? If so, can you find a way to recharge them?

4. Show enthusiasm when an employee suggests an innovation in procedure or a new project aimed at achieving goals. You may have to act as the devil's advocate, forcing the employee to think through to operational consequences what at first appears to be a bright idea. You may have to help an employee modify a good idea to make it workable and acceptable. Never shrug off an innovative suggestion because you think it won't work. Help the employee think it through and see for himself why it won't work. Encourage him to try again.

5. As employees drop off nonessential work, delegate essential work from your workload. (See Chapter 14 on delegating.)

6. Conduct achievement evaluations with emphasis on contribution to success. (See Chapter 10, "Upgrading Achievement.")

GETTING READY FOR CHANGE

Many attempts to change a situation, procedure, or performance fail because the leader neglected to correctly diagnose the need for change or he did not communicate the need adequately to those involved in the change. Successful changes have the following features:

1. They result in improvement of the object of the change. Change for the sake of change hardly ever is successful. Change for the sake of betterment can be successful.

2. They are understood by those affected as being useful and desirable.
3. They are presented positively. Positive suggestion is more readily accepted than negative criticism.
4. They are presented in small installments. People are willing to alter their habits only slightly.
5. They are presented by a supportive individual whom the affected person views with trust and respect.

The first step in getting ready for change is to define the desired improvement. Figure 19–1 is a form you can use for implementing change. At the top of the form define the desired improvement in specific terms. State it in much the same way that you would state a goal or objective.

Break down the desired improvement into small steps and list these in the left-hand column of the change implementation form.

Next determine who is affected by the desired change and list these individuals in the next column, opposite the appropriate step you have listed. Imagine resistance that any of these people might have to any part of the change. Consider the source of any such resistance. Is the resistance valid? Do you need to alter any part of the desired change you are contemplating? If you imagine resistance that is not valid, can you conceive a convincing rebuttal?

After you have thought through the desired change and the small steps toward accomplishing it, and after you have thought about each individual person who will be affected by the change, confer with the people affected, either individually or in a group, whichever seems to be most desirable. When you have your conference or conferences, point out the value and consequences of the desired change. Encourage two-way communication. Listen to opposing viewpoints. Reason together to eliminate differences. Be as flexible as you can be. Arrive at a group decision if at all possible. People are more committed to a task if they have helped to formulate it.

Be enthusiastic about the desirable effects of the change. Your enthusiasm will be catching.

With the help of the individuals involved, enter the date when each step will be implemented and the date when you all expect the implementation to be completed.

The column headed "Date of Conference" is for you to enter the date when you confer with the individual(s) involved in

CHANGE IMPLEMENTATION				
Define Desired Improvement:				
Steps toward Desired Improvement	Person Affected	Confer Date	Implement Date	Complete Date

Figure 19-1

each step. This is merely for your own reference in case you need this information later.

Monitor the change as it progresses. Encourage individuals to report to you any problem they are having in implementing the change. Help them work through these problems or, if necessary, adjust the step so that implementation can occur.

Handling Uncertainties that Arise with Change

When a major change is about to occur, such as the moving of an office from one location to another, or the reorganization of a company or department, the presence of the immediate leader can help the group withstand anxieties that build up in times of uncertainty. You, as their leader, can undergird them. You can give them facts and thus prevent harmful rumors from taking hold and adversely affecting your staff.

If, after analyzing your own leadership style, you determine that a change in your approach is advisable, find a way to explain it to your followers. The change in your approach can be upsetting to them if they do not understand it.

MISTAKEN ASSUMPTIONS
IN THE MANAGEMENT OF CHANGE

There are some common mistaken assumptions that people make when they contemplate initiating a change. But there are good reasons for not making these assumptions.

1. The assumption that process is simple and does not need leadership.

   People generally resist change regardless of how simple or small it is. They must be helped to understand why the change is beneficial. They must understand the change itself and how it affects them. They must be committed to it. All of this takes leadership.

2. The assumption that the present organizational structure can be automatically transposed to manage the change.

   The present staff may or may not have the ability to handle some changes. The organizational structure may be inappropriate for certain changes. Outside consultant(s) may be needed to analyze the situation and give direction.

3. The assumption that people are committed because they give lip service to the change.

They may give lip service to it to please you. Avoid presenting your plan completely worked out to the last detail and then attempting to "sell" it. It is better to present the problem or situation that needs changing and let those involved help work out the change process. People will be more committed to a change process they have helped develop.

4. The assumption that a good plan means good implementation.

Much more is involved in implementing a change than good planning. It takes not only a good plan, but also understanding and commitment on the part of those involved. Plus it takes follow-up to see that it is working and, finally, evaluation of the change after it has been operative for a while.

20

Discipline:
A Function of Leadership

For many leaders the most difficult part of their job is disciplining their followers. There are few who enjoy taking disciplinary action against an employee who has broken a rule or terminating an employee whose performance is unacceptable. Such unpleasant tasks can be made less difficult if discipline is viewed as correcting a problem rather than punishing an offender.

The traditional approach to discipline stresses the use of increasingly more serious punishment, such as warnings, threats, reprimands, suspensions, and demotions. These may bring about short-term improvement, but often fail to solve the discipline problem and often create more problems. Such punishments can produce hostility, reduced output, and create a desire to "get even." Discipline must create positive motivation in the employee to improve and continue to improve his performance. It should be designed to help employees overcome performance and behavior flaws. It should communicate an expectation of change and improvement rather than an expectation of continued problems and future termination.

THE NEED FOR A SYSTEM

Being soft, overlooking problems, giving chance after chance—these postures don't win popularity. They destroy morale. It is easier for a leader to perform the discipline problem when there is an effective discipline policy in writing and understood by all employees. A discipline policy, to be effective, must have certain characteristics:

- The system should be easy to understand. Rules should be written in simple language, readily understood by every employee.
- The rules must make sense to the employee. He must be able to see that following the rules will make a difference to the organization.
- Rules should be uncomplicated and easy to enforce. A complex rule that is difficult to understand will usually be ignored by most employees.
- Rules must be enforced to be valuable.
- There must be consistency and impartiality in the enforcement of rules.

Components found in most discipline systems include:

- A first warning, which is usually given orally. It serves to remind the employee of the rule that he has broken or is breaking. The warning or reminder should be given privately. The tone should be friendly but firm.
- A second warning, which is usually written, should state that the employee had been warned orally and the date on which the oral warning occurred. The written reminder should call for specific improvement by a specific date. The written reminder should be handed to the employee, rather than being delivered by mail or other means. This will give the leader an opportunity to again discuss the breach of rule with the employee. The employee should be given an opportunity to explain his behavior. If the employee has, in the opinion of the leader, an honest reason why he has been unable to obey the rule, the leader should make every effort to help the employee solve the problem.
- Some organizations, after one or two written reminders, put the employee on a decision-making leave with pay. This gives the employee a day away from the workplace to consider his infraction of rules and the ultimate consequence of the continuance of such behavior. The leader places the employee on leave following an interview with

him in which the purpose of the leave is explained to the employee. Giving a day off with pay might seem like a reward for disobeying rules. However, leaders have found that employees usually return with a better attitude than the hostile, upset attitude of those suspended without pay.

- Following the leave, the employee usually returns and reports his decision to continue working for the organization and to observe all the rules. At this point, in organizations using this system, the leader expresses his pleasure and confidence in the employee, at the same time letting him know that any future violation of rules will result in termination.

  It sometimes happens that the employee decides not to continue working for the organization. When this is the case, the leader processes the necessary paperwork for a voluntary termination or resignation. If the employee does not return at all following the leave, his employment with the organization would be terminated.

CAUTIONS TO OBSERVE

There are cautions leaders must observe relative to any disciplinary matter:

1. If the organization has discipline policies and procedures, the leader should follow them to the letter.
2. If the organization has a contract with a union, the leader should be familiar with the disciplinary provisions of the contract. Organization procedures relating to discipline and disciplinary provisions of the contract should harmonize.
3. A written record should be made of all disciplinary actions taken and a copy placed in the employee's personnel file. If the employee should attempt legal action against the organization or his leader, it would be well to have the discipline action documented.

REASONS FOR TERMINATION

A leader may have employees who, after going through the discipline system of the organization, still do not perform or behave in an acceptable manner. These employees ought to be discharged, for the following reasons:

- If they are not discharged, the minimum standard of performance for the group is lowered. Each time undesirable work or behavior is accepted the minimum standard is lowered. Lowering the minimum standard has a degrading effect on the motivation to achieve in other employees.
- If a leader continues to put up with low achievers, he will be spending his time helping them, correcting their mistakes, and solving problems they create. This is an unproductive use of a leader's time, which should be spent maximizing the output of high achievers.
- To paraphrase an old cliché that says a chain is only as strong as its weakest link: a staff is only as productive as its least productive member allows it to be. A nonachiever in a group will always pull down the total achievement of the entire group.
- A leader risks lowering his leadership image if he does not take decisive action when it is necessary.
- When a leader accepts the below-standard performance and poor behavior of one employee, he is unjust to the other employees who must carry the load of the nonachieving employee.

ABSENTEEISM AND TARDINESS

By far the most common discipline problem that leaders face is that of absenteeism and tardiness on the part of employees. It is perhaps the most costly problem in terms of money, morale, and production. An automobile dealer found that the cost of absenteeism among all employees was running as high as $300 per employee per year.

The dissensions and frustration caused when other employees have to fill in for late and absent employees lowers morale among all employees. Production also suffers when employees are absent or tardy. The cost of this discipline problem warrants constant effort to keep it under control. Here are some ways achieving leaders attempt to keep absenteeism and tardiness under control:

1. Insist on prompt notification when someone must be absent unexpectedly. Set a deadline, such as within one hour of the time the individual is supposed to report for work. If the deadline is not observed, ask for an explanation when the employee returns to work. By asking for an explanation you impress on the employee the importance of the rule.

2. Unless the absence is due to an unexpected emergency,

require employees to discuss pending absences with their immediate supervisors prior to the absence.

3. Have standard operating procedures for each job in writing so someone else can fill in for the absent employee. Have a back-up list of employees that is available to all employees so they will know for whom they are to fill in in case of absences.

4. Keep a running record by employees of absences on Mondays and Fridays and on the day before and the day after holidays. Have some employees established a pattern of extending weekends and holidays by choosing these times to be absent? Some organizations have a policy that a day's pay is forfeited for absences on such days unless the employee can produce proof of legitimate reason for absence, such as a doctor's certificate.

5. Without prying, show an interest in the personal lives of your employees, especially those who are frequently absent or late. They may have personal problems that could be solved by counseling.

6. Look for safety hazards in equipment and operation and for poor housekeeping that can cause accidents, such as the bottom drawer of a file cabinet being left open.

7. Require all injuries, no matter how minor, to be reported. It is the leader's responsibility to see that injured employees get proper first aid treatment to avoid serious aftereffects.

8. Let employees know you appreciate good attendance. Let them know they are missed when they are absent. Most employees will make an extra effort to be at work if they know their presence really makes a difference.

9. Monitor lunch and rest breaks. Talk privately to those who habitually take extended lunch and rest breaks. Point out the reasons why you rely on them to be prompt, how their tardiness affects the productivity of the group, and how lower productivity will eventually affect them.

10. Monitor lunch and rest breaks of employees of other departments. You can hardly expect your employees to return on time if others can take extra time. If this is what is happening, discuss the problem with other leaders in your peer group or place the problem on a leadership meeting agenda.

11. Be a model for your employees to emulate. This may mean that you will have to hold yourself more strictly accountable for observing rules than you hold your employees, but it will pay off in fewer discipline problems for you to handle.

CIVIL WAR

Conflict can arise when two or more people work together. It can arise between individuals, between groups of individuals, between employee and employee, and between employee and leader.

Jealousy, justifiable or not, can cause conflict between employees. Aggressiveness on the part of an employee to advance can cause conflict. A supervisor who demands strict compliance with rules but ignores the same rules himself can cause conflict. The manager who feels he does not get a proportional share of the organization budget tends to be uncooperative with the manager who seems to get more than his share. A delay in one department holds up the work in another department and conflict results. How can an achieving leader deal with these types of conflict within the organization or department?

First, let us look at some of the inappropriate approaches to conflict:

- *Ignoring the conflict.* This includes listening to a complaint and not investigating the other side, assuming the employee will learn to deal with the problem.
- *Sugarcoating the conflict.* Encouraging the employees to do better, hiring an assistant for one, or defending one against the other.
- *Punishing*—such as reprimanding, suspending, holding back wage increases, giving undesirable tasks.

These approaches do nothing to resolve the problem that caused the conflict. They tend rather to increase the intensity of the conflict or send it underground.

Achieving leaders approach conflict by realizing that some conflict is inevitable, recognizing conflict as a positive force that can be used effectively by the organization, and managing the conflict.

When conflict arises in a staff, it will not go away by itself. If ignored, it will grow and do greater damage to the organization. It must be managed in order to be resolved and in order for the organization to profit from it.

Achieving leaders deal with conflict in these ways:

1. Deal with it promptly. If it goes on for an extended time unresolved, it cannot be used effectively by the organization.
2. Strive for creative, acceptable, and relative resolutions.

3. Focus on the problem, not the people involved.
4. Strive for resolution of conflict where both sides win and no one loses.
5. Give empathetic support to hostile feelings. This is important in getting the parties to express the real differences between them.
6. Listen patiently.
7. Know the situation and the feelings of the principals involved in the conflict in order to pace the confrontation. If the leader knows a possible conflict situation exists and the stance of the parties involved, he may be able to bring the conflict out into the open at the most suitable time.

five

MAKING LEADERSHIP SEEN, HEARD, AND FELT WITH CREDIBILITY AND POWER

21

Communicating Leadership

Because leadership deals with human relationships, it follows that being able to communicate well is a prerequisite to achievement leadership. Leaders are called upon to communicate in numerous ways: person to person, person to group, leader to superior, leader to subordinate, leader to peer, leader to family, leader to civil representative, and so forth.

USING LEADERSHIP WORDS

Communicating for achievement leadership is more than using correct grammar. It's more than knowing what to talk about or who to talk to, or when to talk and when not to talk. All of these aspects of communication are important. But leadership communication is much more than that. Words can detract from your image or they can enhance your image. So the choice of words is vitally important to your leadership image. The words you used during high school and college days are not the words you are likely to hear in executive leadership circles. Your word choice can reveal your age, the extent of your education, whether or not you are well traveled, and whether you read a lot or very little. Consider the following words.

Ordinary Words	Words that Can Enhance Your Leadership Image
honeymoon	wedding trip
blackboard	chalkboard (They're not all black any more)
drapes	draperies or window covering
stewardess	flight attendant
maiden name	birth name
the Sahara Desert	the Sahara ("Sahara" means desert)
ex-husband	former husband
bathing suit	swim suit
cake of soap	bar of soap
colored, Negro	Black or Afro-American
cuss	curse
graduated	was graduated from (The action is done to the graduate)
groom	bridegroom
got married	married
icebox	refrigerator
vet	veterinarian
the missus, the mister, my old man, my old lady	my wife, or Mrs. Doe, or Jane my husband, or Mr. Doe, or John
Sierra Mountains	Sierra
you claim	you say ("claim" indicates you do not believe what the other person says)

Unless you are referring to a specific product or manufacturer, do not use tradenames. For example:

Don't use	Say
Coke	cola

Don't use	Say
IBM	computer
Jello	gelatin
Ping Pong	table tennis
Scotch Tape	cellophane tape
Xerox	copier

When speaking of a member of the clergy, do not say "the reverend." Say, "pastor," "minister," "priest," or "rabbi." When addressing a member of the clergy in writing, use "The Reverend Mr. Baker" or "The Reverend Dr. Baker."

To say, "Chief Justice of the Supreme Court" is incorrect. Say, "Chief Justice of the United States."

You can think of other words and phrases to add to this list. To improve your leadership image by correct word usage, keep your own personal list in a pocket-size notebook that you can refer to while waiting for a plane, commuting to work, or whenever you have a few minutes to spare. Another way to upgrade your conversation is to ask a friend or family member to help you. Have the person evaluate your speech and tell you when you could have used a better choice of words.

HOW TO BE HEARD
WITH CREDIBILITY AND POWER

Here are some more ideas for getting others to pay attention to you when you speak:

- Do not speak in generalities when you have something specific in mind. For example, don't say, "We need to reorganize our office layout" when all you want to do is turn a desk around. Turning a desk around may make a big improvement in the work flow in the office, but "reorganize our office layout" sounds like such a major change that it might receive a negative response.
- Emphasize the benefits of your proposal from your listener's viewpoint.
- Get feedback from the other person by asking questions.
- Do not use a questioning intonation at the end of a phrase or a sentence. This causes you to sound doubtful even when you are not.
- Banish "kinda," "I think," "justa," "sort of," and "it seems" from

your vocabulary. Such indefinite phrases cause you to appear to lack confidence.

- Do not ramble or repeat yourself. Come to the point quickly. Repeat only if the other person has not understood you, or for emphasis. When you do repeat, express your thought in different words than you used the first time.

PUBLIC SPEAKING

Leader power is probably most visible when the leader is making a speech. If the speaker has not organized his speech well, if he has not tuned his speech to his audience, if he is a victim of stage fright, if he does not have mastery of his subject, his leadership image suffers loss of credibility.

Organizing the Speech

The organization of your speech is the most important part of your speech for getting the audience to understand your message. The first step in organizing a speech is to know your reason for making the speech. To put your speech objective firmly ... mind, fill in the blanks to this sentence:

"I want _____ to _____
      (who)   (always—what; sometimes—when, where,

_____ because _____ ."
or how)   (why)

Tuning in to Your Audience

The audience is the second most important part of your speech. Analyze your audience before you prepare your speech. Ask yourself: Why should they be interested in my topic? How can what I have to say benefit them? What does the audience probably already know about my topic? How does the audience probably feel about my topic? How does the audience probably feel about me?

After you have thought through the answers to these questions, you can fit your information to your audience. Begin your information at the point of new or fresh information for them. Don't tell them what they already know. If you suspect that the audience is not particularly excited about your topic, can you think of ways to interest them in it? Can you establish a relationship between your subject and your audience? Can you point out ways that your objective will benefit your audience? If you feel the audience has a negative attitude toward you, pay special attention to the way you will present yourself. Would the audience respond more positively if you appeared to be humble? strong? persuasive? demanding? Your audience will be more willing to accept you and your message if you attempt to tailor yourself to the audience by careful choice of words and phrases. Use words your audience can understand. If you are talking to a group of assembly-line workers, you would not use the same words you would use if you were talking to a group of diplomats or top-level executives.

Consider the physical comfort of your audience. If you have a choice of place for your presentation, choose a setting that is uncrowded and pleasant. Let the audience know you are concerned about their welfare. Can they hear you comfortably? Is the air conditioning making the area too cool? Or is it too hot? Does everyone have a place to sit? Can everyone see clearly (if you are using visual aids)?

Speaker's Credibility

Audiences believe speakers whom they feel are competent, trustworthy, well meaning, dynamic, and likable. They usually disbelieve speakers who are, in their opinion, incompetent, dishonest, self-oriented, timid, or obnoxious.

Your credibility with your audience is established with your audience before you speak, if they have had previous experiences with you, by your reputation, by your rank in the organization, and by the similarity of your and your audience's attitudes and values.

If you are addressing an audience whom you have never addressed before and to whom you are unknown, you can enhance your credibility as the speech progresses in the following ways:

- By showing an understanding of the audience's needs
- By appearing well informed and fair-minded
- By expressing yourself dynamically

- By appearing to like the audience
- By having mastery of the subject about which you are speaking

Controlling Stage Fright

Fear produces energy. That is why people experiencing stage fright usually have quaking knees, trembling hands, a quivering voice, and so forth. If you suffer from stage fright, don't attempt to eliminate it. Instead, attempt to channel the energy it produces to help you make a more effective speech. Here are some methods achievement leaders have found helpful:

- Do some physical exercise. Expend some energy before getting up to speak. If you are an after-dinner speaker, excuse yourself briefly just before it is time for you to be introduced. Walk out of the room. Walk quickly the length of a hall a couple of times, or up a flight of stairs. The exercise will release a great deal of tension. Don't eat heavily just before you are going to make a speech. You can think more clearly if your digestive tract is not overloaded. Take several deep breaths just before speaking.
- After you stand up to speak, wait a few seconds before speaking. Look over your audience. Smile at them. If someone smiles back, you will feel some tension leave your body. If you find it difficult to smile when you are experiencing stage fright, do what one acquaintance of ours does. He visualizes the entire audience minus their noses, or with crossed eyes, or some other ridiculous appearance.
- While speaking, move around. Don't appear to be glued to one spot. The movement will use energy and help you to relax. Your audience will appreciate it, too. It is monotonous to the audience when the speaker stays in one spot.
- Gesture as you speak. However, be certain that your gestures are meaningful. A continuous flailing of the arms can distract the audience.
- Vary your voice tone appropriately.
- Use eye contact. Select several persons seated in different areas of the audience and talk directly to them. It helps to pick out people who appear to be interested in what you are saying. Their interest encourages you to relax and talk naturally.

The Speech Itself

The introduction is very important. It is during the introduction of your speech that you can rouse the audience's interest. If the introduction is well done, the audience will be inclined to listen to what follows. If the introduction is not done well, the audience will not likely give the remainder of the speech much attention.

Introduction. To get the audience's attention during the introduction, you can use any of the following methods which will involve the audience mentally:

- Ask a series of rhetorical questions.
- Relate a brief narrative—one that will rouse the audience's curiosity about your subject.
- Many speakers like to begin by telling a funny story. If you do, be sure the story is more than funny. It should be relative to your message, the occasion, or the audience.
- Some speakers begin by complimenting their audience. If you can do this sincerely and for a specific attribute of the audience, it will give the audience a warm feeling toward you. However, it is easy to overdo a complimentary introduction. For example, if the audience is a group of persons with similar status, such as all secretaries, they get a little bored hearing speakers tell them how important they are to their bosses, for example, or how attractive they are. Such generalities have an insincere ring to them.
- A reference to the occasion will establish common ground for speaker and audience.
- A reference to your own experience will interest the audience. However, it should be an experience relative to your subject or the occasion.
- The surest way to get audience attention in the introduction is to relate the topic directly to the audience. Let the audience know what the information you are going to give them will do for them. Will it help them achieve something they desire? Will it help them improve their situation, or avoid something undesirable? First, analyze your audience's motives and then state, in your introduction, how the topic relates to them.

The Body of Your Speech. Have about four or five points you will make to reinforce the objective of your speech. If you have too many points, it will make your speech run too long. It is better to have a few well-prepared arguments than many poorly prepared ones. For each point, look for an example or an anecdote that will prove the point. An illustration related conversationally will not only prove your point, but will add entertainment value to your speech.

Closing Your Speech. Do not belabor the ending of your speech. When you have made all your points, summarize in a sentence or two the objective of your speech. If you want your audience to take some action on what you have told them, provide them with the information they need to enable them to take the action you desire. Then sit down—you are through. Don't be like the houseguest who arrives at eight, visits for thirty minutes, and spends from eight-thirty to ten leaving.

Someone has aptly said that the best speech outline is:

1. Tell them what you are going to tell them: Introduction.
2. Tell them: Body.
3. Tell them what you have told them: Conclusion.

The Question Period

Many situations allow time for the audience to ask the speaker questions following his presentation. This is an important time. If this session goes badly, much of the impact of the speech will be lost. Prepare for the question period ahead of time by knowing a great deal more about your subject than you will present in your speech. Try to predict what parts of your speech your audience will find particularly interesting. Be sure you are well versed on those parts. What areas of your speech will you cover only briefly? Will the audience have questions concerning these areas? What additional facts will the audience want?

Be prepared to handle the question period professionally. Do not allow one or two people to monopolize the time. Consider the entire audience so everyone has an opportunity to ask questions, or as many as time will allow. Here are some suggestions for the question period:

- Admit ignorance rather than faking answers to questions for which you have no real answer.
- React to all questions. If you cannot answer the question now or the answer would be too involved, postpone the answer until a later time, or offer to meet with the questioner after the session.
- Avoid confrontations with hostile questioners. Respond in a friendly manner.
- Repeat questions or rephrase questions for the audience so they can relate the answer to the question.
- Analyze "loaded" questions for the audience to prevent misunderstanding.

Evaluating Yourself as a Speaker

Robert Burns wrote, "Oh wad some power the giftie gie us to see ousels as others see us!" The most effective evaluation of your speech is made by your audience. The trouble is that an audience will not always tell you how well you did except in a very general way by applause or by verbal compliments following the program. Some leaders use a critique sheet with their audiences to ask them to comment specifically on various aspects of their presentations. Figure 21-1 is a critique sheet developed by Mike Stanfield of Computer Galaxy, Norwalk, California. You, too, may find it useful. You can have copies put at each place, or distributed after the presentation. It would be wise to put your name and address on the form so it could be mailed to you later.

Another effective way to evaluate your speechmaking ability is to videotape your presentation. You can readily see any flaws in your presentation and work to improve in those specific areas.

MEETING THE MEDIA

Executive leaders are newsworthy subjects especially when they are associated with a large organization in times of stress or major change. Sometimes they have only a few minutes to prepare to meet the press, a television camera, or a radio audience. Their main concern is being able to represent their organization in a truthful and favorable light.

On the other hand, news reporters who interview executive leaders are skilled at asking provocative questions to get provocative, interesting, and controversial answers. When a reporter or correspondent asks questions, he is working for *his* reading and listening audience. His goal is not to give favorable or unfavorable exposure to the executive or the executive's organization. His goal is to unearth a newsworthy story that will stimulate his audience.

Some leaders dread being interviewed by the media. They fear being "tricked" into saying something that will put the executive or his organization in an unfavorable light. Other leaders, however, welcome such interviews as opportunities to tell their organization's story to a large audience. They consider any exposure to be good public relations. It is not that simple. Achievement leaders know that if the interview is going to be good for the organization, they must make it so. They know that every reporter's objective is to

```
                    CRITIQUE SHEET

    I would sincerely appreciate your help in improving myself as a
    speaker.  Would you listen to my speech and briefly evaluate me
    on the following?

    1.  What was I trying to say?



    2.  How could I have made it clearer?



    3.  What strengths do I have in delivery skills?



    5.  What areas of delivery should I work on to improve?



    5.  Add any comments, suggestions, or criticisms you might have.










    Thanks again.


    _____
    Your name
```

Figure 21-1 *(Used by permission of Mike Stanfield, Computer Galaxy, Norwalk, California.)*

uncover a "story" for his reading or listening audience. Achievement leaders are aware of this but they do not look upon the news media as being hostile to them. Rather, they understand that the news media are merely doing their job. Achievement leaders face the reporter or the camera with a friendly, candid attitude.

Here are some guidelines you can use when called upon to meet the press or to be interviewed on television:

- Do not fear the tape recorder. Reporters are using tape recorders more and more to ensure the accuracy of their quotations.
- Prepare carefully for interviews. Anticipate questions, research facts, and prepare effective answers. Have the answers in your mind so you do not have to refer to notes during the interview. Referring to notes may make you appear too "prepared" and make you seem less candid. Don't memorize your answers word for word, but have the facts firmly in your mind so you can answer without hesitation.
- Talk from the public's viewpoint, not from your organization's viewpoint. For example, suppose you are an executive of a utility company asked to tell why you require a deposit from new customers. You might reply like this, "We don't like to ask for deposits because they annoy our customers and they're a nuisance to us. Also, we have to pay interest on the money. But we don't think it fair that you should have to pay part of someone else's electric bill when he fails to pay. And that's what happens: the cost of his service is passed along to other users in higher rates. If a new customer pays his bills promptly for six months, we refund his deposit, and we're glad to do it."
- Talk in terms the public understands. Every industry has its own terminology which is understood only by people in the industry. Translate this kind of language into words used and understood by lay people.
- When possible, use the pronoun *I* rather than *we* or *the company*. The terms *we* and *the company* reinforce the public's image of corporations as being impersonal and lacking in individual employee responsibility. You can say, "I was a member of the team that. . . ."
- Talk about the work of the organization you are involved in. For example, if you are a local representative for a corporation headquartered in another state, don't attempt to talk about corporate matters. Talk about your work as it relates to the people in your city. You will gain more credibility that way.
- Do not make a statement that you don't want quoted. "Off the record" does not exist in a reporter's mind. He may not attach your name to the quotation, but your words will likely turn up elsewhere as "Meanwhile, it has been learned from other sources that . . ."
- State the most important fact first. Then you can follow with reasons or explanations. In this way your most important fact will not be edited out of the news story or the radio/television script because of lack of space or time.

- Keep cool and never argue with a reporter. You may win an argument, but you will lose the debate. Remember it's the reporter who will write the copy. The published story will reflect his feeling toward you.
- Beware of any reporter's attempts to put words into your mouth. He may ask a question containing words you do not care to use. Do not repeat those words when answering the question. For example:

Question: Mr. Smith, wouldn't you describe the discipline at Junior High as out of hand?

If Mr. Smith answers, "No, the discipline at Junior High is not out of hand," he has associated "discipline" with "out of hand" and the story may come out with this headline: "District Administrator Says Discipline at Junior High Not Out of Hand." Mr. Smith could have answered the question like this: "We have some discipline problems at Junior High, but the principal and staff have the situation under control."

- Do not become defensive when a reporter relates a so-called fact and asks you to comment on it. If you are not familiar with the reporter's source (which may or may not be real), say so. Then answer the question in a positive way.
- Avoid answering reporters' questions with simple yes or no answers. Amplify your answers by explaining your organization's point of view. Your answer should respond to the yes-or-no question but in such a way as to give the reasons for the response. This is your opportunity to tell your organization's story in a positive way.
- Tell the truth and be tactful. If you attempt to hide the truth, you will lose credibility with the press and the public later when the truth is discovered. When telling the truth will hurt someone or make you or your organization open to legal action, tact is needed. For example, suppose one of the high officials of your organization has been discharged and a reporter asks, "I've heard that Mr. Jones was responsible for the union problems your company experienced last year. Is that true?" You might reply something like this: "When there is employee unrest, companies sometimes make management changes, and that's what we've done."
- Do not exaggerate the facts. You will be asked to explain later when exaggerated predictions do not materialize, and that could be difficult to do without appearing foolish.

22

Leadership Ethics

In the Book of Genesis there is the story of Cain and Abel. Cain was jealous of his brother, Abel, and murdered him. Later the Lord asked Cain, "Where is thy brother?" To this Cain replied, "I know not. Am I my brother's keeper?"[1] There are few people who think highly of Cain's philosophy concerning ethics.

"Am I my brother's keeper?" That is a question that each person has to answer to determine his own ethical standard. Ethics has to do with the relationship between people.

Peter Drucker says:

> Businessmen, we are told solemnly, should not cheat, steal, lie, bribe, or take bribes. But nor should anyone else. Men and women do not acquire exemption from ordinary rules of personal behavior because of their work or job. Nor, however, do they cease to be human beings when appointed vice-president, city manager, or college dean. And there has always been a number of people who cheat, steal, lie, bribe, or take bribes. The problem is one of moral values and moral

---

[1] Genesis 4:9.

education of the individual, of the family, of the school. But there neither is a separate ethics of business, nor is one needed.[2]

While it is true that the same ethics apply to everyone, leader and follower, most people agree that a position of leadership confers a heavier burden of responsibility to adhere to ethical behavior than lesser positions do. Most people still expect their leaders, especially their public officials, to be ethical. Few would knowingly elect a member of organized crime, for example, to a high political office.

Achievement leadership requires exceptional standards of personal morality, accountability, influence, loyalty, and dependability.

PERSONAL MORALITY

The "everybody's doing it" syndrome leads to "acceptable" practices that are compromises of ethical standards. Most people know it is wrong to tell lies, steal, kill, and so forth. Most people can recite the Golden Rule, but there are few who strictly live by it today. Man is a rational being and seeks to justify his actions whenever conscience tells him he is falling below his moral standard. And so he tells the "little white lie" and even at times requires it of those he leads—for example, the secretary who is called upon to tell a visitor her boss is "out of the office" when, in truth, he is in his office only a few feet away.

In 1975, the American Management Association estimated that the annual loss to business by employee theft was $10 billion. Business leaders are concerned about this tremendous cut into profits every year. But how many of these same business leaders think they are doing wrong when they pad an expense account, make a long-distance personal phone call at their employer's expense, or take extra time off?

Achievement leaders *do* live by the Golden Rule and they encourage their followers to do the same. Those who achieve and enjoy their achievement are those who have thought through their moral standard and are prepared at all times to make ethical choices

[2]Peter Drucker, *Management: Tasks, Responsibilities, Practices*, New York, Harper & Row, 1973, p. 366.

based on their predetermined moral standard. They do not wait until the moment demands it to decide what their standard will be.

Followers are quick to perceive the moral caliber of their leaders. If they sense that their leader does not have very high moral standards, if they note that he preaches one way and practices another, they will feel free to do likewise.

The Need for Candor

Achievement leaders who want their followers to display a high standard of morality must first adhere to a high standard of morality themselves. Followers usually emulate what they see in their leaders. But it is not enough for a leader to have a high moral standard. His actions can be misjudged in a complex situation. Even though a leader's actions are based on high moral principles and are fair from his viewpoint, his followers can easily misinterpret the leader's actions if the leader's reasons for his actions have not been communicated to the followers.

For example, take the case of Manager L. P. who reorganized his department. One of his better employees, Fran, was being favorably considered for promotion by the organization. Fran, who was not aware of this, returned from vacation to find her desk had been placed in an adjoining hall along with the desk of Jim Peters who would retire in a month's time and whose position was going to be discontinued and his work divided among the remaining employees. Fran assumed that her position, too, was about to be discontinued and that she would be laid off. She knew she had performed well, better than most in her department, and felt that her manager had treated her unjustly. She went higher up to complain about her unfair treatment.

The mistake was quickly corrected by dialogue, but not before some unpleasantness had occurred. If Manager L. P. had earlier created an atmosphere of candor and two-way openness with his staff, Fran would have asked what was going on rather than jumping to a false conclusion. Furthermore, in the minds of the remaining employees, a seed of doubt has now been planted. How can they be sure Fran's assumption had not been correct and that her complaining to upper management had not forced their manager to reconsider?

How can a leader promote candor in his organization? Here are some ways achievement leaders do it:

1. Achievement leaders encourage critical feedback from subordinates. Fran Tarkenton, former NFL quarterback and founder-president of Behavioral Systems, Inc., says, "The best thing my receivers can do for me is to tell me exactly how my passes are perceived by them and how they match their ability to get down field. If there is something wrong with my passing, I need to know."[3]

2. They ask for and are able to accept negative feedback as well as positive feedback. Leaders who want to be surrounded only by "yes men" are soon "found out" by their employees and they will receive only positive feedback even though it may be dishonest feedback.

3. They are consistent in the way they deal with feedback. They're always open to employees' comments. They let employees know they are interested in their thoughts and are glad they offer them.

4. They give employees the opportunity to convey their thoughts. They're available to them. They don't limit their contacts with employees to crisis or emergency situations.

5. If they can act upon an employee's suggestion, they do so. If it is not feasible to act on an employee's suggestion, they explain why they cannot act on it.

6. They never "pass the buck" up or down. If they act on an employee's suggestion and it doesn't turn out well, they don't blame the employee for making a poor suggestion. The decision to act was theirs and they are accountable for the results of their own actions. Similarly, if they must announce bad news to their employees, they don't imply that those higher up are responsible or to blame for the bad news.

7. They involve employees in problem solving and decision making. A feeling of involvement encourages candor.

8. They never, by their response to suggestions, create feelings of guilt or inadequacy in an employee.

9. They show respect for their employees. They expect them to be honest and assume that they are. Giving a person a high reputation to live up to is one of the best ways to bring out the best in that person.

ACCOUNTABILITY

Alfred North Whitehead, English mathematician and philosopher, once said, "A great society is a society in which its men of business think greatly of their functions." Leadership in any field

[3] Aetna Life and Casualty Insurance Company, Hartford, *Honesty from the Bottom Up*, Career, Fall, 1979, p. 14.

should not be taken lightly. Through the thoughtfulness of the opinions they express, the positions they advocate, and their business activities, leaders have opportunities to exert a profound effect on their organizations, on society, and on the nation as a whole.

Jesus said that to whom much is given, much shall be required. Leadership evokes accountability. To be accountable one must achieve. To achieve one must be committed to the task.

Achievement leaders are totally committed to excellence—excellence in their own functions, in their employees, and in their organization. They have their priorities in order. They are committed first to themselves, to be the best person that they can be; secondly, to their function in the organization, to do the best that they can; thirdly, to their employees, to provide for them opportunities for growth and commitment; and fourthly, to the organization, to help shape its goals—goals that uphold a high moral standard.

INFLUENCE

Leadership implies influence over other people. The story is told of a particularly foggy night in Southern California. The fog was so thick one could see only dimly the taillights of a car not more than 3 or 4 feet ahead. Two cars crept slowly along Pine Avenue. The driver of the leading car was in his own neighborhood and could sense his whereabouts. But the driver of the following car was in strange territory. He could not see the parked cars along the edge of the street nor the line down the center of the street. All he could see were the two red taillights of the car ahead. Feeling lost and alone the driver of the following car found comfort in those two red dots and followed them, rationalizing that the driver of the car ahead surely must know the way. The left-turn signal of the car ahead began to blink dimly and the two cars made a sharp left turn. Almost immediately the first car stopped and the red dots disappeared. The driver of the second car slammed on his brakes and stopped just behind the blurry shadow of the car he had been following. He got out and shouted excitedly to the driver of the first car, "Why did you stop? Where are we?" To which the driver of the leading car replied, "I don't know about you, Mister, but I'm in my garage. This is where I live."

Many people follow their leaders as blindly as the driver of the second car followed the taillights of the first car. "He knows because he's the boss," they rationalize. And they follow the leader, not only in the performance of their jobs, but also in their general attitudes and beliefs. What a responsibility is placed on leaders that their influence over those who follow them is of the highest ethical quality!

Achievement leaders do not leave the quality of their influence to chance. They make sure their followers know where they are being led, the route that is being followed, and why they should want to get there.

LOYALTY

Leadership is concerned with loyalty in three directions: upward, downward, and laterally.

Loyalty from Leader to Superior

From a moral point of view, loyalty can be good or bad, depending on its subject. Loyalty to Hitler before the collapse of the Third Reich and loyalty to Jim Jones at the mass suicide in Guyana are examples of misplaced loyalty. Many of the victims of the Guyana tragedy came from our own environment, and we find it difficult to understand how such a tragedy could happen to people like ourselves. But there are people in all fields of endeavor who follow persons they mistakenly feel deserving of their loyalty.

How can a person know who is really deserving of loyalty from a moral standpoint? The answer must go back to the person's own moral code. Leaders cannot afford to be lazy thinkers when it comes to morality. It is dangerous to bask in the reflected morality of another person and not establish one's own moral code.

Achievement leaders do not blindly follow their superiors. They give their loyalty first to their own beliefs, then to the organization, and thirdly to their leader. Whenever serious differences appear between his own moral standard and that of the organization or his superior, and he is unable through his influence to reconcile the difference, an achieving leader must determine within his own conscience and according to his own beliefs and values the course of action he must take.

Loyalty from Leader to Employees

Loyalty from leader downward to employees is as important as loyalty upward from leader to his superior. A leader can make himself deserving of his employees' loyalty by his own adherence to high moral and ethical standards. It is important that employees know they have the backing of their leader. Achievement leaders prove their loyalty to their followers in many ways:

- They treat their followers with respect. They never talk down to them or belittle them privately or openly.
- They give credit to their followers when credit is due them. And they do it publicly.
- If negative criticism is necessary, they offer it in private.
- They do not place blame when something goes wrong, but instead work with the employee to correct the situation.
- They do not take credit for employees' ideas and suggestions.
- They back their employees when they are acting within the function of their positions. When they delegate a task or a function to an employee, they also delegate the authority to enable the employee to carry out the task or function.
- They take a personal interest in each employee and are always open to employees who want to talk things over.
- They keep personal confidences that employees entrust to them.
- They never make an employee a scapegoat for their own mistakes.
- They do not place an employee in a position where the employee must choose between being loyal and compromising personal ethics.

Loyalty from Employees to Leader

There are effective and ineffective ways that leaders can win the loyalty of employees. Effective ways include observing all the suggestions listed above under "Loyalty from Leader to Employee," because loyalty is reciprocal. If the leader shows his loyalty to his employees, his employees will usually return the loyalty, often several times over.

An ineffective way to win loyalty of employees is by infection. The following example illustrates how infectious a leader's behavior can be; and if that behavior is damaging to the organization, it can defeat the leader and even his followers.

In a large computer organization the manager in charge of Forms conceived the false impression that, through reorganization of the division, his department would be consolidated with Policy, Research, and Procedures. He imagined himself being lowered to the level of assistant under the manager of Policy, Research, and Procedures. He was so convinced that this was about to happen that he communicated his suspicion to his staff at every opportunity. Eventually, one by one, his staff became convinced also. All employees under this manager became indignant about the bad treatment of their leader. Some looked for and found positions with another company. Some asked for transfers out of the department. Those who remained became a cohesive group of loyal supporters of their manager. They went to bat for him in a negative way by failing to cooperate with other departments, especially Policy, Research, and Procedures. Soon open warfare existed with all departments in the division taking sides. When upper management finally stepped in to straighten out the mess, the truth came out—the truth, as upper management saw it, was that the two departments should indeed be consolidated. And the Forms manager's suspicions became self-fulfilling prophecy. He had developed a loyal staff but it benefited him very little.

Lateral Loyalty

Lateral loyalty, or "esprit de corps" as it is often called, within a department and among departments is founded on mutual respect and commitment to department and organizational goals. See Chapter 11 for suggestions on building team loyalty.

When individual employee loyalty to the department or organization is strong, there will usually be lateral loyalty among the employees within the department or organization.

Loyalty Based on Coercion

Another ineffective way to promote loyalty of employees is by coercion. Coercion wins very shaky, false loyalty, and is devastating to an organization. For example, an insecure manager had a very high need for recognition. He enjoyed his leadership spot as the head of his department. He wanted the friendship and respect of his employees because it gave him a feeling of importance. He expected his employees to agree with him at all times. If a subordinate manager dared to voice disagreement, he would be treated coolly and eventually some of his responsibilities would be given to someone else until this subordinate manager was only a figurehead, let go under some pretense of inefficiency, or laid off because of lack of work.

Employees soon learned to outwardly agree with their manager, regardless of their inner thoughts. Knowing that their manager enjoyed prestige, they treated him accordingly at every opportunity. Thus they protected their positions and received pay increases and good performance evaluations.

Needless to say, this kind of loyalty is not conducive to productivity and is not good for an organization. Nor is it good for the leader because it has no foundation and eventually will topple, leaving the leader's insecurity exposed.

False Loyalty

False loyalty can occur when employees have high dependency needs. This type of employee would rather accept what the leader thinks than face the responsibility of expressing his own thoughts. Some people are by nature pilots (leaders), while others are by nature passengers (followers) who go along for the ride, preferring not to feel they are in control.

Top management can prevent false loyalty from occurring in a department by supporting individual response and independence of mind in the organization. They can buffer false loyalty by selecting and promoting managers who support individual responsibility and independent thinking. Interdepartmental committees and exchange of information between departments lessen the likelihood of false loyalty developing within a department.

DEPENDABILITY

Dependability is an essential part of an achievement leader's ethical code. He shows his dependability when the following conditions exist:

- His superiors and his subordinates are confident of his integrity.
- People can depend upon him to keep his promises, no matter how insignificant they may seem to him.

- Superiors and subordinates know they can depend on him to keep confidences entrusted to him. Superiors know that organizational information of a confidential nature will not be used in an unethical way. Subordinates know that confidences they have entrusted to him will not be revealed or used against them.
- New employees find that their jobs are as they were represented to be when they were interviewed. Leaders are sometimes tempted to build up a position or to tell only the positive side of it in order to get a promising candidate to accept employment with the organization.
- Others can depend on him being consistent in every situation. The leader who is "high" one day and "down" the next is not dependable.
- He has no prejudices relative to race, color, creed, sex, age, or anything else. People must be able to depend on him to treat everyone with equal personal respect and consideration.

ACHILLES' HEELS
OF ETHICAL LEADERSHIP

There are a number of vulnerable spots that can damage a leader's ethical standards if he is not prepared to handle them. They include conflicting interests, whistle blowing, dissonance, cooperation in wrong-doing, tunnel vision, and many more.

Questions a leader must answer according to his own moral code or ethical standard are:

- Is it wrong to hold an after-hours job if doing so lessens my efficiency on my regular job?
- If I hold stock in a company my employer does business with, and I am a purchasing agent or buyer for my employer, should I tell my employer of my interest in this company?
- If I find that my superior takes part in unethical practices that are harmful to the organization, should I report him to someone higher up?
- If organizational policy conflicts with what my superior requires of me, what should I do?
- If my superior asks me to cooperate in wrongdoing of any kind, such as padding his expense account, should I cooperate?
- If I do not agree with my employer's opinions or methods and I cannot influence him to change, should I remain loyal to him and his opinions and methods?

These are only a few of the questions concerning ethics that leaders may have to answer. Answers are not given here because no two situations are exactly alike. There can be circumstances that would alter a person's reaction to any given situation. Answers are not given also because if we gave answers, they would reflect only *our* moral code or ethics standard. Every leader must react according to his own standard.

The point is that achievement leaders *have* personal standards concerning moral and ethical issues on which to rely when such questions arise. Indecision concerning matters of ethics can be fatal to achievement leadership. As the prophet Elijah asked, "How long halt ye between two opinions?"[4]

[4] 1 Kings 18:21.

23

Enhancing Your Image

A leader may be all he should be, but if his leadership ability is hidden under a cloud of self-effacement, it will not have much influence on others. When promotions are being awarded, such a leader will be passed over unnoticed.

Jesus said, "Neither do men light a candle, and put it under a bushel, but on a candlestick; and it giveth light to all that are in the house."[1]

Imagine a line running from self-effacement to conceit. Somewhere along the line, just a little right of center, is the spot where achievement leaders should place their candles.

This chapter will deal with the candles achievement leaders can light and place on this imaginary line.

HALLMARKS OF ACHIEVEMENTS

Leaders who achieve have certain distinguishing features. The more these features become an integrated part of you, the more

[1] Matthew 5:15.

your leadership will be visible to others. Here are twenty hallmarks of achievement leaders:

1. *Greater-than-average willpower.* Roger Bannister, talking about the time he broke the 4-minute mile at Oxford, May 6, 1954, said, "My body had long since exhausted all its energy but it went on running just the same. The physical overdraft came only from willpower. . . . Those last few seconds seemed never ending."

Willpower to see the goal reached long after the excitement of goal setting has faded is a characteristic of a leader who achieves.

2. *Single-mindedness.* Einstein and an assistant had finished a paper and were looking for a paper clip. They finally found one but it was too badly bent to use. So they began looking for a tool to straighten it. Opening many more drawers, they came upon a whole box of unused paper clips. Einstein began shaping one of them into a tool to straighten the bent one. When the puzzled assistant asked why he was doing this when he had a whole box of new clips, he replied, "Once I am set on a goal it becomes difficult to deflect me."

3. *Self-discipline.* Willpower and single-mindedness are results of self-discipline. The word discipline comes from the word *disciple*, which means a learner or follower. Achievement leaders are constantly aware of their need to learn and train themselves to achieve excellence.

4. *Open-mindedness.* Achievement leaders are not always looking for some hidden, devious meaning in the comments or actions of others. They are willing to accept other's behavior at face value.

5. *Self-acceptance.* Achievement leaders feel good about themselves. They are not conceited, but accept themselves as they are and work toward improvement.

6. *Adaptability.* Achievement leaders are able to face change with the assurance that they can handle it advantageously.

7. *Sense of independence.* They are not afraid to disagree candidly with their peers and superiors.

8. *Sensitivity.* They are not insensitive to the feelings and values of others.

9. *Realistic attitude.* Achievement leaders face facts as they are. They do not look through rose-colored glasses, nor are they overly negative in assessing situations.

10. *Frankness.* They are frank and open in all their dealings.

11. *Curiosity*. Achievement leaders are observant and curious. They ask meaningful questions.

12. *Upward mobility*. Achievement leaders keep their eyes on the next higher job level. They groom themselves for the next job. They think and behave as though they already possessed it.

13. *Subordinate sense.* Achievement leaders are effective subordinates. They know that managing their relationships with superiors is as vital as managing relationships with subordinates.

14. *Knowledgeability*. Achievement leaders are knowledgeable about the organization that employs them and about the industry or profession they are involved with.

15. *Power sense*. Achievement leaders know where the influence lies in their organizations. They know the key people are those whose ideas and advice are sought, regardless of their formal status.

16. *Trust.* Achievement leaders know that basic ethical behavior and integrity are the keys to trust.

17. *Territorial sense*. Achievement leaders know the limits of their responsibilities but they discreetly test questionable boundaries to maximize their contribution. Unless it is otherwise spelled out, achievement leaders take a very broad view of their area of contribution to organizational goals.

18. *Analytical sense*. Achievement leaders avoid generalization. They know the need for objective and discriminate handling of information. They avoid simplistic labels. They recognize that there are gray areas as well as black and white in many facts, ideas, and issues.

19. *Career sense*. Achievement leaders recognize the necessity for honesty, hard work, and productive performance, but realize, too, that these alone are not enough to insure advancement in a competitive world. They have a sense of political reality regarding their own positions. They appreciate the importance of a helpful sponsor.

20. *Empathy*. Achievement leaders protect the dignity of other individuals, whether they are subordinates, peers, or superiors.

OUTWARD SIGNS OF SUCCESS

If you look successful, people generally believe that you are. Well-chosen business accessories can augment your look of success.

Your Business Card

Your business card is important because it represents you. A well-designed business card created by a top graphics firm can be costly. You may choose to be your own designer. Eye appeal is a "must." You can have conventional black on white or color on color. Other variations are in the style of type, artwork, and size. A good-quality card stock will add prestige to your image.

Here are some other ideas you may want to consider in relation to your business card:

- Include name, address (including zip code), and telephone number (including area code). Other data may be appropriate, but keep in mind that too much information detracts from the card's appearance and effectiveness.
- Slogans can attract considerable attention. Slogans are not always appropriate, however. If your organization has a logo or symbol, you may want to incorporate it into your business card.
- If the information you want to include exceeds available space, consider a folded type of business card. It will accommodate about three hundred words about your qualifications and services. The folded business card tends to stimulate more attention than the traditional style. You can use the folded style even without a lot of information printed on it. The outside could merely state your occupation or profession, such as "Doctor of Psychiatry." Inside would be your name, address, and phone number.
- Avery Label has developed a self-adhesive business card. It has many functional uses. It can be used as a name tag at a convention or other large gathering where you mingle with people who will be interested in your specialty. It can be attached to luggage, golf cart, etc. It can be placed in your professional literature, books, and magazines. It can be used as an address label, to fill out hotel registration cards, and on equipment to be loaned or sent for repair.

Your Briefcase

The character and quality of your briefcase tell a great deal about you. The higher up the corporate ladder you move, the less you will need an image-making briefcase. But while you are on your way up, your briefcase is as important in building your leadership image as your business card.

Here are some factors to consider when contemplating the purchase of a briefcase.

- Think first about function. Decide the quantity of files and papers you need to transport; then divide it in half. Most people carry much more than they need. It is usually safe to assume that notepaper and other standard office supplies will be available at your destination.
- A small briefcase is more impressive than an oversized one. Standard attaché dimensions should be your outside limits. Something just a little smaller and thinner is in order. Modesty is the ultimate weapon of the supremely confident.
- Quality is important. Genuine leather is preferred. People in a high-technology field may prefer lightweight aluminum alloy.
- Avoid a lot of hardware, contrasting leather bands, and insets. Also avoid any manufacturer's or store's identification, such as a monogram. They may add to the store's or manufacturer's image, but they detract from your image.
- The stigma of newness should be removed as quickly as possible. The impression you want to convey is that your briefcase has had long use and your current status is not new.

Your Business Photograph

Achievement leaders need two sets of photographs on hand at all times: a formal photograph for business announcements and an informal photograph for feature articles about you and your organization. All photographs should be 5 × 7 inches and should be printed for reproduction, that is, with a glossy finish. Color prints are not necessary unless your photograph is likely to be used on television.

In preparing to have a picture taken, a man should wear a dark suit with little or no pattern and a shirt in a muted color. Prints should not be worn. Bright, white shirts draw attention away from the face. A woman should wear clothes that suit her skin tone and do not draw attention away from her eyes.

Get a good night's rest before having your photograph taken. The camera will exaggerate fatigue. Allow a week for a haircut to grow out before having pictures taken—it will give you a more natural look.

Tell the photographer you want several poses to choose from. Select the photographer by his samples, not his credentials.

To keep up with changing styles, have a new business photo taken every five years.

THE CORPORATE WIFE OR HUSBAND

Perhaps one of the most important considerations that face achievement leaders is that of spouse. Let's consider problems that may be present in various situations:

Husband has career; wife oversees home and children. Sometimes a husband who is striving to reach a career goal has to devote long hours to his job. He may even have to be away from home for weeks at a time. The family may have to move often, which means changing schools for the children, changing churches, changing friends, packing belongings, and moving to another community.

The wife can feel lonely. She can feel left out of a large part of her husband's life. The full burden of managing the home and raising the children falls upon her. She can become bitter. She can feel unappreciated and neglected. Sometimes wives in such situations tend to blame the "company" for the husband's absences, late hours, and the many moves the family must make. She loses sight of the fact that it is not the company but her husband's choice, which he made at the time he chose to reach his career goal, that is the cause of these inconveniences.

Wife has career; husband oversees home and children. All the foregoing problems can be present in this situation—only the roles are reversed. There is an added problem here, however, when the traditional roles of wife and husband are reversed. In our society we are not so far removed from tradition that resentment can't build in either party when traditional roles are reversed.

Husband has career; wife has career. It is becoming increasingly normal for both husband and wife to have their individual careers outside the home. The biggest question in this situation is, of course: Who takes care of the household responsibilities and who cares for the children? There may be additional problems such as when the demands of one partner's career conflict with the demands of the other partner's career. Vacations may not be scheduled at the same time. The husband's or the wife's career may require a change of locale and a determination must be made as to which career will be accommodated, or a solution found where both can be accommodated. One partner may advance in his or her career more rapidly than the other advances. When this happens the slower partner can feel discouragement, inadequacy, self-condemnation. Because of our cultural tradition, this tends to be more of a problem when the wife experiences greater success than the husband.

We cannot give you solutions for the problems noted above. We can tell you, from our research and our experience with many career-minded people we have met in our work, that there are two necessities that help prevent such problems from developing: set clear values and priorities early, and communicate clearly with each other. Here are some suggestions for you to consider:

1. Both parties need to recognize the possibility that such problems can arise. You may think you have such a close relationship and such a strong marriage that no such problem will ever arise between you. Don't bank on it. Such rationalizing is taking your partner for granted. Marriage counselors will tell you this is one of the most destructive things you can do to your marriage.

2. Together determine your values and your priorities. If you value your home and family more than your career, they should have a higher priority than your career. Determine your values first and then set your priorities.

3. When problems do arise, share them with each other. They cannot be solved without two-way communication. Never assume that your partner can know your feelings without you expressing them.

4. Work out the solution together. Work toward a "win/win" solution, where both partners gain something. When discussing problems and solving problems, always keep your values and priorities in mind. Those you have already agreed upon—they are a good place to begin discussion.

5. Remember that each of you can enhance the other's career by being an outstanding corporate wife or husband. By cooperation at home you can relieve your spouse of nagging homefront problems that take away from his or her concentration on the job. You can build up your spouse's self-image by support and encouragement. You can support your spouse in the presence of super-

iors at organizational functions. You can enhance his or her image by the way you dress, talk, and behave.

THE CORPORATE CLIMB

Your climb up the corporate ladder may not end in the same organization it began in. Whether you remain with the same organization or not, you should expect to change positions every three to five years. Each change should be an upward step on the corporate ladder. To change positions more often than every three to five years may not be a point in your favor; however, to remain more than seven years in the same position usually results in career immobility and stagnation.

Changing Jobs

Some changes of position you may initiate yourself, while others will be initiated by the organization that employed you. You may be laid off or fired. If you are dismissed, here are some thoughts that can help you make the best of the situation:

1. Vent your anger in a recreational activity, such as golf, or take a brief vacation. Don't display anger to the employer who dismissed you. It could have a bad effect on your future employment opportunities.
2. Allow your spouse to share in the traumatic experience. She or he will be able to accept the situation and make necessary adjustments if you can communicate your feelings. It will help you if you have the support of your spouse and other family members.
3. Review the positions you have held in the past. Determine your strengths and weaknesses. Get a clear focus on your job preferences and the type of job you are best qualified for.
4. Make a list of the organizations you think can use the skills you have developed so far in your career. Find contact people in these organizations. If you don't know anyone, perhaps a friend or relative does. If you ask someone to introduce you, use a positive approach. Assure him that introducing you will reflect well on him.
5. Prepare a marketing plan for yourself. List the skills you have that a particular employer could use. Emphasize these when you plan the presentation you will make to a prospective employer.

6. Revise your résumé to include additional abilities and experience you have gained since you first wrote your résumé. If you never have had a résumé, write one now. See the next section of this chapter for suggestions relating to your résumé.

Some employers help former executives to find new positions through "outplacement" services. If your organization has an outplacement service, it could be a help to you in your search for a new position. However, let your leadership shine by taking the initiative in marketing your assets.

Carl W. Menk, president of Boyden Associates, one of the country's largest executive search firms, says recruiters look for a pleasant degree of self-assurance, ease, articulateness, and honesty in applicants.[2] The spouse's appearance is important if the job is in a small community or overseas. It is not as important if the job is in a large city.

Some executives make themselves visible, inside and outside their organizations, by writing articles for trade journals. Some make themselves available as speakers for service clubs and at functions where they can gain recognition in their field.

In deciding where to apply, bear in mind that you can gain a wider range of experience in a small company. In larger companies there is more competition. However, large companies will expose you to more sophisticated ways of doing things.

Your Résumé

A résumé is a sales tool designed to get you an interview. Achievement leaders keep an outline of their résumé up to date at all times. They keep a running record of positions held and what they accomplished in each position. If you were particularly successful with a specific project, write down the details about it. You will need this information to help sell your experience and accomplishments later on in your career. At that time, unless you have written it down, you may not be able to recall enough of the details to enable you to use it as a selling point. (See "Career History" later in this chapter.)

From this outline or running record of experience and accomplishments, achievement leaders design a résumé to fit the specific position for which they apply. Your résumé will be one of many

[2] "A Top Headhunter Tells How to Get Ahead," (interview with Carl Menk), *Money*, December 1979, pp. 92-94.

received. If you apply through an executive-recruiting firm that receives thousands of applications a year, yours will have to stand out to be noticed and placed in their data bank.

Your résumé should be designed to make your potential employer want to know more about you. Do not tell all about yourself in your résumé. A résumé should be brief—not more than two pages. A page or page-and-a-half is an ideal length for a résumé.

The color of paper for your résumé is important. Ivory and pale blue are attractive colors for résumés. White does not stand out from other papers enough. Pink does not look sophisticated. Use a quality bond paper, but not too slick or expensive-looking paper because the person looking at it may not trust it.

If the résumé is mailed, it should be accompanied by a covering letter. The covering letter should state specifically how your qualifications match the requirements of the position.

If you mail your résumé, address it to the chief personnel officer by name. If you want to send your résumé to the department head in charge of the position to be filled, wait several weeks after you have sent your résumé to the chief personnel officer and then send a copy to the department head. You wouldn't want to run the risk of antagonizing the personnel officer by letting him suspect that you think he doesn't know what positions are open in his organization.

Figure 23-1 is a classified ad from a newspaper. Figure 23-2 is a sample résumé sent in answer to the ad.

Note the following points about the résumé in Figure 23-2:

Figure 23-1 *Classified Ad*

```
          PERSONNEL DIRECTOR

No. 80-9. Salary $2000 - $2400
Final filing date April 18, 1980
Requires knowledge of public
personnel laws, policies and
procedures and skill in employee
negotiations, recruitment and
selection, management and
supervision and handling employee
benefits and worker's compensation
program.
          CITY OF NEWTOWN
     300 Centennial Way, Newtown
          714/489-9999
```

```
                              JOAN DOE

Address:   123 Main Street                Phone:  (213) 468-9251
           Newtown, CA  90650


Objective:               Personnel Director

Experience:              Assistant Personnel Director, Newtown School
                         District, from 1976 to present

                         Responsibilities include:  recruitment,
                         selection, management of non-teaching
                         personnel; annual salary and fringe benefits
                         studies and recommendations for non-teaching
                         personnel

Special Qualifications:  As assistant personnel director, I am a member
                         of the district's negotiating team.

                         I keep the administrative staff posted on all
                         current legislation relating to public
                         employees.

Education:               MA in Personnel Administration, University of
                            California, Irvine, 1975
                         BA, University of California, Irvine, 1973

Personal Data:           Married; daughter 7, son 5
                         Born: August 14, 1950
                         Health:  Excellent
```

Figure 23-2 *Résumé*

1. It is brief—it fits on one page.

2. The applicant's name is at the top, in capital letters, easily located on the page. The prospective employer does not have to look for it. Address and phone number are also easily located.

3. "Objective" states the position the applicant is applying for. The same title is used that was used in the ad. (If you are not answering an ad, use the title that best signifies the type of position you want.)

4. Experience is listed next in Figure 23-2 because it is the most important part of your résumé. Joan Doe's experience pretty well matches the qualifications called for in the advertisement, and this fact makes it the most important part of her résumé. If Joan Doe

had had no such experience—say, if she had just graduated—she would have listed her education first and enlarged upon it, pointing out some special aspect of it that ties in with the qualifications the advertisement suggests. For example, she may have written her thesis on the subject of laws pertaining to public personnel.

Most recent experience is listed first (function, employer, dates of employment). Each entry should be followed by an explanation of responsibilities that clearly coincide with what the prospective employer is looking for. If possible, use strong words like *accomplished, organized, managed*, and *directed*.

List all positions you have held, going back about ten years, and explain the responsibilities of each position. Always keep in mind what the prospective employer wants.

Account for any time between jobs—for example, if you had taken a sabbatical, or if you didn't work in order to care for your family. In our sample résumé for Joan Doe, only one position is listed because she had only one position since graduation.

5. Special qualifications are listed next. This is where you list additional things you have done that have a bearing on the qualifications sought in the ad. You may have served on a task force that gave you valuable experience along the line the prospective employer wants. Do not say you directed the project unless you did.

Other special qualifications could include community service, foreign travel, and service organization experience. Include any of these kinds of qualifications that would add to your credibility in relation to the position you are applying for.

6. Under "Education" include college, graduate schools, and technical courses with degrees and dates. Don't list any schooling below that. High school is not pertinent unless this is your first job and your education does not extend beyond high school.

7. It is not necessary to include personal data, but it gives the prospective employer a more complete picture of you. If you include it, keep it brief as in our example.

Additional points to keep in mind concerning your résumé are:

- Personalize your résumé with a covering letter. (See Figure 23-3.)
- Be truthful. You should be able to substantiate everything you say in your résumé and covering letter.
- Don't use initials of organizations or trade and brand names—or any

terminology that might not be familiar to the résumé reader.
- Don't copy phrases from other people's résumés or use trite expressions. You will be branded as unimaginative if you do.
- It is not necessary to include salary on your résumé. This can be negotiated during the interview.
- If you have been awarded special recognition or honors relating to your qualifications, include them in your résumé and explain them.
- List professional licenses, if any are necessary for the position, and publications and professional associations.
- References are optional on your résumé. If your prospective employer wants references, he will ask for them.
- Proofread your résumé for typing and other errors.
- You can have your résumé written by a professional résumé writer. If you decide to go this route, be sure the résumé sounds like you and contains accurate information.
- Always follow up your résumé with a phone call.

The Interview

When you go for an interview, look like a person who already has the level of position for which you are applying. Dress appropriately and imagine that you already have the job. Your prospective employer will be able to visualize you on the job. You will feel self-confident and your prospective employer will see you as a self-confident person.

The interview begins in the outer office. Your attitude—the way you walk in and talk to the receptionist or secretary—is noted by these lower-echelon people. They are often asked how you came across to them. You must make as professional an impression on them as you do on those with whom you talk in the interview behind closed doors. Achievement leaders behave consistently regardless of who is watching them.

If you are interviewed by a panel of interviewers, make a note of each one's name so you can use their names when answering questions. At the end of the session thank each one individually using their names.

Follow up the interview with a letter of appreciation to each individual interviewer. Offer to come back and answer additional questions. Mention something in your favor that you might have overlooked during the interview.

```
                              123 Main Street
                              Newtown, CA  90650

                              April 10, 1980


Mr. Jack Smith, City Administrator
City of Newtown
300 Centennial Way
Newtown, California  90650

Dear Mr. Smith:

For the past four years I have been employed as assistant personnel
director in charge of all non-teaching personnel of the Newtown
School District.  As you will see by my resume, which is enclosed,
my responsibilities at the school district coincide very closely
with the qualifications of the position you advertise.  I am,
therefore, applying for the position of Personnel Director for the
city of Newtown.

In connection with my work at the school district, I have developed
a unique indexing system for public personnel laws, policies, and
procedures that comprise, not only a history of these laws, but an
up-to-date reference of current laws including bills in the legislature
at the present time.  This has been a real time-saving help to us here
at the city offices; and I believe it would be equally beneficial to
city employees who must work with these laws.

Sincerely,



Joan Doe

Enclosure:  Resume
```

Figure 23-3 *Covering Letter*

Salary should not be an unsurmountable barrier, unless it is far below what you believe it should be. Remember that salary includes fringe benefits. The total package may add up to more than you expected.

```
                         Education
  Date:  June 1973

  Achievement:  BA

  University/Other:  U. C., Irvine


  Date:  June 1975
  Achievement:  MA - Personnel Adm.
  University/Other:  U. C., Irvine


  Date:

  Achievement:

  University/Other:
```

Figure 23-4 *Career History—Education*

Career History

An effective way to keep a permanent record of your career history is to purchase a 5 × 8-inch record book, about ¼ inch thick. Divide the book into four sections: Education, Work Experience, Recognition, and Other Accomplishments. Leave more pages in the "Other Accomplishments" and "Work Experience" sections than in the other sections. You can separate the sections by using paper clips.

Set up the "Education" pages as shown in Figure 23-4, "Work Experience" as shown in Figure 23-5, "Recognition" as shown in Figure 23-6, and "Other Accomplishments" as shown in Figure 23-7. Use of each section is self-explanatory.

INVESTING IN YOUR IMAGE

You can get professional help to enhance your leadership image. There are public relations specialists who will teach you how to put your best foot forward. There are speech specialists who

```
                    Work Experience

    Date: August 10, 1976
    Position: Ass't Personnel Dir, Newtown Schools
    Superior's Name and Title: Dr. John Franks
    My responsibilities:      Personnel Director
    Recruitment and selection of non-teaching
    personnel; annual salary and fringe benefits
    studies; supervise office staff; work with
    negotiating team.
    Special Assignments:

    Keep Adm Staff posted on legislation
    affecting public employees - Designed
    indexing system for same.
```

Figure 23-5 *Career History—Work Experience*

```
                    Recognition

    Date: May 1974
    Type: Teacher of the Year Award
    Given by: Newtown Teachers Association
    For: - Achievement with third graders
         - Participation in Association work
    Date:

    Type:

    Given by:

    For:
```

Figure 23-6 *Career History—Recognition*

```
                    Other Accomplishments

        (Include memberships in professional organizations,
        service clubs; community projects; offices held,
        committees chaired, etc.)

        Date:  Sept 1974

              Elected president of faculty
              Club, Newton School District
```

Figure 23-7 *Career History—Other Accomplishments*

will help you overcome speech defects and make you an accomplished public speaker. There are image consultants who will tell you how to dress and behave. There are seminars you can attend to make yourself more assertive. There are books on subjects relating to image building.

Join a professional association in your field and take part in their meetings. It will give you practical help for performing your on-the-job duties.

Help out in voluntary organizations. Assist in the many tasks that are necessary. Take part in fund drives. This is a safe place to get valuable experience doing things that you may have to do later in your organization.

Subscribe to a trade journal in your field. They often contain many excellent articles relating to achievement leadership.

Find a mentor in your organization who will help you succeed.